To my frien Andrew with (handwritten)

If A Name Means Anything

A dictionary of Christian names

2nd Edition

DAVID WINTER

PERISSOS MEDIA

Published by
Perissos Media
An imprint of Perissos Group UK
www.PerissosMedia.com

ISBN: 0992667704
ISBN-13: 978-0992667702

For a FREE sample from this book,
direct your family and friends to:

www.IfANameMeansAnything.com/sample

CONTENTS

If A Name Means Anything

A dictionary
of Christian names

2nd Edition

DAVID WINTER

FOREWORD

I am always interested when a mature, responsible and respected servant of God tells me that God has said something to him. After all, we believe that God has lips as well as ears – He speaks as well as listens! I am aware that such a thrilling reality can be abused and so can become self-gratifying and dangerously human. In fact, it can descend into the foolish and bizarre. However, David Winter is someone I have known for many years and I honour him as a man of God molded and shaped in the furnace of life. You will note that this book was born out of God's initiative, and has not been written simply because of circumstances but in obedience.

Names have always fascinated me. Since the morning of time, in the book of Genesis, when God gave man the responsibility for all living creatures and naming them He has demonstrated His interest in names. In fact, as the great drama of redemption began to unfold, it is God who gives the world's redeemer His name. God's messenger said to Mary, the mother of our Lord: "You will be with child and give birth to a son, and you are to give him the name Jesus." Luke 1:31.

Names in the Bible have great significance. They often identify the person in his character and conduct or speak prophetically about his ministry and mission. Names clearly matter to God and so should also matter to us. Naming a child is no trivial pursuit. Apart from the social implications involved, there is also something of a spiritual destiny. Sadly, as society has become de-Christianised the reality of this has lost its significance. Official documents increasingly no longer speak of 'Christian names' but rather 'first' names or 'given' names. David Winter, by strong implication, confronts this trend and challenges it. In this book he puts a tool into our hands to help us to recapture this Christian and spiritual dimension.

Years ago I heard of a man doing a census-survey in one of the highly populated, run-down districts of Glasgow. He knocked on the door in a dark, bleak, soul-less tenement building in that city. A woman responded. He asked her how many people lived there in that one apartment. "Well", she said; "there's Willie and Tom and Margaret and Hughie and Tina and Bella…" The census man interrupted. "Missus" he said, "I'm not interested in names, I'm only interested in numbers!" "Well" she said, "they may only be numbers to you, but they're names to me!" and continued to name her family! Names personalize. They express hope, relationship, love – and, no doubt, other things as well. I am impressed that in the gospels we find Jesus beginning with a company or crowd of people and before the end of the incident He is relating to only one person. That occurs on nineteen occasions. Individuals matter to God, and names individualize us.

Society has not only become de-Christianized; it has increasingly become de-personalized. At the time of the industrial revolution people were called "hands" – to do the work. As society progressed we became "heads" – to be counted. Now we seem to be "numbers" (account numbers, insurance policy numbers, credit card numbers etc.) – so that we are identified! All that is within us cries out; "I'm a PERSON created in the image of God – by God and for God." My name recalls something of that distinctiveness and destiny.

As you use David Winter's book it is certainly the yearning of my heart that you will reflect on the name you bear and realise its dignity and that you will desire, with God's help, to become the kind of person your name declares. Of course, our humanity will constantly get in the way, but God by His Holy Spirit, wants to help us with our humanity – not to become religious freaks, but to become truly human. And for those who will turn to this book to select a name for their, as yet, unborn child, may you be filled with wonder as you realise that you have been co-operating with God in the creating of a new life. As you choose a name let it express your faith, not in the life that is about to be born but in the God who wants to take that life and express his love, grace and purpose through it and so make our world a better place than it was before your child was born.

Jim Graham
Director of External Ministries
Gold Hill Baptist Church
Buckinghamshire

PREFACE TO THE 2ND EDITION

For some years now the first edition of my book "If a Name Means Anything…" has been out-of-print, and I do apologise to all those of you who have patiently waited for this new edition.

The truth is I have not been very well. In 1998 I had a major heart attack and, as a result, was fitted with an ICD (Implanted Cardioverter Defibrillator). In 2013 it was due a battery change but the hospital advised me to have an upgraded version – so I now have a CRT (Cardiac Resynchronisation Therapy Device)! Oh well, such is progress! The result of this wonderful machine is that I feel so much better and have been applying myself to various tasks that have hitherto gone undone.

The final 'push' for this 2nd edition came when I saw one of my books on a second-hand book site (which I sold for £5.95) advertised at £130!!! This is absolutely true - if you doubt it I will gladly give you details of the site.

Sadly, Joshua, to whom I dedicated the book originally, died in 1998 – hundreds attended his funeral – many of them young people that he had influenced in his short 13 years. The other sad event was that my son-in-law and daughter decided to part company, and as he was responsible for the excellent original cover, we had to find a new artist.

I have been fortunate enough to have recruited James Dawson (the brother of my PA Jason Dawson who worked with me for four years as my assistant presenter on Revelation TV). James has done a wonderful job with the new cover; he is a very talented graphic designer. You can access more of his superb work at www.IfANameMeansAnything.com.

In particular you may want to order framed posters of individual names as gifts for your friends and relatives. The wordings are taken from this book and the posters are beautifully designed and framed.

The Rev Jim Graham readily agreed to allow me to retain his excellent Foreword and I am indebted to him for this kindness – as I am to the other original helpers listed in the Introduction.

I have discontinued the list of scripture references at the back of the book because I am not at all sure that this was helpful to anyone – the list contained every one of the scriptures quoted in the book. If you would like a copy, I will gladly send you one.

So much has happened in the years since the book was first published, but strangely, we still have names – and those names have meanings – and God still calls us by name – telling us that we are very precious to Him.

He knows your name!

David Winter 2013

INTRODUCTION

This book is dedicated to the memory of Joshua Pannell the son of some friends who were members of our Church.

One Tuesday afternoon we received an urgent request on the 'Prayer Chain' - we were asked to pray for Joshua who, in spite of all that he had been through, was now having difficulty feeding. That very evening I was leading an 'Introduction to Hebrew' Course and was surprised and delighted to discover that the word we were to be studying in Hebrew was 'Yeshua' the short form of 'Yehoshua' - the same word that our friends Steve and Sarah had chosen as their son's name when he had been born just two months previously!

The pregnancy, the birth and the months following Joshua's arrival were very traumatic for Steve and Sarah. Early in the pregnancy it became clear that things were not going well. The doctors at Guys Hospital, London told them that the baby's heart was deformed and that to their certain knowledge no baby had ever survived this condition. The suggestion was that they consider termination - they already had six very lovely, healthy children at home. However, when Steve caught sight of the image of a tiny foot on the ultra-scan it seemed to make an indelible impression on his mind that could not be erased. The following day the Lord showed both Steve and Sarah, quite independently, that the pregnancy should be allowed to run its course.

During the weeks following this experience Steve and Sarah sought help from Christian friends who believed in God's power to heal and on the 1st August 1995 Joshua was born normally. The doctors were amazed at the way in which his heart had developed - but it was not completely healed and within 36 hours Joshua was undergoing open-heart surgery for a repair to the left valve of his heart. During this time both Steve and Sarah felt a great sense of God's peace and the assurance that all would be well with this tiny bundle of life that was their latest son. After nearly five weeks in intensive care Joshua was discharged and allowed to go home.

God had not only proved His power to heal but had also given two very strained and tired parents the strength and determination to go on. You can imagine their dismay just over a month later, when they found that Joshua couldn't take his food! Once more it was back to the hospital and more tests, treatment and medication. It was at this point that we were asked to pray for Joshua. The following morning I was sitting at my computer thinking and praying about the amazing 'co-incidence' of being asked to pray for a modern-day Joshua whilst at the same time taking a class of students who were studying the same 3,000 year-old name. To me there was no doubt that God was trying to tell ME something too - but what?

I decided to type out the story of the original Joshua rereading it from the early books of the Bible and, particularly, from the book of Joshua. Once again I was thrilled and captivated by the exploits of this incredible man. Moses had recognised Joshua's potential whilst he was still young and had made him his Commander-in-Chief. At the same time Moses changed his name from Hoshea to Yehoshua which means literally; "Yahweh is salvation". Some 1200 years later a baby was born in Bethlehem and the instructions from the angel were: "you are to give him the name Jesus (Yehoshua), because he will save his people from their sins." Mt.1:21. As I began to type the story of Joshua I thought that it would make a nice poster for his parents and so I typed the name in English and Hebrew at the top and at the bottom concluded with the verse: "But as for me and my household, we will serve the LORD." Joshua 24:15.

I printed out the 'poster' on a plain piece of paper and presented it to Steve and Sarah at the first opportunity. They were overcome and later Steve said: "...it is the most valuable piece of paper we have ever owned". The 'poster' was framed and displayed on the wall of Joshua's bedroom where it remained to the day of his death.

Sadly, Joshua died on the 8th January 2008 - just a few weeks before his 13th birthday. His life had been a testimony to the love and grace of his Saviour and his funeral was attended by hundreds of young people whose lives he had influenced.

Two weeks after I had given them the 'poster' I was approached by Steve and Sarah who wanted to thank me again for the poster and to report on Joshua's progress. In the conversation Steve said: "You realise that all the other six children are jealous of Joshua's poster - would you consider doing one for each of them?" So the poster ministry was born - and now everyone wanted one! A few months later the Christian Resources Exhibition was being held at Sandown and I was challenged to "bless many more people" by exhibiting there. By then I had only 400 names on my poster list but decided to 'test the market'. In the event we were overwhelmed by the demand and I was working from early in the morning till late at night trying to satisfy requests. Eventually the story reached the local paper and following this I was interviewed twice on BBC West Midlands and several times on Premier Radio. We opened a small 'stall' in a craft centre in Chelmsford and now attended various shows and exhibitions selling the attractive posters. Some Ministers present our 'Name Posters' to candidates at Baptisms, Dedications and Confirmations. During an exhibition I found myself opposite a Publisher's stand - the rest they say, is history...

My purpose in this book is to help readers realise that they are SPECIAL to God by demonstrating that their name has meaning and that they have significance. Our names are important - not just because they have meaning and history but because they identify the individual. The Bible tells us that God KNOWS our names and CALLS us by our name; "I have called you by your name - you are mine" Is. 43:1. The Lord Jesus reinforced this when He said; "He calls His own sheep by name..." John 10:3.

The Lord Jesus was at Caesarea Philippi when Peter made that momentous statement "You are the Christ the Son of the living God" Jesus replied; "Blessed are you Simon Son of Jonah, for this was not revealed to you by man, but by my Father in heaven" Mt.16:16&17. I think it was one of those occasions when He had a twinkle in His eye! He knew that the Hebrew word 'Jonah' is also the Hebrew word for 'a dove'? He was aware that God reveals things to men through His word and through the Holy Spirit - the symbol of which is a dove.

Your name may mean something startling and wonderful or, it may have a very ordinary and mundane meaning. It does not matter, God knows your name and calls you by it. This is one of the reasons why I have tried to be as accurate as possible in giving the meaning and history of each name. You may have read alternative meanings and I am ready to concede that these do exist. However, where there is doubt about the meaning or history I have sought two independent sources to corroborate my facts. Nowhere have I given facts that I know are not completely true. Where you have seen names that are given fanciful and other 'astrological-type' meanings - be careful! There is an occult art known as 'Onomancy'.

We have a great tradition in the west of 'Christian names' and I would like to encourage my readers to help guard this valuable heritage. It is NOT your 'first' name, nor is it your 'given' name, it is your 'Christian name'. The reason behind this is simple: We owe it to the Christian Church for introducing the double-name as a means of identifying people more accurately.

Additionally, there was a time in Britain when every child was required to have the name of a saint or a Biblical character as their Christian name. Following the Reformation new names were introduced, and today we have many other names to enrich our choice.

I have used the New International Version of the Bible because I have found that this translation is the most widely accepted version in the English-speaking Christian world today. Occasionally I have quoted from the King James Version where I feel that the wording is more suitable (e.g. "Beulah") in these cases the entry is marked "KJV". The text following the name/s is one which I have considered, after prayer, to be the most appropriate - I am anxious that no-one becomes obsessed or places any undue significance on the verse, it is just the verse of Scripture that I felt is relevant to that particular name or subject. I have also retained the upper-case versions of the word "LORD" because this normally indicates the distinctive name of God 'Yahweh' in scripture.

The names are listed alphabetically with what I consider the most common usage first followed by alternative spellings and other cognates and associated names and forms.

I am particularly indebted to friends who have assisted me by checking and correcting the proofs. In particular my friend John Thomson (a retired solicitor) who has given many hours of his valuable time going through the MSS and making many good positive suggestions, I have tried to incorporate them all. Mrs Sam Eldon-Lee, Mrs Christine Sparrow and Mrs Sue Ducat have also assisted me. The language consultants: Dr Tony Charalambou (Greek) Mrs Margaret Grant (Scottish Gaelic) and Mr Hefin Williams MA (Welsh) have all given freely of their time and expertise. It has been difficult to locate folk who are fluent in Breton, Cornish and Irish Gaelic. The Chelmsford Branch of the Essex County Library has been helpful by obtaining dictionaries in these languages. For all this assistance I am very grateful but retain the right to take the blame for any errors, omissions or inaccuracies.

My grateful thanks to my good friend the Rev. Jim Graham, late of Goldhill Baptist Church, for writing the foreword. The cover design is by my friend and colleague James Dawson of 'Visual Elements', and he and the lovely individual name posters can be accessed through our website, www.IfANameMeansAnything.com.

Please feel free to contact me with suggestions, corrections or additions.

David Winter
PO BOX 10349
Danbury
CHELMSFORD
Essex, CM3 4YH, UK
iouyeshua@yahoo.co.uk

Aaron Aron Arran

The name means 'lofty teacher' the older brother of Moses who used him to speak on his behalf. He became the High Priest and founder of the priestly line.

Aaron first appears in the Bible in the book of Exodus after his brother returns from meeting God in the burning bush. Moses had protested to God that he had "never been eloquent" Ex.4:10. God replied: "What about your brother Aaron? ...he can speak well." Ex.4:14. Aaron has his ups and downs but he loves God so much that he is made High Priest and responsible for entering the 'holy of holies' once a year with the blood of the sacrifice for the sins of the people.

"God is exalted in His power. Who is a teacher like Him?" Job 36:22.

Abagail - see Abigail

Abbie - see Abigail

Abdul Abdullah

From Arabic meaning 'servant of God'. The theme of Isaiah and the Lord Jesus Christ.

A large part of the book of the prophet Isaiah is devoted to the concept of 'the suffering servant'. This has been interpreted in several ways: some scholars see it as referring to the nation of Israel - the Jews; others suggest that it outlines personal and individual traumas, whilst a third view is that it foretells the suffering of the Messiah. This third view is most popular because of the fulfilment of passages such as Isaiah chapter 53 in the life of the LORD Jesus Christ.

"...and sang the song of Moses the servant of God...Great and marvellous are your deeds, Lord God Almighty. Just and true are your ways, King of the ages." Rev.15:3.

Abe - see Abel or Abraham

Abel Abe

From Hebrew meaning 'breath' or 'vapour'. Adam's second son who was killed by Cain out of anger and jealousy.

Abel was a righteous man (see Mt.23:35, Heb.11:4) and when he brought an offering from his flocks God was pleased with it and accepted it. When Cain brought his offering of the fruits of the soil God rejected it and this made Cain angry and jealous of his brother. When they were in the fields Cain attacked and killed his brother and then denied that he was responsible for him (see Genesis chapter 4). God judged Cain for his sin. God was not unfair to Cain because He had clearly told him what was required (see Gen.4:6-7). The principle had been laid down from the beginning.

"By faith...he was commended as a righteous man when God spoke well of his offerings." *Heb.11:4.*

Abigail Abagail Abbie Gail Gayle

Hebrew for 'her father rejoiced' and in the Bible she is one of King David's first two wives.

Fathers do tend to rejoice over their daughters - even when the daughters don't deserve it!

One daughter really did give her father cause for rejoicing - she saved her entire household from the vengeance of David's men and when her husband died she married David. The full story is told in the later chapters of 1 Samuel.

More importantly, we want our 'heavenly Father' to rejoice - and He will give us the ability to please Him.

"...his wife's name was Abigail...she was an intelligent and beautiful woman." 1 *Sam.25:3.*

Abner

From Hebrew meaning 'father of light'. The cousin of King Saul and Commander in Chief of his army.

The latter days of King Saul's reign were difficult and bloody. David had already been anointed king by the prophet Samuel but Saul was still reigning. After the death of Saul, Abner led a short rebellion against David but eventually submitted to him. Shortly afterwards he was killed in an act of revenge. The full story is in 2 Sam.2&3. Both David and Solomon commended Abner as a better man than the man who killed him (2 Sam. 3:34).

"Every good gift and every perfect gift is from above, and cometh down from the Father of lights, with whom is no variableness, neither shadow of turning." *Jas.1:17 KJV.*

Abraham Abe Ibrahim

From Hebrew meaning 'father of many nations'. One of the first men of faith.

One of the best summaries of the life of Abraham is in Acts 7:2-8. He is revered as a man of faith by the world's three great religions. He trusted God when he was commanded to leave Ur of the Chaldees and move to a land that God would show him. Again he trusted God when he was told that he would father a great nation. The greatest test of his faith was when he was called upon to sacrifice his only son - the one through whom God had promised so much. It is little wonder that he is described as 'a man of faith' by the writer of Hebrews (11:8-12).

"Abraham believed God, and it was credited to him as righteousness." Rom.4:3.

Ada Adela Adelaide

From the German 'adelheit' which means 'nobility'. The name of many famous people and places.

Ada came from the German for 'nobility' and was first translated as 'Adelaide'.

This was the name of King William IV's queen in the nineteenth century and from her the town in Australia was also named. She was a devout Christian.

There is also a possible link with the 'Adahs' in the book of Genesis. One was the wife of Lamech (Gen.4:19) and the other was one of the wives of Esau (Gen.36:2). In Hebrew 'Adah' means 'a decorative thing of beauty'.

"All...know...you are a woman of noble character." Ruth 3:11.

Adah

In Hebrew this lovely name means 'he adorned her'. It is the name of one of the wives of Lamech and also of Esau. The mother of Jabel and Jubal.

It would not be surprising if the names of these two children rang a bell with you because they both have interesting legends surrounding them. It is said that Jabal 'invented' civilized society and that his brother 'invented' the harp and the pipe! That must have been a happy home - I wonder which invention came first? A person may not be musical or very well organised but that doesn't prevent them being 'beautiful inside'.

"Your beauty should not come from outward adornment...Instead, it should be that of your inner self, the unfading beauty of a gentle and quiet spirit, which is of great worth in God's sight." 1 Peter 3:3-4.

Adam

In Hebrew means 'man' and is closely related to the Hebrew words for 'red' and 'ground', perhaps referring to the colour of his skin or the colour of the 'dust of the ground' from which he was formed.

The Bible is more concerned with 'why' than it is with 'how','where' and 'when'. We are told that "God created man in His own image" Gen.1:27. This means that every man, woman and child bears the imprint of the creator and in some mysterious and wonderful way is like Him.

"as we have borne the likeness of earthly man, so shall we bear the likeness of the man from heaven." 1 Cor.15:49.

Adeel Adeela Adil

From Arabic meaning someone who is 'upright and honest'. ('an ornament of God'. 1 Chron. 4:36 .).

As in so many other attributes, God sets the standard Himself - He is the only one who can rightfully claim to be 'upright and honest'. The Psalmist asked: "How can a young man keep his way pure - By living according to your (God's) word" Ps.119:9. He then went on to say "I have hidden your word in my heart that I might not sin against you." Ps.119:11. The Lord Jesus Christ also indicated that it is man's heart which is the root of the problem (Mt.15:18-19). Once our hearts are cleansed and filled with God's word we are able to be upright and honest - as He is.

"He is the Rock, his works are perfect. A faithful God who does no wrong, upright and just is he." Deut.32:4.

Adela Adelaide - see Ada

Adil - see Adeel

Adnan

The name is from Arabic and of unknown origin - according to tradition he was the ancestor of the North Arabians (this would include the Arabian Gulf and Southern Iran).

This may also have encompassed the area of Sheba - where the Queen of Sheba lived. She was the Queen who made a journey of some 2,000km to visit King Solomon and declared that ' the half had not been told her' of his wealth, glory and wonderful temple. The full story of her visit is told in 1 Kings 10 and 2 Chron. 9. The Lord Jesus Himself speaks of her in Mt.12:42 where her willingness to suffer the discomfort and danger of a long journey in order to find wisdom is contrasted with the unwillingness of His hearers to repent and believe.

The Queen of Sheba: "Praise be to the LORD your God, who has delighted in you..." 2 Chron.9:8.

Adrian Adrienne

Latin 'Hadrianus' which means 'a man of Adria'. Builder of a barrier between England and Scotland.

The 'man from Adria' was in fact, a famous Roman Emperor, soldier, and traveller called Hadrian. Whilst he was alive the Roman Empire was at its greatest and he left a valuable legacy of building and social reforms. During a visit to Britain in or around AD125 he commissioned the then Governor

Platorius Nepos to build a row of forts linked by walls to mark the northern boundary of the Empire and this is known as 'Hadrians Wall'. It stretches 110 km (73 miles) from the Tyne to Bowness on the Solway.

The "Adriatic Sea" is mentioned by Paul in Acts 27:27. During a storm on the sea Paul dreams and hears a voice. As a result of this he tells the men with him in the boat that they will be safe and that it is important to:

"...keep up your courage...have faith in God.." Acts 27:25.

Aengus - see Angus

Aftab

A light to the world!

From ancient Persian meaning 'the light of the sun' Like many names with a Persian ancestry this name uses one of the great natural forces of the universe. Not only does the sun give light and heat, but without it, the world would die in a moment!

"His face was shinning as the sun in all its brilliance. When I saw Him I fell at His feet…" Rev.1:16-17

Agatha

From Greek meaning 'good'. A 3rd century martyr. A famous detective story writer.

History is full of stories of those who have given their lives for the faith. St Agatha was almost martyred but as they were about to light the fire there was a huge earthquake - she died later in prison. She is the patron saint of Catania, Sicily. There are at least four churches named after her in Britain.

The 20th century writer Agatha Christie died in 1976. She excelled in detective stories and is as popular today.

"A woman who fears the LORD is to be praised." Prov.31:30.

Agnes Annes Annice Annis

From Greek meaning 'pure' and also possibly from the Latin 'agnus' meaning 'a lamb'. The name of a Christian martyr.

The 4th century martyr St Agnes had as her symbol a lamb because her name sounded like the Latin word meaning a lamb. She died because she refused to renounce her Christianity. In another sense she was a lamb - she was only thirteen years of age. In Scripture Jesus is described as 'the lamb of God' and in the book of Revelation He is called 'the lamb' some 30 times. Hundreds of years ago Isaiah had depicted Him in this way: "He was led like a lamb to the slaughter..." Is.53:7.

"Look, the lamb of God, who takes away the sin of the world!" John 1:29.

Aidan

Irish Gaelic for 'fire'. The name of a 7th century Bishop and missionary.

In AD633 Oswald, King of Northumbria won a decisive victory at Hexham and following this he wanted the people to learn about Christianity. He requested that someone come from the isle of Iona to be a missionary to his people. The first man was not successful so Aidan was sent instead. He is called 'the Apostle of England'.

Aidan lived and expounded the virtues of simplicity, humility and gentleness and his mission was a resounding success. He made his home on the small island of Lindisfarne which is now called 'Holy Island' as a result. It is situated on the east coast between Newcastle and Berwick-on-Tweed.

"...we went through fire and water, but you brought us to a place of abundance." Ps.66:12.

Aiesha Aisha Aishah Ayesha Ayisha Aysha

From Arabic meaning 'prospering' or 'alive, fit and well'. H.Rider Haggard used the name in his novel "She" adding the phrase: '...who must be obeyed!'

From the root Arabic word 'asha' meaning 'to live'. The name of Muhammad's third and favourite wife.

The ancient Greeks placed great emphasis on physical health and fitness, as the Olympic Games demonstrated. Physical prowess was worshipped and those who proved themselves as athletes or fighters were greatly honoured. In comparison, the Bible has little to say about physical attributes but a great deal to say about the health of the spirit.

"For physical training is of some value, but godliness has value for all things holding promise for both the present life and the life to come." 1 Tim.4:8.

Aileen Eileen Ilene Ilona - see also Elaine, Evelyn and Helen

From unknown Irish Gaelic roots in the 12th century. Brought to England in the 19th century by Irish folk fleeing the effects of the potato famine.

These names are quite obviously of Irish origin and possibly share their roots with names such as Elaine, Evelyn and Helen. The very pronunciation brings a vision of the beautiful green of Ireland with its incredible scenery and warm-hearted people. Why such a lovely place should have so sad a history is a mystery. The potato famine of 1847 meant that many Irish folk made their home in Britain and the USA - thus spreading such lovely names.

"All you have made will praise you O LORD; your saints will extol you." Ps.145:10.

Ailsa Ilsa

From the rocky island in the mouth of the Firth of Clyde called 'Ailsa Craig'.

335 metres high and composed of micro-granite the rocky island of Ailsa Craig stands like a sentinel at the entrance to the Firth of Clyde. The material is rare and it is quarried to make 'curling stones' and paving slabs.

The rock is thought to have been present since the Ice Age and is almost completely inaccessible to humans - although a few rabbits and goats make their home there. Gannets and other sea-birds also inhabit the area. A lighthouse warns approaching ships of the danger. There is a small cave on the north side.

"The LORD is my rock, my fortress and my deliverer...in whom I take refuge, my shield...my salvation." 2 Sam.22:2.

Ainsley Ainslie

Old English for 'a meadow' (from Ains-lea). 'Ains' was probably the name (or nickname) of the person who owned the meadow.

Most of us need a quiet spot where we can go to think and pray. The Psalmist must have had something like this in mind when he wrote; "He makes me lie down in green pastures, He leads me beside quiet waters, He restores my soul..." Ps.23:2-3.

This reminds us that it is not only external situations that give peace but also an internal sense of rest that we get from the ministry of the Holy Spirit.

"Come to me...and I will give you rest." Mt.11:28.

Aisha - see Aiesha

Aishah - see Aiesha

Ajay - see also Jay

From Sanskrit meaning 'I am invincible'. The dictionary definition: "unconquerable, not possible to overcome".

The truth is that no-one is that strong. Each of us is weak in certain areas and all of us are weak in the area of our ability to 'conquer' ourselves and our sinful nature and tendencies.

This is the reason Jesus came - to show us that only GOD on earth could live the perfect life and die for us. We need Him and His power - which He gives freely.

"Jesus said; I have given you authority...to overcome all the power of the enemy." Luke 10:19.

Al - see Albert

Al - see Alexander

Alan Alain Alana Allan Allen Alun

A very old name with origins in French and Celtic. It also means a Welsh stream. Streams are very prominent in the Bible.

The Bible opens with the story of creation where there was "a river watering the garden" Gen.2:10 and it closes with "the river of the water of life" Rev.22:1. In Psalm 1 we are told that a righteous man "...is like a tree planted by streams of water..." and in Psalm 23 the writer says: "He leads me beside quiet waters..." Ps.23:2.

"Whoever believes in Me...streams of living water will flow from within him." John 7:38.

Alasdair Alastair - see Alexander

Albert Alberta Al Bert Bertie Halbert

From Old English and meaning 'noble and bright'. The name of Queen Victoria's consort and many other famous people.

The ancient form of 'Albert' was 'Ethelbert' and that was the name of the King who welcomed St Augustine when he came to convert us Anglo-Saxons to Christianity in AD597.

The name was made popular in the 19th and 20th centuries by Prince Albert, Albert Einstein the great physicist and Albert Finney the actor.

"I, Jesus, have sent my angel to give you this testimony...I am...the bright Morning Star." Rev.22:16.

Aldo Aldous

From Old German meaning 'mature'. In most of Europe it is normally spelt 'Aldous'. It has been used in Eastern Europe since the 13th century. The name of many famous people.

In the New Testament the Greek word for maturity also means 'complete' or 'whole' .

The atheistic philosopher Aldous Huxley who wrote "Brave New World" and "Brave New World Revisited" died in 1963 after experimenting with drugs - hardly a 'mature' thing to do!

Popular in East Anglia and in Italy. Surnames such as 'Aldhouse', 'Aldiss' and others have come from this name.

"Perseverance must finish its work so that you may be mature...not lacking anything." Jas.1:4.

Alethea

From the Greek meaning 'truth'. One of God's great and enduring attributes. An absolute and consistent virtue.

Many people claim that truth is relative - if it is true for you then it is true -

but that is not what God says. He says that it is something which is real, complete and unchanging. Here are a few thoughts;

The Christian faith is true (Gal.2:5), Jesus mediates the truth (Jn.1:17), the Holy Spirit leads men into it (Jn.16.13), Jesus' disciples know it (Jn.8:32), and do it (Jn.3:21), the new birth rests on it (Jas.1:18), and it is God's word which must be obeyed (Rom.2:8).

"Jesus answered, 'I am the way, the truth and the life..." John 14:6.

Alexander Al Alex Alexandra Alistair Alister Alix Sandra Sandy
Gaelic form: Alasdair Alastair; Russian form: Sacha Sasha

Originally a Greek name which meant 'a defender of men'. It is interesting to see that his father carried the cross for Jesus (Mark 15:21).

Can you imagine what it must have been like for Alexander? His father would have told him the story about the day he had carried the cross for Jesus. Perhaps as they sat round the fire in the evening he would begin by saying: "...it started like any other day. I had to go into Jerusalem to buy some bread. There were crowds of people and they were all shouting 'Crucify! Crucify!' They made me carry His cross...I had never seen a crucifixion and I wondered what the man had done to deserve such a cruel death..." It's not surprising that Alexander became a Christian - his father had played a vital part in the last moments of the Saviour's life.

"I want to know Christ and the power of His resurrection and the fellowship of sharing in His sufferings..." Phil.3:10.

Alexis

From the Greek 'alexius' 'to defend' or 'protect'. A 5th century saint.

Little is known about the fifth century St Alexis of Edessa except for the fact that he had a reputation for being 'a man of God'. Edessa was an ancient city of west Mesopotamia - today it is called Urfa and is on the border of Turkey and Syria. It has some association with Abraham and was also the site of a Christian Church from the 2nd century.

Our ability 'to defend' or 'protect' will depend on how much we have allowed God to defend or to protect us.

"...our God has not deserted us...He has given us a wall of protection..." Ezra 9:9.

Alfred Alf Alfie

Old English and meaning 'good counsel'. An attribute of God and the name of a King of England.

Alfred the Great reigned in the 9th century and is famous for saving England from the Viking invasion, promoting education and personally translating many of the great Christian classics into Anglo-Saxon. He is credited with the founding of the English Navy. He set an example of what a Christian king should be like.

The advice that Jehoshaphat gave to Ahab is relevant today; "First seek the counsel of the LORD" 2 Chron.18:4.

"You guide me with your counsel, and afterwards you will take me into glory." Ps.73:24.

Alice Alicia Alison Alix Alyson Elisa Elke
From Old German meaning 'nobility'.

When the Apostle Paul wrote to the Corinthian Christians he said: "Not many of you were wise by human standards; not many were influential; not many were of noble birth." 1 Cor.1:26. We should be thankful he said "not many" - he didn't say "none". There have been some Christians of 'noble' birth and they have made a considerable impact upon their world. However, everyone who is a child of God is a 'child of the King' and therefore born into a 'royal' family.

"The nobles...assemble...for the kings of the earth belong to God; He is greatly exalted." Ps.47:9.

Alistair Alister - see Alexander

Alison - see Alice

Alix - see Alexander Alice

Allan Allen - see Alan

Allegro Allegra
From an Italian word which means 'cheerful' and a musical term which has come to mean 'at a lively pace'. Also the name of a brisk, sprightly movement in a symphony.

Cheerfulness is a constant theme in Scripture. The writer of Ecclesiastes even tried hard drink to achieve it! (Eccl.2:3.)

The book of Proverbs has the answer when it says: "A cheerful heart is good medicine, but a crushed spirit dries up the bones" Prov.17.22, and "A happy heart makes the face cheerful" Prov.15:13.

"...Cheer up!...He's calling you...he jumped to his feet and came to Jesus." Mark 10:49-50.

Alma
Originally from Latin and meaning 'bounteous'. Similar to an Spanish word for 'soul'. A river in Russia notorious since a famous battle in 1854.

An illustration of the use of this name is found in the phrase 'Alma-mater' meaning my present or past school. The exact translation being 'bounteous mother' or 'midwife'. It became popular after the Crimean battle of 1854 when the British and their allies defeated the Russians at the river Alma. A similar word in Spanish means 'soul'; this may be purely coincidental, but it is given this explanation in the 1948 play "Summer and Smoke" by the writer Tennessee Williams.

"...my people will be filled with my bounty, declares the LORD." Jer.31:14.

Alred

The name is from Old English and means 'noble' (or possibly, 'old counsel').

When the Apostle Paul wrote to the Corinthian Christians he said: "Not many of you were wise by human standards; not many were influential; not many were of noble birth." 1 Cor.1:26. We should be thankful he said "not many" - he didn't say "none". There have been some Christians of 'noble' birth and they have made a considerable impact upon their world. This name means 'noble' and everyone who is a child of God is a 'child of the King' and therefore born into a 'royal' family. Let us pray for those born of 'royal' birth who make a bold and uncompromising Christian witness.

"My heart is stirred by a noble theme as I recite my verses for the king..." Ps.45:1.

Alun - see Alan

Alyson - see Alison

Amabel Amabella

From the Latin meaning 'lovable' (from 'amabilis') and Spanish or Italian meaning 'beautiful'. Who could ask for more in a name which even sounds lovable and beautiful.

There is something about every single child that makes it loveable and beautiful and perhaps God made us like that so that we would have that extra protection when we are at our most vulnerable. As we grow older that innocent sweetness seems to disappear but it is then that we find that everyone is lovable and beautiful in one way or another. God is love and proves His love for us - what matters most is that we allow Him to make us beautiful on the inside.

"Nowhere in all the land were there found women as beautiful..." Job 42:15.

Amanda

From Latin meaning 'to be loved', 'lovable' or 'deserving love'. Three possible definitions for one lovely name.

'To be loved' is very easy and enjoyable - we were made by God to receive love and it is a basic human need which each of us has - sadly, we are not always 'lovable'. This is why we are told so often to love others and so seldom to love ourselves. 'Deserving love' - is it possible? The good news is that God loved us when we didn't deserve it.

"...God demonstrates His own love for us...While we were still sinners, Christ died for us." Rom.5:8.

Amar Amarjit

Amar is an ancient Sikh word which means 'life' or 'to be set free, to live forever'. It was a name that was often attributed to martyrs.

Since the beginning of time man has longed for the ability to live for ever. When our first ancestors sinned and disobeyed God they forfeited that right. From that sinful act mankind lost eternal life because he was cut off from the source of life. But there is a way to regain that lost estate. "For since death came through a man, the resurrection of the dead comes also through a man. For as in Adam all die, so in Christ all will be made alive." 1 Cor.15:21-22.

"Now this is eternal life: that they may know you, the only true God, and Jesus, whom you have sent." John 17:3.

Amber Amberley

A yellow translucent fossil resin used in the manufacture of jewellery. A pre-Celtic river and valley in the Peak District. When it is used in connection with traffic lights it means 'be prepared'.

In prehistoric times Amber resin exuded from trees and became fossilised. The brittle yellow-brown lumps have a distinct but not unpleasant odour and are often found in the Baltic countries. When Amber is burnt it has a bright flame. Some British villages have been called Amber - such as Ambergate which is 23 km (15 miles) north of Derby in the Peak district where you will also find the Amber river and the Amber valley.

"...be prepared to give an answer to everyone who asks you...the reason for the hope that you have." 1 Pet.3:15.

Amelia Emily Emmeline Milly

Latin 'Aemilius' meaning 'worker'. Made popular in the 14th Century by the Italian writer Boccaccio. One of the most famous Amelia's of recent years was the Suffragette Emmeline Pankhurst. She lived from 1858 to 1928 and worked tirelessly for a woman's right to vote - this was granted just ten years before she died.

Work was ordained by God and was an integral part of the activity in the garden of Eden before the fall of man. Even the Lord Jesus worked as a carpenter and Christianity has always condemned idleness.

"May the favour of the Lord our God rest upon us...yes, establish the work of our hands." Ps.90:17.

Amin Amina Amena

From Arabic for 'trustworthy', 'honest' or 'reliable'. Popular with Muslim families because it was the name of one of the prophet Mohummed's parents.

Any of these three definitions indicate a very praiseworthy attribute and most of us would be very happy if we were described in this way. A reputation in these areas takes years to secure and only moments to loose. The book of Proverbs includes admonitions concerning these virtues and Jesus said; "Trust in God, trust also in me." John 14:1.

"...a trustworthy saying...Jesus came into the world to save sinners" 1 Tim.1:15.

Amos

Hebrew meaning 'a man strong enough to carry a burden'. All we know of him he wrote himself.

Amos lived in a difficult time (probably about 760BC) when the nation of Israel was far away from God. The rich had forgotten the poor and all the people had forgotten God. With the help of five great visions Amos cried out his message to return to justice and righteousness. It was because the people had turned their backs on God that He would judge them but there would be a restoration in the future which GOD would bring about.

"Seek good not evil that you may live...Then the LORD God Almighty will be with you." Amos 5:14.

Amy Aimi

From the French 'Aimee' which means 'loved'.

To be loved is very easy - we all long for loving and unconditional acceptance. That is the way God made us - so that we can receive His love.

To love is not always easy because there are people who we find it very difficult to love. People remind us of God because we are all created in His image - this may also be the reason we find it hard to give Him our love.

God solved this problem by showing us how much we are worth to Him and how dearly He seeks our love.

"...the son of God, who loved me and gave Himself for me." Gal.2:20.

Anastasia - see Stacey

Anabel – see Annabel

Andrew Andrea Andreanna Andy - see also Drew

The name from the Greek 'Andreas' means 'strong, manly' and it is the name of one of the twelve disciples. Andrew was always bringing people to Jesus. The patron saint of Scotland.

He had been a fisherman in Bethsaida on the shores of the Sea of Galilee when Jesus challenged him to be a 'fisher of men' (see Luke 5:9-10). He responded to the call and among those he brought to Jesus was the boy with five loaves and two small fish...

He was the first Home Missionary (John 1:42) and the first Foreign Missionary (John 12:21-22). Tradition says that he was crucified for his faith.

"The first thing Andrew did was to find...Simon...and he brought him to Jesus." John 1:41-42.

Anetta - see Ann

Angela Angel Angelica Angelina Angeline
From the Greek 'Angelos' which means 'a messenger'.

Angels are powerful beings who live and work in the spiritual realms. When the angel appeared to Mary and announced the birth of Jesus, he said; "I am Gabriel. I stand in the presence of God..." Luke 1:19. It is clear that God uses these beings to convey news and make proclamations. There are many accounts of angels in the Bible both in the Old Testament and in the New Testament. Angels always do God's will - they bring blessings and good news. There have been a number of books written about the ministry of angels today.

"See, I am sending an angel ahead of you to guard you..." Ex.23:20.

Angus
Scottish Gaelic form: Aeneas Aengus Aonghas Oengus
From Scottish Gaelic meaning 'one choice'. Once a county in Scotland. A breed of beef cattle.

The old county of Forfarshire which incorporated Dundee was renamed Angus in 1928, but it is now part of the new administrative area of Tayside.

The black 'Aberdeen Angus' beef cattle were originally native to the county of Angus.

When the prophet Elisha challenged the prophets of Baal on Mount Carmel he gave them 'one choice' - to serve God or Baal. Many years later Jesus challenged people to be either 'with Him' or 'against Him'(Mt 12:30) - today that challenge remains.

"...choose this day...as for me and my household, we will serve the LORD." Josh.24:15.

Ann Anna Anne Anetta Annetta Annette Annie
(Ann, Anna and Anne are also prefixes and suffixes).
Spanish form: Anita

26

From the Hebrew 'Hannah' which means 'God has graciously favoured me'.
Hannah was the wife of Elkanah and the mother of the great prophet Samuel.
She was a woman of prayer and one day after she had been praying and
weeping in the Temple she promised God that if He gave her a son she
would dedicate him to His service. God granted her wish - see 1 Sam.1.
Her husband was very fond of her and; "he gave her a double portion -
because he loved her" 1 Sam.1:5.
"Greetings, you who are highly favoured! The Lord is with you." Luke 1:28.

Anice

From the Greek 'Aneketos' - 'to conquer'! Also similar to the names 'Aniceto'
in Spanish, Italian and Portugese. Maybe the source of the brand name 'Nike'.
The basic Greek word for this lovely name also means 'unconquered' or
'unconquerable'. It is also the source of 'Nike' and 'Nikita' - the preferred
Russian cognate. One Russian priest in the 17th century with this name
illustrated its meaning, he conquered everything in his rise to power as the
'Grand Sovereign' but ultimately failed because he couldn't 'conquer' his
own temper! He had never discovered the secret which Paul knew;
"No, in all these things we are more than conquerors through him who loved us. For I
am convinced..." Romans 8:37-38.

Annabel Anabel Anabell Annabella Annabell Annabella

From Latin meaning lovable ('amabilis') and Italian meaning beautiful. Who
could ask for more in a name?
Every man, woman and child has two rights: the right to love and the right
to be loved. Somewhere there is someone who loves you and someone you
can love - that's the way God made us. The Apostle Paul could say "...the
Son of God who loved ME and gave Himself for ME" Gal. 2:20. Someone
once wrote "I asked the Lord how much He loved me and he stretched out
both his arms and said 'this much'".
"How great is the love the Father has lavished upon us." 1 John 3:1.

Annastazia - see Stacey

Annes Annice Annis - see Agnes

Annetta Annette Annie - see Ann

Anthea

From the Greek word 'anthea' which means 'flowery'.
The Oxford dictionary defines 'flowery': "abounding in flowers, full of fine

words, full of compliments." For someone whose name means 'flowery' that could be a great ideal - people are beautiful because God made them in His image - and there are no exceptions. God has created a wonderful world - our task is to make even more wonderful by learning to blossom where He has planted us!

"O LORD, our Lord, how majestic is your name in all the earth!" Ps.8:1.

Anthony Antony Toni Tony Antonia Antonious
Russian short form: Nina

Originally from a Latin word meaning 'of great value'. Perhaps the best known Anthony of all time is the Roman Mark Antony of "Antony and Cleopatra" and "Julius Caesar" by Shakespeare.

St Anthony was the first Christian monk around the fourth century. He is noted for his battles with temptation as he lived as a recluse near the Red Sea.

The 'h' was added in the sixteenth century - possibly through Greek influence. Shakespeare uses the 'original' spelling.

"Look at the birds of the air...are you not much more valuable than they?" Mt.6:26.

Aonghas - see Angus

April - see Avril

Arabella Arbelia Bella Belle

Derived from the Latin word 'orabilis' meaning 'obliging' and 'beautiful'.

There is something very lovely about a person who is 'obliging'. The dictionary gives alternative meanings: 'to aid', 'to assist'. When the one who obliges is also 'beautiful' - then that is an extra bonus. Both attributes can be acquired so we must remember that "beauty is only skin-deep". It is more important to be 'beautiful inside' (1 Pet.3:3-4).

"I am obligated...That is why I am so eager to preach the gospel..." Rom.1:14-15.

Archibald Archie

From Old German 'Ercanbold' meaning 'noble and bold'. Used from before the Norman Conquest.

'Noble' people are featured in the Bible on many occasions. In the New Testament the Apostle Paul says "...when you were called...not many were of noble birth." 1 Cor.1:26. Whereas being 'noble' is an accident of birth, being 'bold' is an acquired attribute. When the early Church was under great pressure the disciples prayed; "Now, Lord, consider their threats and enable your servants to speak your word with great boldness." Acts 4:29.

"The wicked flees though no-one pursues but the righteous are as bold as a lion" Prov.28:1.

Arezu

From the Pharsi word 'wish'. Also, in the ancient language eastern Iran, it was the name Avestan (600-400BC), which was once used of a volcanic mountain!
To 'wish' for something can be both negative and positive. If you 'wish' in the sense that you 'dream' for things - they may never happen. However if you 'wish' in the sense of 'wanting or willing' then there is a possibility that you can make them happen and the Lord Jesus can help you!
"If you remain in me and my words remain in you, ask whatever you wish, and it will be given you." John 15:7.

Armin Arminus Herman

An ancient Germanic name with connections to the time of Christ!
This name has recently been revived – there are records dating back as far as AD21. He was an army chief who actually defeated the Romans. A modern equivalent might be 'Herman' which has been popular with German families – particularly those with socialist leanings.
"Endure hardship with us like a good soldier of Christ Jesus." 2 Tim. 2:3.

Arnold Arnaud Arnie

From Old German and Norman French 'the power of the Eagle'.
'The power of the Eagle' has been very evident throughout history - the great Roman Empire used it on its standards because it symbolised supremacy. Eagles range throughout the world and they are renowned for their stately soaring flight, their keen vision and powerful talons. When the young eaglets are learning to fly the mother will often use her body as a 'safety-net' allowing the trainee to land on her back and slide to land without harming itself.
"...how I carried you on Eagle's wings and brought you to myself." Ex.19:4.

Arran Aron – see Aaron

Arthur Art Artus

Celtic for 'bear'. First recorded in the Latinised form 'Artorius'. The famous 'King' Arthur.
Whether or not the famous 'King' Arthur and his 'Knights of the Round Table' ever lived is open to some considerable doubt - certainly there was a man who lived in or around the 6th century who fought the Saxon invaders and according to tradition is buried at Glastonbury.
Bears feature prominently in the Bible - Isaiah, Daniel and John all had visions in which Bears played a part.
"He is the maker of the bear(constellation)..." Job 9:9.

Ashima

From Sanskrit meaning 'my prayer' or 'my benediction' or from the tribe of Asher meaning 'happy'.

If it is true that "seven prayerless days make one weak" then it is also true that people of prayer are happy people. In fact, Jacob's final benediction on Asher spoke of his prosperity, particularly in the area of cuisine! (Gen.49:20).

If indeed it is from the tribe of Asher and means happiness then the owner needs to be aware of the fact that happiness is often a subjective experience. True joy comes from knowing and following Jesus.

"But may the righteous be glad and rejoice before God; may they be happy and joyful." Ps.68:3.

Ashleigh Ashley

From Old English meaning 'a burnt field' (ash-lea). The name of a great Christian reformer.

The first day of the Christian fast of Lent is called Ash Wednesday. This follows from the Old Testament practice of using ashes as a sign of penitence and mourning (dust and ashes).

Earl Ashley or as he was later known Lord Shaftesbury was one of the great Christian social reformers of the 19th century. He did much to help the working classes and children and was also involved in the YMCA, the British and Foreign Bible Society, the London City Mission, the Church Pastoral Aid Society and many other organisations.

"The LORD watches over the alien and sustains the fatherless and the widow..." Ps.146:9.

Ashraf

From Arabic meaning 'noble' or 'honourable'.

Very often we know what the noble and honourable things are - but we fail to do them. This is because our nature is sinful and fallen. The Apostle Paul has an exhortation; "Finally, brothers, whatever is true, whatever is noble, whatever is right, whatever is pure, whatever is lovely, whatever is admirable - if anything is excellent or praiseworthy - think about such things." Phil.4:8. "The LORD, the God of Israel declares...those who honour me I will honour, but those who despise me will be disdained." 1 Sam.2:30.

"But the noble man makes noble plans, and by noble deeds he stands." Is.32:8.

Astrid

From Old Norse meaning 'divine beauty'. An exquisite name with earthly and heavenly connotations.

'Divine' means of God with all the attributes that go with Him and His Majesty.

'Beauty' is an earthly word which describes some of the things made by God which appeal to our senses and cause us to feel elated or satisfied. Eventually, things of earth which satisfy us here and now will pass away and be replaced by eternal things of greater beauty and substance.

"You have set your glory above the heavens..." Ps.8:1.

Aubrey

From Old German and meaning 'elf counsel ruler'. Shakespeare used it as 'Oberon' in "A Mid-summer Night's Dream." Also J.R.R.Tolkien in "Lord of the Rings" (1954 55).

'Elves' don't always have a very good history or a good press! Traditionally they are the 'baddies'. They are usually mischievous. However, in Tolkien's 'Lord of the Rings' they are noble and show ancient wisdom.

In the real world we know that bad things are caused by people and not imaginary beings. Men and women are sinful and in need of a Saviour. God, in His love and mercy has provided that Saviour.

"To God belong wisdom and power; counsel and understanding are His." Job 12:13.

Audrey

From the old English 'Etheldreda' 'noble strength'. Also a Saint of the 6th century.

St Audrey was known by the Latinised form of her name 'Etheldreda'. She died from a tumour on the neck - which she endured all her life assuming that it was a divine punishment for her love of necklaces. A number of churches and Ely Cathedral are dedicated to her so clearly, many appreciated her 'noble strength'. The cathedral was built in 1080 on the site of the old wooden building which preceded it. Parts of it are clearly Norman and there are some lovely carvings in the nave and choir. The west front is particularly imposing.

"The LORD is my strength and my song; He has become my salvation." Ex.15:2.

Austin Austen

Originally from the Latin for 'venerable' or 'distinguished'. Two Church leaders, a novelist and a motorcar.

This name shares its history with other 'august' and famous people because it comes from the same root word as 'Augustine'. There were two famous Church leaders named Augustine - one was an African Bishop who was called Augustine of Hippo and the other was the one who converted the heathen Anglo-Saxons at the end of the 5th century.

Jane Austen (1775-1817) was the daughter of a Christian Minister and her novels were about ordinary people.

One of the most valuable vintage motorcars is the Austin 7. When it was made in 1922 it was the perfect family car.

"With my mouth I will greatly extol the LORD; in the great throng I will praise him." Ps.109:30.

Aveline - see Evelyn

Avril April Averil

From the French for 'April' also the name of a 7th century Saint.

The Latin word 'aperire' which looks and sounds like 'April' means 'to open' and presumably this is a reference to Spring and the 'opening' of the buds etc. Certainly, April is a wonderful spring month. The first day of the month is known as "April-fools Day" and the traditional practice is to send people on a 'fools' errand or deceive them in some way.

The Bible has a lot to say about fools and foolishness particularly in the book of Proverbs.

"The fear of the LORD is the beginning of knowledge but fools despise wisdom." Prov.1:7.

Avtar

A Sanskrit word meaning 'an incarnation'. The Oxford dictionary definition includes: "The process of forming new flesh", "an embodiment in flesh" and "an impersonation of another living human".

In the west when one speaks of "the Incarnation" it normally refers to the Lord Jesus Christ - God made man. It is also used when we want to describe someone who is an exact likeness of someone else - "he is the incarnation of..." The fact is that we are all made in the 'likeness' of God - but the Lord Jesus Christ was unique - as was His incarnation.

"So God created man in His own image, in the image of God He created him." Gen.1:27.

Ayesha Ayisha Aysha - see Aiesha

Ayrton

From Old English meaning; 'a farm on the river Aire'

'Airtone' was originally called 'Airtone in Kirby Malham' but the villages are now two distinct communities.

The racing driver Ayrton Senna was a committed Christian – on the racing circuit he was one of the most daring. His death at 186 mph during the San Marino Grand Prix plunged his home nation into deep mourning.

"… like a champion rejoicing to run his course." Psalm 19:5.

B

Balaji

From an ancient Sanskrit word meaning 'strong'. The name of a famous Peshwa in the 18-19 century.

This name comes from ancient Sanskrit – which was Indo-European literary language of India. The word 'Sanskrit' comes from two words 'Sans' which means 'put together' and 'karoti' which means 'he creates'.

The Peshwa (ruler) was a 'strong' man in many ways – but that did not stop him seeking the protection of the British in 1802 through the treaty of Bassein.

The strongest man who ever lived sought God in his hour of need. In one last desparate act Samson cried out to God to help him – and his prayer was answered!

"Samson prayed to the Lord, 'O sovereign LORD, remember me..." Judges 16:28.

Balvinder

From Sanskrit 'strong'. The strongest man that ever lived was weak in at least ONE area.

One of the first definitions of 'strong' is "...having the power of resistance..." Accepting this definition means that the 'strongest man who ever lived' was, in fact, one of the weakest. Samson was attracted to beautiful women and his weakness for them was to prove his downfall. Physical strength is a great gift but strength of character is a greater gift. A person may be able to run, jump, lift etc., but is he strong inside?

"O Sovereign LORD, you have begun to show to your servant your greatness and your strong hand. For what God is there in heaven or on earth who can do the deeds and mighty works you do?" Deut.3:24.

Barbara Babette Barbie Barbra

From a Greek source suggesting 'unconventional and foreign'. The earliest record is the 3rd century.

The 3rd century story of St Barbara is of a young girl who defied her father by becoming a Christian. When her father heard of this he personally tortured and executed her. He was struck by lightning as he returned home and died immediately. Barbara is the patron saint of miners and artillerymen.

There have been many martyrs down through the centuries but few people realise that there have been more in the 20th century than in the total of all the previous centuries.

"The islanders (in Greek:'barbaroi') showed us unusual kindness..." Acts 28:2.

Barnabas Barnaby

Hebrew meaning 'son of consolation' or 'encouragement' (Acts 4:36). A companion of St Paul.

Luke says that Barnabas was "a good man, full of the Holy Spirit and faith." Acts 11:24. He was always there when he was needed - sometimes at very critical points in the development of the fledgling Church.

However, one of Barnabas' greatest strengths lies hidden in the text of the book of Acts. Up to the 13th chapter of Acts it is "Barnabas and Saul", after Cyprus it is always "Paul and Barnabas". Such was the stature of the man that when the time came for him to take second place he was able to do it with grace and humility.

"...the God who gives...encouragement give you a spirit of unity...as you follow...Jesus" Rom.15:5.

Barrie Barry

Irish Gaelic 'one who is fair-haired'. Sir James Barrie the author who wrote of Peter Pan.

A whole variety of Celtic names form the basis of the word for fair-haired and these are two of them.

There is also a Welsh connection - the district and Island of Barry in South Wales were named after the hermit who lived there very many years ago.

Sir James Barrie wrote the popular stories of the boy who never grew up. There is a statue of Peter Pan in Kensington Gardens as a memorial to him.

"..anyone who will not receive the kingdom of God like a little child will never enter it." Mark 10:15

Bartholomew Bart

Surname of Nathanael, Hebrew meaning 'son of Talmai' (Talmai was a giant).

He met Jesus and Jesus saw that he was a good man. The story of Nathanael whose second name was Bar-tholomew and his meeting with Jesus is told in the 1st chapter of John's gospel. He was from Cana in Galilee and was brought to Jesus by Philip. When Jesus met him He told him things that revealed He was God's son - the Messiah. Nathanael recognised Jesus as the Son of God and the King of Israel. Later on, Nathanael was one of the witnesses to the resurrection of Jesus.

"...Nathanael declared, - Rabbi, you are the Son of God; you are the King of Israel." John 1:49.

Basil Bas
Russian form: Vassili Vassily

From Greek 'basileios' meaning 'kingly'. A 4th century Bishop. A sweet-smelling herb.

It was possibly brought to Europe by the returning Crusaders.

Great Basil was a 4th century Bishop who lived in Caesarea and in spite of strong Roman opposition and heretical influences maintained a firm Biblical faith.

Basil is also the name of a sweet-smelling herb of the mint family used for seasoning food and for its fragrance.

"But you are a chosen people, a royal priesthood..." 1 Pet.2:9.

Beatrice Bea Beatrix Beat Trixie - see also Benedict

From Latin (Beatrix) meaning 'one who brings blessings'. Literary connections.

Both Dante and Shakespeare used the name, and more recently it has become famous through the writer Beatrix Potter - who will ever forget "The Tales of Peter Rabbit"? Even royalty are now calling their children 'Beatrice'.

In Dante's "Divine Comedy" it was Beatrice who guided the poet through Paradise and no doubt, Dante had in mind the Latin root of the name 'one who brings blessings'.

"...I have set before you life and death - choose life...love the LORD your God..." Deut.30:19-20.

Becca Beccie Becky Beckie - see Rebecca

Belinda Linda

Spanish for 'pretty' and similar to an Old German word which means 'wise and supple'.

A combination of Spanish and Old German meanings for this name seem to cover everything. If they are listed in order of importance; 'Wisdom' - Solomon was commended by God because he asked for "wisdom and knowledge" 2 Chron.1:10 - someone has said that wisdom is 'education in action'. 'Supple' - or bodily fitness. The Apostle Paul says that this benefits - a little (see 1 Tim.4:8). 'Pretty' - or good looks. Scripture is full of warnings about physical appearance being the sole criteria for judging people - it is more important that we are 'beautiful inside'.

"Man looks at the outward appearance, but the LORD looks at the heart." 1 Sam.16:7.

Benedict Benedic Benito Bennet

From the Latin 'Benedictus' which means 'blessed'. A 5th century Italian Saint

and an alternative title to "Much Ado About Nothing".
Few people realise that "Much Ado About Nothing" was once performed under the title of "Benedict and Beatrice". This was in 1613 and in the presence of King James.
The most well-known 'Benediction' is the 'Aaronic blessing' recorded in Num.6:22-26.
"The LORD bless you and keep you; the LORD make his face shine upon you..."
Num.6:24-25.

Benjamin Ben Bennie

From Hebrew meaning 'the son of my right hand'. The tribe which had a reputation for bravery.
The story of the birth and life of Benjamin is one of the most fascinating in Scripture. His father Jacob was deeply in love with his mother Rachel from the moment he met her until the day she died whilst giving birth to Benjamin. This meant that Benjamin always held a very special place in his father's heart. The full story is told in Genesis chapter 35.
Today we speak of someone being "my right-hand man". God's 'right-hand man' is Jesus.
"Sit at my right hand until I make your enemies a footstool for your feet." Heb.1:13.

Bennet - see Benedict

Berenice Berenitz

From the Greek 'Pherenike' meaning 'the one who brings victory'.
'Victory' in the Bible is always God's - although He often uses men to achieve it. Sometimes He brings victory in so-called impossible situations such as the time when David met the giant Goliath. On that occasion David's proclamation was; "...the battle is the Lord's..." 1 Sam.17:47. The purpose of this is to demonstrate His glory. This is similar to the New Testament where the people of God enter into His victory through faith .
"...thanks be to God! He gives us the victory through our Lord Jesus Christ." 1 Cor.15:57.

Bernard Bernadette

An Old German name which means 'as brave as a bear'. Also the name of a number of 'Saints'.
One of the saints was St Bernard of Menthon and it was he who gave his name to the Saint Bernard dogs. Another was St Bernard of Clairvaux who is credited with the hymns "Jesus the very thought of Thee" and "Jesus, Thou joy of loving hearts". He was a dominant and controversial figure in the 12th century.

In Bible times the bear was more feared than the lion and this is why the prophet Amos said it was impossible to escape the judgement of God.
"It will be as though a man fled from a lion - only to meet a bear" Amos 5:19.

Bert - see Albert Herbert Robert

Bertha

From Old English meaning 'noble and bright'. The male form 'Albert' was the name of Queen Victoria's consort.
The ancient form of 'Bertha' was 'Ethelbert' and that was the name of the King who welcomed St Augustine when he arrived in England to convert the Anglo-Saxons to Christianity in AD597.
The male form of the name was made popular in the 19th and 20th centuries by Prince Albert and it is said that Queen Victoria and he were so in love that she never quite recovered from his death. The Albert Memorial opposite the Royal Albert Hall was built by her to perpetuate her love and remembrance of him.
"Those who are wise will shine like the brightness of the heavens, and those who lead many to righteousness, like the stars for ever and ever." Dan.12:3.

Bertie - see Albert, Herbert or Robert

Bertram Bertrand

From Old German meaning 'bright raven'.
The first part of the name has been made popular in the 19th and 20th centuries by Prince Albert, Albert Einstein the great physicist and Albert Finney the actor.
The Raven is a significant bird in the Bible. It was the first bird that Noah sent out from the Ark (Gen.8:7), man is forbidden to eat it (Lev.11:15), Elijah was fed by the ravens (1 Kings 17:4) and God provides them with food (Job 38:41).
"Consider the ravens: They do not sow or reap, they have no storeroom or barn; yet God feeds them. And how much more valuable you are than birds!" Luke 12:24.

Beryl

From the Greek 'beryllos' the name for a mineral - from which we get the emerald. A very precious commodity.
The mineral called 'beryl' is a valuable gem substance and the chief commercial ore of beryllium. Pure beryl is colourless and transparent. Emerald, one of the most valuable gems, is a green-coloured variety. The other varieties are less valuable and they include the blue, the golden and the rose beryl.

The Bible speaks of beryl: It formed part of the decoration for the priest's breastplate (Ex.28:17). It is part of the eternal Jerusalem coming down out of heaven from God (Rev.21:20).

"....four rows of precious stones....a beryl...." Ex.39:10.

Bess Bessie Bessy Betsy Bette Betty - see Elizabeth

Bethany

This is the name of a beautiful village on the slopes of the Mount of Olives where Jesus loved to spend time with His friends Mary, Martha and Lazarus. The Hebrew word means 'the house of unripe figs'.

The meaning of the name and other indications confirm that the 'Mount of Olives' was more thickly wooded than now. Bethany was also the place where Jesus raised Lazarus from the dead and visitors can see the house where this is reputed to have happened. John 11:35-44. It was at Bethany that the woman anointed the feet of Jesus with expensive perfume. The disciples were unhappy about this but Jesus said she had done it to prepare Him for burial.

"...to the vicinity of Bethany, He lifted up his hands and blessed them." Luke 24:50.

Beulah

From Hebrew meaning 'rejoicing over you'. Applied to the land of Israel. John Bunyan called it 'the land of heavenly joy'. The title of a novel.

An ancient hymn says; "Oh Beulah land, sweet Beulah land, as on the highest mount I stand; I look away beyond the sea where mansions are prepared for me..."

The Old Testament says; "as a bridegroom rejoices over his bride, so will your God rejoice over you." Is.62:5.

Augusta Evans Wilson wrote a best-selling novel entitled Beulah. John Bunyan used the name in his famous book The Pilgrim's Progress.

"Thou shalt no more be termed Forsaken; neither shall thy land any more be termed Desolate: but thou shalt be called Hephzibah, and thy land Beulah: for the LORD delighteth in thee," Is.62:4 KJV.

Beverley Beverly

From Old English and meaning 'a beaver-meadow(lea)'.

The Old English 'bever-lea' is a wonderful and very descriptive name. 'Lea' is the name for a meadow and this would normally mean a modest field where one man could graze his animals and grow the crops he needed to support himself and his family.

The beaver is an aquatic creature so he would not be in the field unless there was a stream running through it. What a lovely peaceful picture - a

small meadow, a stream running through it and beavers.
"You will keep him in perfect peace...because he trusts in you..." Is.26:3.

Bill Billie Billy - see William

Bjorn

Norwegian word meaning 'a bear'.
The bear is a large carnivorous animal closely related to racoons, pandas and the dog family. Although classified as flesh-eating, most species (other than the polar bear) are mainly vegetarian - but they will eat almost anything.
The bear in the Bible is most likely to be the Syrian Brown Bear which is now very rare - the last one in Israel was killed in the 1930s. David killed bears whilst guarding his father's sheep (1 Sam.17).
The Great Bear or Plough is also a constellation. It includes the two stars which we use as 'pointers' to find the Pole Star.
"Better to meet a bear robbed of her cubs than a fool in his folly." Prov.17:12.

Blake

From Old English meaning 'a dark complexion'.
There have been many famous 'Blakes' in English history. Admiral Robert Blake (1599-1657) fought for the right of English democracy under Cromwell. William Blake (1757-1827) was one of our finest artists and poets although not really understood in his lifetime. His final work, "The everlasting Gospel" was never completed. Both of these men were Christians.
The 'Song of Songs' or 'Song of Solomon' is a group of love-poems which are sometimes erotic but describe a purity of love which is often purer than ours. In the first chapter dark skin is clearly an attractive feature.
"Dark am I yet lovely O daughters of Jerusalem..I am dark because I am darkened by the sun." S.of S.1:5-6.

Blaise

From the French region of Blois or a Latin word for a speech impediment. A famous philosopher.
This name was first recorded early in the 4th century when a Bishop of this name was martyred in Armenia. More recently, the Christian philosopher Blaise Pascal (1623-1662) made his impact on the world of physics, literature and Christianity. His arithmetical machine was built to assist his father in his work as a tax official but laid the basic principles for digital computers that were to come many years later. In 1654 he had a personal experience of Jesus Christ and was an evangelical Christian for the

39

remainder of his short life.
"The mouth of the righteous man utters wisdom, and his tongue speaks what is just."
Ps.37:30.

Blodwen

From Welsh meaning 'white flower in bloom' derived from the name of a beautiful woman in Welsh medieval romance. A lovely Welsh opera.
One of the loveliest languages is the Welsh tongue spoken, or preferably sung, by someone who is Welsh. This side of heaven there is rarely a more beautiful sound. The annual International Eisteddfod is held each year at LLangollen and attracts some of the best choirs in the world as well as poetry, dancing and other Welsh folk arts. The first Welsh opera to be performed was called "Blodwen" by Dr Joseph Parry in 1879.
"Like the crocus, it will burst into bloom..." Is.35:1.

Bob Bobbie Bobby - see Robert

Bonnie

A topical word from Scotland - sometimes known as 'Bonnie Scotland'! Made famous by the films 'Bonnie and Clyde' and 'Gone with the Wind'. From the Spanish 'Bonita'.
The Spanish word means 'physically attractive' and the first word to come from it was the English word 'bonny' which means healthy, robust and looking good! These may be very welcome exterior qualities but the New Testament writer thought that real beauty;
"...should be that of your inner self, the unfading beauty of a gentle and quiet spirit..."
1Pet.3:4.

Boyd

From Scottish Gaelic meaning 'from the isle of Bute'. A name with a fascinating history.
Scotland is a very beautiful country of some 5 million people who are warm-hearted and generous. From north to south it measures some 435 km (274 miles) and is 250 km (154 miles) wide. Nowhere can you be more than 65 km (40 miles) from the coast. It includes 186 islands and many Lochs. One of its most interesting islands is the island of Bute in the Firth of Clyde - separated from the mainland by a winding strait called the Kyles of Bute.
"Sing to the LORD...you who go down to the sea...you islands, and all who live in them." Is. 42:10.

Bradley Brad

From Old English. In the West country a 'broad-lea' is a wide field. Bred-leah' is a source of wood.

This name forms part of many local village and town names e.g. Braddock, Bradfield, Bradninch. It is also a name in its own right in Derbyshire and Wiltshire. 'A wide field' speaks of space and affluence - normally a man would only own enough land to support himself and his family. It would be difficult to imagine a field without trees. Trees provide so much that is essential to our well-being and survival. Growing or being fashioned they are beautiful - is it so surprising that Jesus was a carpenter?

"...isn't this the carpenter? Isn't this Mary's son?" Mark 6:3.

Brandon Brendan Brenda

From 'Brendon' a Welsh source meaning 'a royal child'. It is also found in the Shetland Islands where it means 'a sword'. The Old English means 'a hill where broom grows'.

There is a legend which says that St Brendan discovered America in the 6th century. He was Irish and is credited with very many other adventures. This legend was re-enacted in the 1970s by a man called Severin, who sailed a two-masted oxhide curragh from Ireland to Iceland and Newfoundland - so proving that it could have been possible.

Sir Walter Scott used the Norse translation 'Brand' in his novel "The Pirate".

A royal child, a sword or a broomstick, like everyone else you have a choice - which will you be?

"I the LORD will be their God, and my servant...will be prince among them." Ez.34:24.

Brett

From Latin meaning 'a Briton'.

There some things in life that we can change but there are many that we cannot. Our nationality is one of the things which we cannot change. Most people are proud of their country and happily boast about its climate, achievements, standing or size. When something happens that makes us ashamed of our country, we try to excuse its shortcomings.

The Bible speaks about 'dual nationality' - the people who know and love Jesus have another passport!

"..our citizenship is in heaven. And we eagerly await a Saviour...the Lord Jesus Christ." Phil.3:20.

Brian Brien Brion Briony Bryan Bryony

Celtic name for 'hill of strength'. Brian Boru was an Irish King in the 11th century who was constantly fighting the Danes.

The Psalmist cries: "I will lift up mine eyes unto the hills..." Ps.121:1 and the prophet Isaiah says; "Though the mountains be shaken and hills be removed, yet my unfailing love for you will not be shaken...says the LORD." Is.54:10.

The words for 'hills' and 'mountains' are inter-changeable in scripture. They often speak of the difficult times in life but are also identified as one of the oldest parts of creation. ('Bryony' is also the name of two climbing plants).

"I lift up my eyes to the hills...My help comes from the Lord." Ps.121:1-2.

Bridget Bride Bridgid Brigid Brigit Brigitta Bridgitte Britt

From Irish Gaelic and meaning 'strength (of character)'. The name of a 6th century saint.

St Bridget lived in the 6th century and is the saint of pity and mercy. She was born to a slave in Dundalk. Later she gained her freedom and founded a shelter for refuge and prayer at Kildare.

When we speak of someone being 'a strong character' we usually mean that they have a determination which is above average. Some people in history have been physically weak but spiritually strong.

"...the weakness of God is stronger than man's strength." 1 Cor.1:25.

Brien - see Brian

Brin - see Bryn

Briony Bryony Brion- see Brian

Britt - see Bridget

Bronwen Bronwyn

From Welsh meaning 'white and fair'. A Welsh name with lots of history.

This name, has long been a great favourite in Wales and has many associations with folk legends there.

'White and fair' is a good description of a lady. Particularly when white is a description of her conscience and fair is a description of her character. "White as snow" is a Bible term for God's promised forgiveness and cleansing in Is.1:18. 'Fairness' is a characteristic we all strive to achieve - God promises that we can acquire it if we will first of all trust Him and His word (Prov.2:9).

"Though your sins are like scarlet they shall be as white as snow..." Is.1:18.

Brooke Brook
Meaning 'a small river'. A source of life and a thing of beauty.
Rivers run through the Bible. We are told that one of the features of the garden of Eden was "a river that flowed from Eden.." Gen.2:10. This was the source of life for the plants because 'rain' had not yet begun to fall (Gen.2:5-6). In the middle of the Bible we have the book of Psalms. Psalm 1. says that a 'righteous' person is "...like a tree planted by streams of water..." Ps.1:3. In the closing chapter of the Bible we read "..the angel showed me the river of the water of life..." Rev.22:1.
"..this is what the LORD says; I will extend peace to her like a river..." Is.66:12.

Bruce
Originally French 'de Bruis' from Cherbourg around 1066. Also a descendant who was equally brave for a greater king.
The first Robert Bruce came over with William the Conqueror and he died around 1094. He founded the Scottish Bruces in the area of Dumfries and Galloway. For over 200 years they fought the English for the Scottish throne and founded the Stuart house of Scottish kings who later became kings of England as well.
Five hundred years later a descendant of the original Robert Bruce also named Robert Bruce had a deep spiritual experience whilst studying law in Paris. Within a few years he was made Moderator for the Church of Scotland. His bold preaching brought him into conflict with King James IV (1473-1513) and he was confined to Inverness for his last 30 years.
"Therefore, since we have such a hope, we are very bold." 2 Cor.3:12.

Bryan - see Brian

Bryn Brin
Welsh for 'hill' and the name of a number of places in and around Wales.
Brynmawr is the largest town in Breconshire - it owes its presence to the mining and smelting industries of the 19th and 20th centuries. Bryn Mawr College is a famous college in Pennsylvania - presumably named by a home-sick Welshman. Bryn Paulin is the hill on which the smallest cathedral in the UK is built - St Asaph's in Flintshire.
Hills feature prominently in the Bible - most of God's great transactions were carried out on a hill or mountain.
"Praise awaits you, O God, in Zion...the hills are clothed with gladness." Ps.65:1-12.

Bryony - see Brian

Caius - see Gaius

Caitlin – see Karen

Caleb Kalab

From Hebrew meaning 'whole-hearted' or 'intrepid, bold' or 'from the heart' (an uncertain origin). An outstanding man who would not be intimidated by giants.

There are four 'Calebs' in the Old Testament but the most famous of them was Caleb ben Jephunneh of Numbers 13 and 14. He was one of twelve spies that Moses sent to spy out Canaan and one of two that brought back a positive report. Because of his loyalty to God he was rewarded by being allowed to survive the wandering in the wilderness and to enter the promised land. At the age of eighty-five he conquered Hebron.

"Only do not rebel against the LORD. And do not be afraid of the people of the land, because we will swallow them up...the LORD is with us. Do not be afraid of them." Num.14:9.

Callum Calum

An original Irish name with a Latin source meaning 'a dove'. Adopted by Scotland around the 6th century through St Columba and changed to form the basis of many other Scottish names.

The dove has always been the symbol of peace. In the Bible it is also the symbol of the Holy Spirit. It was a dove that Noah sent out from the ark in order to find out if the waters had receded (Gen.8). It was a dove that formed the basis of the sacrificial offering in the wilderness (Lev.1:14). The Psalmist cried "Oh for the wings of a dove" Ps.55:6. The Apostle John said; "I saw the spirit come down from heaven as a dove...on Him." John 1:32.

"The peace of God...will guard your hearts and minds...in Christ Jesus." Phil.4:6.

Calvin

The surname of the 16th century French reformer John Calvin (1509-1564). Popular in Scotland.

The next time you hear someone talking about 'Election' be careful - they may not be talking politics! 'Election' is one of the five points of

'Calvinism'. Calvin was a young student in Paris when he began to see the many faults in the established church. He was so radical that he had to seek refuge in Strasbourg. He finished in Geneva which was quite a corrupt city in those days. Through his efforts the city was reformed and he dominated it for some years. As well as spiritual input he spearheaded major social reforms. By the age of 55 he was burned out for God. Just 25 days before he died he wrote; "It is enough that I live and die for Christ."
"For to me to live is Christ and to die is gain." Phil.1:21.

Cameron

This name has Gaelic origins and is the name of a famous Scottish clan.
Scotland covers an area of nearly 97,000 square kilometres (30,000 sq.miles) but this includes some 186 islands in three main groups - the Hebrides or 'Western Isles', the Orkney Islands and the Shetland Islands. All-in-all it is a beautiful land with many lochs and mountains. The clans are no longer as powerful as they once were but still form a part of the traditional culture. The clan was originally composed of family members with a single head or 'Laird'. The Scots are deeply religious people and this comes from a Puritan ethic dating back to the 16th century and the influence of John Knox and of Calvin.
"Then we will not turn away from you; revive us and we will call on your name." Ps.80:18.

Camilla Milla

Roman origin - from a legend where she was a great fighter and a swift runner.
As long ago as 1205 the name Camilla was used in Britain. It has a warm friendly feel to it and is an ideal choice for a lady because, like the originator, many ladies have hidden and undiscovered talents which only emerge in difficult or trying situations.
The male form of Camilla is 'Camillus' and he was a soldier in the Venetian army in 1574. When he received an incurable wound he was discharged and left to die. He became a Christian, recovered and now is the patron saint of sick people and nurses.
"The race is not to the swift or the battle to the strong...but time and chance happen to them all." Eccl.9:11.

Cara

From Latin meaning 'dear' and from Italian meaning 'beloved'. A 'sweet' name with meaning.
'Dear' is a well-known expression of love and affection but it means more than that - it means precious and valued. It is something someone says about someone else.

When we say 'beloved' it is a little different. To be beloved means that I not only receive love but that I also give it. That is not always easy because some people are very hard to love and even the nicest people are hard to love sometimes.

"But God demonstrates His own love for us in this: while we were still sinners, Christ died for us." Rom.5:8.

Carina

From Latin meaning 'dear' and from Italian meaning 'beloved'. A very sweet name with a deep meaning which will be difficult to live up to!

'Dear' is a well-known expression of love and affection but it means more than that - it means precious and valued. It is something someone says about someone else.

When we say 'beloved' it is a little different! To be beloved means that I not only receive love but that I also give it! Now, that is not always easy because some people are very hard to love and even the nicest people are hard to love sometimes.

"But God demonstrates His love for us in this: While we were still sinners, Christ died for us." Rom.5:8

Caris - see Grace

Carl Karl - see Charles

Carla Carly
Feminine form of 'Charles', 'Carlo' or 'Carl'.
From the Greek word 'Chara' (pronounced 'khar-ra') which means 'joy'.

Joy is in the Bible many times as a description of the feelings of those who love and follow God. The words 'joy', 'joyful' or 'joyfully' occur nearly 250 times and there are as many in the Old Testament as there are in the New.

Joy is different from happiness. JOY is not the absence of suffering but the presence of God. So Paul and Silas could rejoice having been beaten and thrown into prison (Acts 16). They knew they were doing what was right. An old acrostic of 'JOY' spells Jesus Others Yourself.

"..the joy of the LORD is your strength." Neh.8:10.

Carlisle Carlyle

'Strong in God' from the fourth century (Roman) with Norman-French and Welsh connections. A town in Cumbria.

The complex history of this name dates from Roman times when a town in Cumbria was called 'Luguvalio' or 'Luguvallium' which meant 'strong in the god'. The Normans wrote the sounds which they heard and so it became

'Cair Luel' - 'Cair' being the ancient Welsh word for a fortified city and 'Luel' being the way 'Luguvalio' was pronounced in the 8th century. Today Carlisle stands on the border of England and Scotland at the western end of Hadrian's Wall and has a population approaching 100,000. Its charter dates from the twelfth century.
"We have a strong city; God makes salvation its walls and ramparts." Is.26:1.

Carol Carola Carole Carolina Caroline Carolyn Carric

These names are associated with hymns sung at Christmas time but the name 'Carol' began as the name of a 'round dance' in the 15th century. The author of Alice...

Charles Lutwidge Dodgson, a mathematician, was very fond of his friend's daughter and decided to write a story for her which he called "Alice in Wonderland". Because he was a famous mathematician he felt that he should use a pseudonym and he chose Carroll - Lewis Carroll. He, his family and his friend were all Christians. He may have been influenced by the 'carols' which were being sung at that time which were dance tunes.

In fact today, not all hymns sung at Christmas are carols and there are carols for other times of the year.

Have you noticed that Christianity is the only 'singing' religion? Paul and Silas even sang in prison (Acts 16).
"An evil man is snared...by his sin...a righteous one can sing..." Prov.29:6.

Caron - see Karen

Carrie - see Carol

Carter

An ancient craft-name. The 39th President of the USA. An English village.

A 'carter' was an ancient carrier whose services were keenly sought. Today we still speak of "putting the cart before the horse" (getting things round the wrong way), a "cart-track" (a poor road), a "cart-load" (a heavy load).

Jimmy Carter the 39th President of the USA lost the Governorship of Georgia in 1966. Shortly afterwards he had a 'born-again' experience and won the Governorship in 1970 and was made President in 1976. Before that time he was an 'unknown' candidate from the Deep South.

Carterton (Carter-town) is an English village 18 miles west of Oxford. It was founded by a Mr Carter in 1901.
"You crown the year with your bounty, and your carts overflow with abundance." Ps.65:11.

Carys

From a Welsh source meaning 'love'. The greatest of the three great and lasting attributes!

The very nature of God and the heart of the Christian message.

'God is love' - almost everyone will know this timeless phrase although not everyone may appreciate its depth of meaning. God demonstrated His love for us when He sent the Lord Jesus Christ to die on the cross for us - now when people ask God how much He loves them He shows them His son with his arms outstretched on the cross and He says "this much"! All human love whether it is for Him or for others has its source in God.

And now these three remain: faith, hope and love. But the greatest of these is love. 1 Corinthians 13:13.

Casey

From an ancient Irish surname meaning 'vigilant in war'.

There have been a number of Caseys in history - from the ballad of Casey-Jones to the famous coach of the New York Yankees in 1975 (who actually called himself 'Casey' by taking the initials of his home town Kansas City!).

The Bible picture is of Nehemiah who, in spite of intense opposition, rebuilt the walls of Jerusalem; "Those who carried materials did their work with one hand and held a weapon in the other." Neh.4:17.

"Be on your guard; stand firm in the faith; be men of courage; be strong." 1 Cor.16:13

Catharine Catherine Cathleen Cathy Catriona - see Karen Cecil Cecilia Celia

From Latin meaning 'unseeing'.

Originally, it was the name of a Roman family and became popular in the 19th century because English aristocracy thought that it sounded fashionable. Cecil Rhodes who gave his name to Rhodesia (now Zimbabwe and Zambia).

St Cecilia was a pagan woman who became a Christian and then brought her husband to Christ. As a result they were both martyred together sometime in the 3rd century. She was a very fine singer and it is said that she sang hymns whilst being tortured for her faith. Because of this she became the patron saint of musicians.

"Greater love has no-one than this, that one lay down his life for his friends." John 15:13.

Cedric

From Welsh 'Cedrych' meaning 'a pattern of generosity'. A close association with the aristocracy.

Sir Walter Scott may have made a slip when he wrote the title character of his novel 'Ivanhoe' - instead of calling him 'Cerdic' he created the new and exciting name of 'Cedric'. Later, Mrs F.H. Burnett had no doubt about the name of the hero in her book 'Little Lord Fauntleroy' - it had to be 'Cedric'. The Welsh origin is a great ideal - but generosity does not come naturally, it has to be cultivated. The first two chapters of the book of Ephesians have some good examples of generosity of language and of love. Paul stretches the bounds of language to describe God's generosity in sending Christ to be our Saviour.

"...like the working of His mighty strength which He exerted when He raised Him from the dead..." Eph.1:19-20.

Celina Celine - see Selina

Ceri Keri

Probably from the Welsh word 'Carwen' which means 'fair love'.
The 'C' should always be pronounced as a hard 'K'. This name is from the Welsh word Carwen meaning 'fair love'. Alternatively, it could also be an abbreviated form of the welsh name 'Ceridwen' which also means 'fair' and was the name of the goddess of inspirational poetry in Welsh mythology.

"As the Father has loved me, so have I loved you. Now remain in my love." John 15:9.

Chander Chandra Chandrakala

Sanskrit meaning 'the moon'. The great 'lesser light'. A sign of the coming King (Luke 21:25).
The moon was created by God and it is called "the lesser light - to govern the night" Gen.1:16. From the beginning of civilisation man has sought to worship the created rather than the Creator and the moon has been the object of veneration by many tribal groups. In particular it was a god in Ur (the city that Abraham moved from) and significantly, a crescent-shaped moon has been found carved on statues of ancient deities. We are not to worship the creation - see Deut.4:19.

"...the sun to govern the day, His love endures forever. The moon and stars to govern the night; His love endures forever." Ps.136:8-9.

Chantal Chantalle Chantel Chantelle

From French meaning 'a stone'.
Because of its French origin this name must always be pronounced 'Shan-tal'. The source is uncertain but we do know that there was 16th century saint by the name of Jeanne Francoise de Chantal. Like many other surnames, this is now a popular Christian name and it has a lovely French 'ring' to it.

Stones and the significance of 'stone' is used for a number of purposes in Scripture.

"Now to you who believe, this stone is precious. But to those who do not believe, The stone the builders rejected has become the capstone." 1 Pet.2:7.

Charis - see Grace

Charles Charlene Charlie Charlotte Charmaine Charmian
German form: Carl Karl

From the Greek word 'Chara' (pronounced 'khar-ra') which means 'joy'. The French feminine form was made popular by the daughter of George IV, Princess Charlotte.

The words 'joy', 'joyful' or 'joyfully' occur nearly 250 times in the Bible and there are as many in the Old Testament as there are in the New Testament. It has been said that 'JOY is not the absence of suffering but the presence of God'. So Paul and Silas could rejoice when they had been beaten and thrown into prison (Acts 16). They knew they were doing what was right.

"There, in the presence of the LORD your God, you and your families shall eat and shall rejoice in everything you have put your hand to, because the LORD your God has blessed you." Deut.12:7.

Charon - see Karen

Chelsea

A very popular and fashionable part of London. Name of the daughter of President Bill Clinton.

Chelsea was originally a riverside village but was made fashionable during the reign of Henry VIII when his Lord Chancellor lived there. The artists Turner, Whistler and Rossetti also made their homes there. Henry VIII liked it so much he had a small palace built there - this is no longer in existence. Today it is one of the more expensive parts of London and the artistic connection survives through art galleries and boutiques. The main thoroughfare is the Kings Road where you will see many avant-garde and outlandish costumes being paraded. You may also have time to browse through the many museums and antique shops.

"The great street of the city was of pure gold, like transparent glass..." Rev.21:21.

Cher Cherie Cherrie Cheryl
Phonetic: Sherene

From the French word for 'darling' or 'dear'. Also a Spanish word which also means 'dear'.

'Dear' or 'Dearest' are words which we normally reserve for people very close to us - our "nearest and dearest". It can be just a form of greeting - such as the one we use when we start a letter. The word 'darling' is an extra special word normally reserved for one particular and special person who is the sole object of our affection and trust. The word is mentioned nine times in the Bible and all nine are in the Song of Songs. It would appear that most are a prophetic description of the Lord Jesus Christ.

"How beautiful you are, my darling! Oh, how beautiful!" S.of S.4:1.

Chester

From Latin meaning 'a fortress camp'. A fine city and the county town of Cheshire.

It is no accident that the city of Chester is called by this name. Situated on the river Dee and close to the Welsh border below the Wirral, the town is the ancient Roman Deva or Castra Devana. There is an Amphitheatre and many Roman ruins - the two main streets are unique, they cross each other at right angles and are cut out of rock below the level of the surrounding houses and shops. The city was captured by William the Conqueror in 1070 and received its first charter in 1176. Entrance to the city is by four gates through the Roman walls. In nearby Wales other sites of Roman civilisation have the prefix 'Caer' to their name (i.e. Caernarfon) and the Welsh name for Chester is 'Caer'.

"The angel of the LORD encamps around those who fear him, and he delivers them." Ps.34:7.

Chirstie Chirsty - see Kirsten

Chloe

A Greek female name meaning 'verdant (flourishing) bud'. She was an informant to the Apostle Paul in Corinth (1 Cor.1:11.). It is clear that she was concerned about the purity of the gospel message.

She may have been a visitor to the area and possibly an attendant or slave to an Ephesian lady who was travelling through. She may also have shared with Paul the other concerns that he addresses in chapters 1-6 of 1 Corinthians. We can assume that she is a Christian from her concern about the purity of the Church's testimony.

The Scottish Psalter translates the second verse of the 23rd Psalm: "Where streams of living water flow My ransomed soul He leadeth, And, where the verdant pastures grow, With food celestial feedeth." Francis Rous.

"I am...flourishing in the house of God; I trust in God's unfailing love for ever and ever." Ps.52:8.

Christopher Chris Christian Christina Christine Cristian Kristopher

A Greek name meaning 'one who bears (carries) Christ'.

It was Gentiles at Antioch who invented the name 'Christian' as a 'nickname' for those who followed 'the way' as it was then known. The word 'Christian' is used three times in the New Testament: Acts 11:26, Acts 26:28 and 1 Pet.4:16.

Anyone who has this name is constantly reminded that it meant 'Christ's - one' and of course this can be true for everyone because the God who made us all sent the Lord Jesus Christ to die for us all on the cross.

"...if you suffer as a Christian, do not be ashamed...praise God that you bear that name." 1 Pet.4:16.

Ciara Ciarra Cinnamon

From Irish Gaelic and meaning 'Dark-haired one'. The name of some 26 Irish saints!

Dark hair was always admired in Scriptural times and white hair was thought worthy of honour. In fact God is said to have white hair in Dan.7:9 and Rev.1:14.

The story of how Samson lost his strength when the crafty Delilah tricked him into to telling her his secret is told in Judges chapter 16. (Incidently, her name means 'hair' too!) The fact is, Samson had taken the Nazirite vow never to cut his hair. The Lord Jesus would also have had long, dark hair!

"Indeed, the very hairs of your head are all numbered. Don't be afraid; you are worth more than many sparrows." Luke 12:7.

Cilla - see Priscilla

Cindy - see Cynthia

Clare Clara
French form: Claire

Latin for 'clear and famous'. One famous Clare was St Clare of the 'Poor Clares' in the 13th century.

Clare was born into a wealthy family in Assisi but was drawn towards a monastic life in the order of St Francis of Assisi. Although she successfully founded a strict contemplative order, she was constantly longing for the more practical work of ministering to the poor and destitute.

"...the LORD has anointed me to preach good news to the poor." Is.61:1.

Clarence

French for 'of Clare' which, in turn is Latin for 'clear and famous'.

In the 14th century Lionel, the brother of Henry IV and the son of King Edward III, married the heiress of the town of Clare in Suffolk. As a result his father made him the Duke of Clarence and this title is now often conferred on younger sons of royalty. Shakespeare tells the story in both "Henry VI" (Part 3) and in Richard III.

Clarence House the home of Queen Elizabeth the Queen Mother was designed by Nash and built in 1825. It is a beautiful and elegant residence even though its postal address is "Stable Yard Gate SW1".

"...He has this name...KING OF KINGS and LORD OF LORDS". Rev.19:16.

Clarissa
Ancient form: Clarice
From Latin meaning 'to bring bright fame'. The heroine of an 18th century novel.
Samuel Richardson was an 18th century apprentice who not only rose to run his own printing firm but also wrote the books he published. "Clarissa; or the History of a Young Lady" ran to 7 volumes and took over a year to complete. It was by far his best work - some say because of the name that he chose for the title and heroine! His later work was "The History of Sir Charles Grandison" in which he presented his ideal of a Christian gentleman.

"I have heard of your fame; I stand in awe of your deeds, O LORD." Hab.3:2.

Clark
Another form of 'clerk' originally meaning a clergyman. From a Greek word meaning 'chosen by lot'.
Many will not remember the early screen idol Clark Gable and will be more familiar with Clark Kent (of 'Superman' fame). Neither of these seem to be very good at office work!

When the Apostle Paul arrived at Ephesus there was a riot and Acts 19 has a graphic description of the event: "The assembly was in confusion: Some were shouting one thing, some another. Most of the people did not even know why they were there." It was the (Town) CLERK who saved the day!

"And in the church God has appointed...those with gifts of administration..."
1Cor.12:28.

Claud Claudia Claudius
From the ancient Roman name 'Claudius'. Popular in Britain since the 1st century.
The Emperor Claudius was ruling Rome when Britain was conquered by the Romans in the first century. He was reputed to be a cruel man but Paul had no problems with him when he landed at Rome and the book of Romans does not suggest that he was particularly wicked. However, he was

the person who excluded the Jews from Jerusalem.

Another Claudius took Paul into custody in Acts chapters 27 and 28. This Claudius had purchased his Roman citizenship but Paul explained that he himself had been born a Roman citizen.

"...our citizenship is in heaven. And we eagerly await a Saviour...the Lord Jesus Christ." Phil.3:20.

Clayton

From Old English - literally 'a farm on clay'. A place-name for many areas of Great Britain. Be careful where - and how you built!

The Old English is 'Clae-tun' and forms part of the names of at least seven areas mainly in north-east England.

In the Bible clay had many uses, sometimes pots were made of clay as were writing tablets. With the latter a smooth white clay was used and whilst it was still damp the letters were 'impressed' into it, the tablet was then baked until hard.

Men and women are often compared to clay which can be molded shaped and even crushed and remolded!

"O LORD, you are our Father. We are the clay, you are the potter; we are all the work of your hand." Is.64.8.

Clemence Clemency Clement Clementina Clementine

From Latin meaning 'mild and merciful'. The name of an early Christian saint.

One of the earliest records of the name comes from the 2nd century and belonged to one of the first Christian scholars, Clement of Alexandria. He wrote many great works and was certainly 'mild and merciful'. His last book was "Who is the Rich Man that shall be Saved?" and tells the story of the Apostle John rescuing a fallen Christian.

"The LORD has heard my cry for mercy; the LORD accepts my prayer." Ps.6:9.

Cleo Cleopatra

The ancient name 'Cleopatra' is from Greek and means 'the glory of her father'.

Cleopatra died some thirty years before Jesus was born. Her life was embroiled with Julius Caesar and Mark Antony when Egypt and the Roman Empire were in turmoil. Although her life was full of intrigue and sadness her devotion to Antony ultimately ennobles her. William Shakespeare, John Dryden and George Bernard Shaw have all written about the life and loves of this beautiful queen of Egypt. The 190 - ton obelisk on the Thames Embankment called 'Cleopatra's Needle' was a gift to the British people by the Egyptian government in the 19th century.

"I have brought you glory on earth by completing the work you gave me to do." John 17:4.

Cliff Clifford

Old English for 'the ford by the cliff'. A famous English family and a village.
The origin of the name is uncertain but the village and baronetcy date from the 13th century. Baron Robert de Clifford won fame for his part in the siege of the castle of Caerlaverock in 1300. There are at least four places with the name 'Clifford' as their name or part of their name in Britain. One of them is the village of Clifford 3 km (2 miles) north of the lovely village of Hay-on-Wye (famous for its many bookshops) on the Welsh border.
"O LORD our Lord, how majestic is your name in all the earth!" Ps.8:1.

Clint Clinton

From an aristocratic surname which means 'farm by the river Glyme'.
If you travel northwest on the A44 from the ancient city of Oxford you will, after a short distance, find Blenheim Palace on your left-hand side. The lake here is fed by the river Glyme which rises further north in the Cotswolds.
Rivers flow through the Bible. From the garden of Eden (Gen.2:10) to the closing of the age (Rev.22:2) they are usually a picture of peace and serenity.
"They feast on the abundance...you give them drink from your river of delights." Ps.36:8.

Clive

From a village in Shropshire called 'Clive', which is in an area of outstanding natural beauty and from which the family of 'Clive of India' took their surname.
Baron Robert Clive of Plassey was born at Stryche Hall, Morton Say some 25 km (15 miles) north of the ancient town of Shrewsbury in 1725. A brilliant soldier and the founder of the British Empire in India, he rose to become the Governor of Bengal in 1755-60 and again in 1764-67. His second governorship was outstanding and during this time he introduced many reforms and restored discipline to the armed forces. He was created Baron Clive of Plassey in 1762 (Irish Peerage) and knighted in 1764. He purchased large estates around Shrewsbury and was the local MP.
"Every good and perfect gift is from above...from the Father...who does not change..." Jas.1:17.

Clodiagh

The name of a river in Ireland or from the ancient Roman name 'Claudius'.
Emperor Claudius was ruling Rome when Britain was conquered by the Romans in the first century. He was reputed to be a cruel man but Paul had no problems with him when he landed in Rome and the book of Romans does not suggest that he was a particularly evil man.
It is more likely to be from the name of a river in a very beautiful part of Ireland.
The Bible opens with the story of a beautiful creation where 'a river watered

the garden' In Psalm(Gen. 2:10) and it closes with 'the river of the water of life' (Rev.22:1). 1 we are told that a righteous person "...is like a tree planted by streams of water..." and in Psalm 23 the writer says; "He leads me beside quiet waters.."

Jesus said ;"Whoever believes in me..streams of living water will flow from within him…" John 7.38.

Colin

From the ancient Greek 'Nikolaos' meaning 'victory to the people'.There is also a similar Gaelic word meaning 'youthful'.

Nikolaos became 'Nicholas' which, in turn, became the French 'Nicolette', and 'Colette' and then finally, the English 'Colin'. After a long and somewhat torturous journey this name has become a popular independent name in its own right and few people would be aware of its origin. The word in Gaelic is 'cailean' which means 'youthful'.

"Even youths grow tired and weary, and young men stumble and fall; but those who hope in the LORD will renew their strength". Is.40:30-31.

Connie - see Constance

Connor Conor

From an old Irish name meaning 'a lover of hunting dogs'. The pen-name of a Christian novelist.

The Christian novelist who used 'Connor' as part of his pen-name was Connor W. Gordon a Minister in the Canadian Presbyterian Church at the end of the 19th century. His books for boys were very popular and they included; "The man from Glengarry", "Sky Pilot" and "Glengarry School Days". His books include vivid accounts of the revival which they were experiencing in the highlands of Scotland. He justified the time and effort spent in writing by saying; "Not wealth, not enterprise, not energy, can build a nation into true greatness but men...with the fear of God in their hearts."

"Righteousness exalts a nation, but sin is a disgrace to any people." Prov.14:34.

Conrad

From the Old German word for 'brave counsel'.

The name of several German kings and a famous British novelist. A name popular in England from the 15th century.

Good advice is always very easy to obtain. Normally we seek out those who will advise us to do the things which we want to do anyway. The difficult task is to give or take advice which is unpopular and few of us have the strength of character to do it. However, Conrad means just that. Scripture is full of examples of people who, under God, gave or took counsel that didn't always pander to men's lower instincts.

"The way of a fool seems right to him, but a wise man listens to advice." Prov.12:15.

Constance Constantine Connie

From Latin and meaning 'firm, resolute'. The name of the first Christian Emperor.

When the Roman Emperor Constantine became a Christian the whole character of the Christian Church changed and Christianity became the state religion. He established Byzantium (which he renamed Constantinople) instead of Rome as his secular and religious capital - it is now called Istanbul.

"...stand firm and see the deliverance the LORD will give you...Do not be afraid..." 2 Chron.20:17.

Coral

From Greek 'korallion' or Semitic origin. A lovely piece of jewellery or a beautiful under-water world.

The origin of the word 'coral' is lost in the mists of antiquity - as mysterious as the processes which produce the wonderful coral reefs in the warm waters of our world. The word is mentioned twice in the Bible. In Ez.27:16 it is a valuable commodity in trade. In Job 28:18, it is listed as one of the valuable things only exceeded by wisdom.

"...who spread out the earth upon the waters, His love endures for ever." Ps.136:6.

Corrine Corrina

Ancient Greek meaning 'a maiden'. A beautiful love-story was dedicated to her by a man who hated violence. Associated with the coming of Harvest.

The origin of this name is lost in mists of antiquity but it is known that the poet Ovid wrote of his sweetheart Corrina around the time of Christ. He had been born to a noble Roman family but fell foul of the authorities because he spurned his official duties and spent his time writing love-poems. In Greek mythology it is the name of someone who 'lost' four months of the year and when she recovered brought the harvest.

"...men and maidens, old men and children. Let them praise the name of the LORD." Ps.148:12-13.

Courtney

From the French area 'de Courtenay' in northern France, meaning 'the domain Curtius', it has an aristocratic history and the Normans used it as a baronial name.

A famous Penzance family called de Courtenay originally took their name from the an area in northern France. Their family tree came to an end in 1918 when the last Baron de Courtenay died. He had been a fine Christian man and many Christian Conscientious Objectors owed their freedom to his fight for their right to abstain from war. Other famous de Courtenay's included one who was Archbishop of Canterbury!

"But you are...a royal priesthood...a people belonging to God, that you may declare the praises of him who called you..." 1 Peter 2:9.

Craig

From Gaelic and meaning 'a rock' or a rocky point or outcrop. It was originally a Scottish surname.

In the Bible 'rock' is mentioned many times and it is often associated with God. The name 'God the rock' is one of the oldest names of God. It symbolises security, refuge and strength. In the New Testament Jesus is called 'a rock of offence' and 'the stone which the builders rejected'.

The land of Israel is very rocky and Jerusalem itself is built on rock - the very centre of the Temple area was the rock on which Abraham almost sacrificed his son Isaac. It is called Mount Moriah.

"...I will put you in a cleft in the rock and cover you with my hand..." Ex.33:22.

Crystal

From Greek meaning 'icicle'. A translucent jewel.

Crystal is mentioned at least four times in the Bible - three of them in the final book of Revelation. The other reference is in the book of Job chapter 28 where it is listed as one of the jewels so valuable that it is only exceeded by wisdom.

One of the facets of crystal is its translucent quality. We use the word today to describe cut glass of beauty.

"Then the angel showed me the river of the water of life, as clear as crystal." Rev.22:1.

Cuthbert

From Old English 'cuth' and 'beorht' which means 'famous and bright'. A 7th century saint.

Cuthbert is a favourite name from the 13th century and one of the few names to survive the Norman Conquest. The 7th century Bishop Cuthbert of Lindisfarne was finally buried at Durham in AD995. After travelling far and wide as a missionary he had attempted to live a life of solitude on one of the Farne islands. In this way and many others he had tried to follow the practices and lifestyle of his predecessor Aidan. Eventually he was persuaded to leave the Farne islands in order to become a Bishop.

"...the LORD...has not left you without a kinsman redeemer. May he become famous..." Ruth 4:14.

Cymon - see Simon

Cynthia Cindy

One of the titles of a Greek goddess and named after Mount Cynthus.

Mount Cynthus was the home of an ancient Cycladic culture and the rocky area housed many foreign gods including Egyptian and Syrian. When the Apostle Paul visited nearby Athens he preached on Mars Hill and said: "Men of Athens! I see that in every way you are very religious...I even found an altar with this inscription: TO AN UNKNOWN GOD...what you worship as something unknown I am going to proclaim to you." Acts 17:22-23.

"O God our Saviour, the hope of all...who formed the mountains by your power." Ps.65:5-6.

Cyril

From Greek meaning 'Lord' or 'Master'. A popular name with an academic history.

Despite the pretentious meaning of the name there have been many wonderful 'Cyrils' down through the ages. One of the most notable was Cyril and his brother Methodius in the 9th century. They took the gospel message to the southern Slavs of Russia. Additionally, they devised what became known as the 'Cyrillic Alphabet'. This alphabet is still used by millions of Serbs, Bulgars and Russians today.

"The greatest among you will be your servant." Mt.23:11.

Daisy Daizy

From the Old English 'days-eye'. One of the loveliest and most profuse of the wild flowers which adorn the countryside.

The French name for a daisy is a form of the name 'Margaret' which means 'a pearl' or 'a child from the light of the moon'.

This small wild garden flower has been so popular in the past that it has generated a number of topical phrases such as "daisy-chain" a string of daisies or an endless pursuit, "pushing up the daisies" to be dead and buried, "daisy-cutter" a horse that doesn't lift its feet or a cricket ball travelling just above the ground.

"Flowers appear on the earth...the cooing of doves is heard." S.of S.2:12.

Dale Dean

Old English for 'valley'. The ending of many place-names.

Similar to the ancient word 'Combe' the names 'Dale' and 'Dean' mean a valley or a small recess. Any place-name which ends with either of these words indicates a current or past feature of the landscape. In the Bible valleys or dales have an additional significance - they speak of human experiences. We sometimes say "that was a mountain-top experience" or "you seem down today".

"Down in the valley or upon the mountain steep; Close beside my Saviour would my soul ever keep." W.Cushing.

"Every valley shall be raised up, every mountain and hill made low; the rough ground shall become level, the rugged places a plain. And the glory of the LORD will be revealed." Is.40:4-5.

Damaris Damara

From Greek 'Damalis' and could mean 'a young lady'. A convert on 'Mars Hill' in Athens.

When Paul arrived in Athens he was saddened by all the gods in this beautiful city. Just in case they had omitted a god the Athenians had an altar to 'an unknown god' and Paul claimed that this was the God he was serving. They heard him gladly until he spoke of repentance and the resurrection; "...he commands all people everywhere to repent. For He has set a day when He will judge the world...by the man He has appointed..."

Some mocked, some believed - and only two of them are named - Damaris being one of them. The full story is told in Acts 17.
"He is not far from each one of us. 'For in Him we live and move and have our being.'" *Acts 17:27-28.*

Dan - see also Daniel

From Hebrew meaning 'vindicated'. A northern boundary of the promised land. One of the tribes of Israel. (A scriptural name in its own right not an abbreviation of 'Daniel').
The town, area and personal name of 'Dan' is mentioned in Scripture many times. Among other things it was the northern boundary of the promised land. The town has been excavated and one of the ancient gates where the elders sat to judge the people can still be seen. The tribe of Dan was noted for its rebellion - so beware!
"'God has vindicated me...and given me a son.' Because of this she named him Dan." *Gen.30:6.*

Daniel Dan Daniella Danielle Danny - see also Dan
Polish form: Danuta

A Hebrew name meaning 'God has vindicated me'.
Daniel was a famous character in the Old Testament remembered mainly for his exploits in the lion's den. There were in fact at least four 'Daniels' in the Old Testament and all we know about this one is in the book of the same name. He was clearly of royal descent and was taken into captivity with the Jews around the 6th century BC. He was a man of great wisdom and righteousness who refused to bow to foreign gods and as a result became the victim of a plot to dispense with him. The rest of the story is well-known (Daniel 6).
"God...keeps His covenant of love with all who love Him..." Dan.9:4.

Danica

From a Slavonic word for 'the morning star'. A famous Danish astronomer of the 17th century. One of the names of the Lord Jesus Christ!
Christian Severin lived from 1562 to 1647, he was a famous Danish astronomer who is best known for his "Astronomia danica" which holds that the Sun revolves around the Earth and the other planets revolve around the Sun. He began the construction of the Copenhagen Observatory in 1632 but died before its completion.
2 Peter 1:19 describes the Lord Jesus Christ as the morning star which outshines the light of the earlier prophetic witnesses.
"I, Jesus...I am the Root and the Offspring of David, and the bright Morning Star." *Rev.22:16.*

Danuta

A Polish name which came either from 'Diana' (perfect light) or from 'Donata' (given by God). Used in the UK from the Middle Ages. The name of a number of martyrs.

It could be said that this name combines two of God's greatest virtues - his light and his bounty!

God is the creator of light and since he commanded it to shine it has shone every day.

God's greatest and most bountiful gift was his son the Lord Jesus Christ. The Apostle John reports him declaring:

"I am the light of the world. Whoever follows me will never walk in darkness, but will have the light of life." John 8.12.

Daphne

From the Greek meaning 'a laurel tree' or 'bush' (also called the 'bay' laurel). A nymph in Greek mythology who was loved by Apollo. A famous writer of the 20th century.

The writer Daphne du Maurier was a romantic novelist who lived from 1907-1989. The name Daphne dates from Greek mythology where Daphne resisted the advances of Apollo and called on the gods to protect her. For this she was changed into a laurel bay tree. Laurel became a symbol of triumph in both Greece and Rome and the Emperor Tiberius believed it would guard him against thunder and lighting so during storms he wore a laurel wreath!

"...the LORD Almighty will be...a beautiful wreath for the remnant of His people." Is.28:5.

Darren Darran Darrell Daryl

From the 13th century and Shakespeare. Exonerated!

The oldest reference to 'Darren' is in an act of Parliament 1555 where that spelling is used for an ancient Norman/French word once used in connection with legal disputes and meaning 'last' or 'most recent' (An earlier [1292] spelling 'Dreyn' probably refers to the same word). A very similar Norman/French word 'darraign' was used by Shakespeare and means to vindicate or to clear someone of a charge against him.

"Who will bring any charge against those whom God has chosen? It is God who justifies." Rom.8:33.

David Davina

Means 'beloved' (loved and loving) - there is only one person with that name in the Bible.

David was the youngest son of Jesse and from the tribe of Judah. He was

Israel's second King and during his reign the nation reached the height of its fame and strength. He is best known for his famous battle with Goliath (1 Sam.17), and the Psalms. The Lord Jesus is described as 'the son of David' in the first verse of the New Testament and, except for the name of the Lord Jesus, the name David is last name in the Bible. Great David's 'greater Son' is King of Kings.

"I have found David...a man after my own heart; he will do everything I want him to do." Acts 13:22.

Dawn Aurora

The colours of dawn are purer and colder than the sunset colours because there is less dust in the air. From deep red to orange - to gold - to yellow as the sun slowly appears over the horizon.

"Have you ever given orders to the morning, or shown the dawn its place?" Job 38:12. The Psalmist says; "He will make your righteousness shine like the dawn." Ps.37:6. We use the word to describe the realisation of something "it dawned upon me". It is also used to describe the beginning of a process e.g. 'the dawn of creation'.

The most wonderful discovery ever made was made at dawn - the resurrection of the Lord Jesus (Mt.28:1).

"The path of the righteous is like the first gleam of dawn shining ever brighter..." Prov.4:18.

Dean - see Dale

Deborah Debbie Debra

Hebrew for 'bee'. A Prophetess and Poet. A major-product producer in the land of the Bible.

Deborah was a judge of some renown at around 1125BC. She played a major part in the battle against Sisera. The exciting story is in chapters 4 and 5 of the book of Judges. Deborah means 'a bee' and honey was vital in the early days of the children of Israel. At least 19 times in the Old Testament they had been promised "a land flowing with milk and honey" (from Ex.3:8). Honey was used for food, (Prov.24:13), cake-making (Ex.16:31), medicine (Prov.16:24), gifts (2 Sam.17:29), as a precious resource (Jer.41:8) and a valuable export (Ez.27:17).

"How sweet are your words to my taste, sweeter than honey to my mouth!" Ps.119:103.

Deirdre Deidre

From Irish and Scottish legend the princess who jilted her betrothed to elope with her lover to Scotland. Popular in Ireland. Immortalised by Yeats and Synge.

Deirdre was the heroine of "The Sons of Uisneach" which is one of the Three Sorrowful Tales of Erin - from which have come many Irish legends and poetry. In 1907 Yeats wrote "Deidre" and around the same time Synge wrote "Deidre of the Sorrows".

"A cheerful heart is good medicine, but a crushed spirit dries up the bones!" Prov.17:22.

Delia

From Greek meaning 'of Delos' - an island and a name shrouded by antiquity and mystery.

Today Delos is just a lump of deserted granite in the Aegean Sea. At the time of Christ it was a flourishing slave market there and there were temples to Apollo and Artemis. The Romans permitted the Greeks to follow their pagan rituals and made some profit from it for themselves. Artemis was also called 'Diana'. There was a riot when Paul preached near her temple. (Acts 19 - 20). This temple was one of the Seven Wonders of the World.

"...your body is a temple of the Holy Spirit...You are not your own..." 1 Cor.6:19.

Demelda Demelza

A lovely Cornish place-name associated with St Columba, the 'Poldark' books and television!

This name came from a place in the Cornish village of St Columba Major called "the hill-fortress of Maeldaf". The Church of St Columba was built there in AD1240. He was a missionary credited with the conversion of Scotland to Christianity in 6th century. The monastery and place where he lived have recently been excavated in Iona.

The name was made more popular by the recent TV series of the Poldark books by Winston Graham - in them Demelza is the heroine!

"The LORD is my rock, my fortress and my deliverer; my God is my rock, in whom I take refuge. He is my shield and the horn of my salvation, my stronghold." Ps.18.2.

Demetrius

This is the male form of the ancient name 'Demeter' who was the earth-god and is often depicted carrying a sheaf of wheat.

The Grand Prince of Moscow was called 'Demetrius' he won a great victory over the Tatars in 1363, as this was fought close to the river Don he was nicknamed 'Don' from then on!

Another Demetrius was a 4th century martyr but before him there was the Bishop of Alexandria who ordained the famous theologian Origen.

One of the great Jewish Passover prayers refers to God's power to bring wheat (food) from the earth.

"The harvest is plentiful but the workers are few." Matthew 9:37.

Denis Dennis Denise Dion Dione Dionne
American form: Dwight
From two sources: the Greek god Dionysios and the patron saint of France.
When Paul arrived at Athens he was saddened by all the gods in this
beautiful city. At the conclusion of his sermon on Mars Hill we are told that
'...some sneered - some believed' Acts 17:32-33 of the latter group only two
of them are named - Dionysius being one of them. The full exciting story is
told in Acts 17.
A 3rd century evangelist of this name became the patron saint of France
and from this we have the modern variations.
*"A few men became followers of Paul and believed. Among them was Dionysius..." Acts
17:34.*

Derick Derek Derrick Deryk
*From the ancient 'Theodoric'. In Greek 'Theo' means 'God' and 'Doric' was a
linguistic and social group in Southwest Asia Minor. From this we could say that
the name means 'God of culture'.*
One of the few places that you would hear the word 'Doric' today would be
in the field of Architecture - it is one of two original Greek 'Orders' and it
denotes the classical Greek column which tapers slightly as it rises. These
columns were used to support the first floors of buildings because of their
strength and beauty.
*"...you too are being built together to become a dwelling in which God lives by his Spirit."
Eph.2:22.*

Dermot
*From Irish Gaelic and meaning 'free from envy'. The principal character in Irish
legends.*
The legendary character by the name of Dermot eloped with Grainne who
was already engaged to General Finn. Finn pursued them and eventually
killed Dermot - so goes the legend. But real life is little different and envy
forces men to do strange and terrible things. The real king of Leinster in the
12th century was also called Dermot.
"Love is patient, love is kind. It does not envy..." 1 Cor.13:4.

Derrick Deryk - see Derek

Desiree
From French meaning 'desired'. Originally the Latin 'Desiderata'.
The dictionary definition is "to long for or to want earnestly". We
sometimes forget that although we have 'desires' God also has them - His

deepest desire is for the fellowship of men and women whom He has created. This is why He created us and then sent the Lord Jesus to die on the cross. One Ancient wrote; "Our hearts are restless till they find their rest in thee." Our deepest desires can be met when we yield them to Him.
"May He give you the desire of your heart and make all your plans succeed." Ps.20:4.

Desmond

From Irish Gaelic meaning 'man from Desmond' (Sth Munster). An ancient Irish kingdom.

In the year AD200 Oilill King of Munster (in southern Ireland), divided his kingdom between his two sons. In those days it was called Des-Mumha. In the 10th century it was united again until 1579 when, after the 'Desmond war' it became part of Co. Kerry. The title 'Duke of Desmond' is still used. The area known as Sth Munster is roughly the old Desmond.

Originally an Irish surname it is a popular Christian name today all over the western world.

"The LORD has established his throne in heaven, and his kingdom rules over all." Ps.103:19.

Devon

A name that means 'a man of rock...'! From the 9th century Old English tribal name for the hard people of a West Country area.

The origin of this name is lost in mists of antiquity! It is thought to originate from the 9th century tribal name 'defnas'. This was a warrior tribe in the area we now call Devon. 'Defnas' became 'Defaniscir' (the district of the 'defnas') and from this we get Devon. The red sandstone rock of the area is also called Devon and is thought to have a marine history of some very many thousands of years - this may well be linked with the name of the area. One of God's oldest names is 'God the rock'.

"But the LORD has become my fortress, and my God the rock in whom I take refuge." Ps 94:22.

Diana Diane Di Dianne

Latin Greek for 'Perfect light'. The cause of a riot when Paul preached near her temple in Ephesus.

Latin: 'luminous' Greek: 'perfect'. The story of Paul's visit to Ephesus is one of the many exciting stories in the book of Acts. His preaching caused a riot and the account is graphically told in Acts 19 and 20. The temple to Diana at Ephesus was one of the Seven Wonders of the World. 'Light' is the subject matter of both the first chapter of Genesis and the first chapter of the gospel of John.

"The LORD is my light and my salvation whom shall I fear?" Ps.27:1.

Dick Dickie Dicky - see Richard

Digby

From Old English meaning 'the settlement by the dyke'. A lovely village between Sleaford and Lincoln.

Close to fenland and in one of the flattest parts of the United Kingdom you will find Digby - a small Lincolnshire village just off the A15. As long ago as 1086 there was a farmstead or a village here. Nearly 600 years later a man by the name of Digby almost escaped trial for being involved in the 'gunpowder plot'. Perhaps he was thinking of the meaning of his name when he hid in a 'ditch' but his captors may have known the meaning as well!

"...he built an altar in the name of the LORD, and he dug a trench around it ..."
1 Kings 18:32.

Dilys

A Welsh name meaning 'sure', 'perfect' or 'genuine'. Of uncertain history before the 19th century but now a popular name all over the western world.

Someone who is SURE is someone who is in modern jargon, 'cool'- they will be confident and self-assured and able to act in an emergency. Someone who is PERFECT will be without faults and everything they do will be right. Someone who is GENUINE will admit that they are neither sure nor perfect!

There has only ever been one person who could justly claim these virtues and He is the LORD JESUS CHRIST.

"... in your great love, O God, answer me with your sure salvation." Ps.69:13.

Dinah

Hebrew for 'He has judged (vindicated) me'. The name of Jacob's daughter through Leah. One of a large family. She is the means of Jacob's return to Bethel.

The story of what happened to Dinah is told in Genesis chapter 34 but God used this incident to bring Jacob back to where he had previously encountered God at Bethel (the 'house of God'). We hear nothing more of Dinah - one of 7 children borne to Jacob by Leah. It seems that she had fulfilled her purpose and then faded from the scene.

Each one of us is precious to God - we may feel that He has so many children He has no time for us but we are told that we all are made in His image and that the Lord Jesus died on the cross for us (Col.2:20).

"...Judge me, O LORD...according to my integrity, O Most High." Ps.7:8.

Dion Dione Dionne - see Denis

Dolly - see Dorothy

Dolores

From Spanish 'Maria de los Dolores' meaning 'Mary of the sorrows'. A reference to the Virgin Mary and her suffering.

A number of names and titles have come down to us from Spanish concerning the virgin Mary such as 'Mercedes' meaning our Lady of the mercies etc. Whilst the worship of Mary is no substitute for the worship of Jesus, Protestants need to be reminded from time to time that the virgin Mary was a unique and singular individual. In some ways she could be called the first believer.

"Gladness and joy will overtake them, and sorrow and sighing will flee away." Is.35:10.

Dominic Dom Dominique Dominick

Latin 'from the Lord' and was possibly originated as the name of children born on Sundays. It was used almost exclusively as a religious name until the 14th century.

Whilst many people are happy to accept that children are 'from the Lord' not all adults are willing to accept that they too are 'from the Lord'. One of the wisest men who ever lived wanted us to know that both good times and bad times are from God and should be an occasion for praising Him. Each one of us is precious - and our creator loves each one of us individually.

"When times are good, be happy; but when times are bad, consider: God has made the one as well as the other." Eccl.7:14.

Donald Don

From Gaelic meaning 'world mighty'. It may have originated in Ireland because it is the name of a number of Irish Kings. In Scotland it became Macdonald one of the fiercest of the highland clans.

One world-famous Donald was Donald Campbell (1921-1967) the motorboat and racing-car driver who, like his father Sir Malcolm Campbell, set world speed records on land and on water. One of the few ways to become 'world-mighty' today is to win a gold medal at the Olympic Games but even then, your fame is only momentary.

"...physical training is of some value...but godliness has value for all things..." 1 Tim.4:8.

Donna

Italian for 'lady'. Recently adopted in the United Kingdom.

'Donna' is a contraction of the original 'Madonna' or 'our Lady'. A number

of names and titles have been given to the virgin Mary. Whilst the worship of Mary is no substitute for the worship of Jesus, we need to be reminded from time to time that the virgin Mary was a unique and singular individual. In some ways she could be called the first believer.
"His mother said to the servants, 'Do whatever He tells you.'" John 2:5.

Donovan

Irish Gaelic meaning 'dark brown'. A popular singer from the 1960s.
The 'pop' singer Donovan of the 1960s did not have dark skin but was a popular 'folk' singer. He was part of the hippie culture of that day. He has exchanged his camper-van for a more permanent residence and his son has taken his mantle. The 'Song of Songs' or 'Song of Solomon' is a group of love-poems which are sometimes erotic but describe a purity of love which is often purer than ours. In the first chapter dark skin is clearly an attractive feature.
"Do not stare at me because I am dark, because I am darkened by the sun." S.of S.1:6.

Dorcas

Greek for 'gazelle' a creature of outstanding beauty. A Biblical character renowned for charity and the object of a miracle. The only woman in the Bible called a 'disciple'.
The name 'Dorcas' appears only once in the Bible in Acts 9:32-43. Her name means gazelle, ibex or roe - all three are used in the Bible to describe very lovely and graceful creatures. The Ibex is today the national symbol of Israel.
Dorcas was called a 'mathetria' in the Greek which is the word for 'a disciple' and she is the only woman who is described in this way. Clearly, she had a unique ministry. The story of how she was brought back to life is told in the closing verses of Acts chapter 9.
"...there was a disciple named Tabitha (which, when translated, [into Greek] is Dorcas)...always doing good and helping the poor". Acts 9.36.

Doreen

From Irish Gaelic meaning 'a daughter of Finn' (characters in Irish mythological history).
General Finn was the man to whom the Irish king gave responsibility for organising the army in AD250. In the process he elected as his lieutenant a man named Diarmait (Dermot) who subsequently eloped with his bride to be - Finn pursued them and in the process killed Dermot and married the lovely Grainne. They produced at least one beautiful daughter whom they called 'Doirind' (Doreen). Finn is surrounded by legend so you are left to decide for yourself how much is fact.

"three daughters...Nowhere in all the land were there found women as beautiful..." Job 42:15.

Doris Dorian

Doris means 'bountiful'. From the Greek people known as 'Dorians'. They originally came from the north of Greece in an area called 'Doris' and the best-known were the Spartans.

Dorian means literally 'from Doris' and Doris means 'bountiful' so it would acceptable to claim that Dorian also means 'bountiful'. The area of Greece where Doris was situated was very productive and this may be the reason for the name.

God is often described as 'bountiful' in Scripture, particularly "abounding in mercy" Eph.2:4.

"My people will be filled with my bounty...declares the LORD." Jer.31:14.

Dorothy Dorothea Dolly

From Greek meaning 'the gift of God'. Name of a legendary martyr.

The names Dorothea and Dorothy have been in use in Britain since the 15th century. Around the 17th century they went out of fashion but the first record of "Dolly" as the name of a child's toy was recorded about that time.

The meaning of the name 'gift of God' dates from the 3rd century Christian usage and in particular from a martyr of that name who led to Christ two women who had been sent to persuade her to renounce the Lord.

"For it is by grace you have been saved, through faith; it is the gift of God." Eph.2:8.

Douglas

From Scottish Gaelic meaning 'dark blue'. The name of many rivers. Capital of the Isle of Man.

Whilst 'blue' was a popular colour in the tabernacle and temple, 'dark blue' is only mentioned once in the Bible (Rev.9:17). The Greek word from which it comes is the same word as our Hyacinth and the orange variety of zircon.

From Celtic times 'Douglas' has given its name to many rivers such as; Dawlish, Dowles, Dulas, Divelish etc.

The town of Douglas on the Isle of Man has a population of 20,000 and is the venue for the annual TT Motorcycle race. It also has Horse Trams and Steam Trains. The Isle of Man is not part of the United Kingdom.

"I...will not forsake them. I will make rivers flow on barren heights, and springs within the valleys." Is.41:17-18.

Drew - see also Andrew

From Old German meaning 'to carry' or 'to bear' or from Old French meaning 'lover'. Also a short form for Andrew which is the name of one of the twelve Apostles.

The two meanings are not so incompatible as would at first appear. In Galatians chapter 6 the Apostle Paul teaches that we should 'bear' or 'carry' each others burdens...and so fulfil the law of Christ (Gal.6:2) This would demonstrate our love for one another. An-drew was a man who was always bringing people to Jesus - he was the one who brought the little boy who had five loaves and two small fish (John 6:8-9). God can multiply what little we do and make it worthwhile.

"Carry each other's burdens, and in this way you will fulfill the law of Christ." Gal.6:2.

Duane Du'aine Dwain Dwayne

From Irish Gaelic meaning 'dark' (tanned). Originally an Irish surname. The discoverer of x-ray.

In 1917 an important discovery regarding the nature and characteristics of x-rays was observed by the scientist D.L. Webster whilst working at the Duane laboratory - this became known as the Duane-Hunt Law and forms part of the basis of all X-ray technology.

"The LORD is thy keeper: the LORD is thy shade upon thy right hand. The sun shall not smite thee by day, nor the moon by night." Ps.121:5-6 KJV.

Duetta

Adapted from the Italian 'duetto' the diminutive form of 'duet' - one of the things that only two can do!

'Two' is a significant number in Hebrew - it is the first number that is a noun (number one is an adjective) and it is used in Scripture a number of times. It was God's plan that two humans (male and female) would form the basis of the family unit. When the law was given to Moses it was on two tablets of stone. The animals were paired and went into the ark in twos. Jesus sent out the twelve and the seventy in twos. Two witnesses were required by law and John says in his Epistle "We accept man's testimony (of two) but God's testimony is greater...for there are three that testify" 1 John 5:6-9.

"Do two walk together unless they have agreed to do so?" Amos 3:3.

Dulcie

From Latin meaning 'sweet and fair'. Origin of a number of surnames e.g. Dowsett, Dowson, Duce etc.

It is always nice to meet a person whose looks and temperament complement each other. In this case either word could be applied to either temperament or looks. The word 'dulcify' is still used in the English language and it means 'to sweeten' or 'to make gentle' (from the Latin 'dulcificare'). The Dulcimer was the forerunner of our modern piano.

We have the invading Normans to thank for bringing the name to Britain.

"Who is this that appears like the dawn, fair as the moon, bright as the sun, majestic as the stars in procession?" S.of S.6:10.

Duncan

From Scottish and Irish Gaelic meaning 'brown warrior'. The name of two Scottish Kings of the 11th century.

From the time that the Israelites entered the promised land they had to fight to gain and retain the territory that God had promised them. In spite of this, David was told that one of the reasons why he would not be allowed to build the Temple was because he was a warrior and had shed blood (1 Chron.28:3). In the New Testament our 'fight' becomes a battle with the forces of evil (Eph.6).

Duncan I and Duncan II were Scottish Kings of the 11th century. Duncan I was immortalised in 'Macbeth'.

"The LORD is a warrior; the LORD is His name." Ex.15:3.

Dwayne - see Duane

Dwight - see Denis

Eamon Eamonn - see Edmond

Earl

From Old English meaning 'a chieftain'. Used as a Christian name mainly in North America but now becoming popular in the UK.

The 'Earl' is third in order of British peerages and comes between Marquess and Viscount. It is the oldest title and was the highest until 1337. It carries no power or authority in itself and is passed down to heirs. An earl is addressed as 'My Lord' and titled: 'Right Honourable'. An Earl's wife is a Countess, also and addressed as 'My Lady'.

"JESUS CHRIST is LORD." Phil.2:11.

Earnest

From Old German meaning 'to be vigorous'. Introduced in the 18th century it became even more popular after Oscar Wilde's play "The Importance of Being Earnest".

This name became popular in the last few centuries - although its origins have been traced to the 11th and 12th century. In 1895 Oscar Wilde wrote his famous play "The Importance of Being Earnest" and from then the name has been even more popular. The double meaning of the name has given rise to many additional uses such as a religious programme entitled "Frank and Earnest" etc.

God loves 'Earnest' people - down through the centuries many of His followers have been enthusiastic, sincere, warm, devoted, serious people - EARNEST!

Eazra Ezra

From Hebrew meaning 'help' - it may be an abbreviated form of 'Ezra-yah' which means 'the Lord God helps'. A fearless man who was concerned about the purity of God's chosen people!

Eazra was the writer of the book of his name, he and Nehemiah were contemporaries. He was a priest who, during the captivity, returned to Jerusalem to assist Nehemiah in the rebuilding of the walls of the city. When he arrived he was horrified to find that many of the other returning Jews had inter-married with the heathen tribes. With weeping and repentance he brought the people back to God.

"Eazra praised the LORD, the great God; and all the people lifted their hands and responded, "Amen! Amen!"" Nehemiah 8:6.

Ebeneezer

From Hebrew and meaning 'a stone of help'. Samuel marked the place of a vital victory.

When Samuel set up the memorial stone and named it 'Ebenezer' he was doing two things; He was creating a memorial to a battle that had been victorious - but he was also underlining the fact that God can be trusted to keep his word. The defeat in 1 Samuel 4 was followed by the victory of 1 Samuel 7. Once again he had learnt that a lost battle is not a lost war.

Here I raise my Ebeneezer, hither by thy help I'm come, and I hope by thy good pleasure safely to arrive at home. (From "Come thou fount of every blessing" by Robert Robinson 1735-1790.)

Eddie Eddy - see Edward

Eden

From the Hebrew word 'y-ead en' meaning 'a lovely place of delightful pleasure'. (It is also an Old English word for 'a rich bear-cub'!)

The Old English origin is from the two words 'ead' meaning 'prosperity' and 'hun' the word for a 'bear cub'. But I prefer the (even older) Hebrew meaning - 'a lovely place of delightful pleasure'. The story of the garden of Eden and how man let God down is told in the first three chapters of the book of Genesis.

There is a Jewish teaching that if Adam and Eve had enjoyed all the lovely pleasures of the garden then they would never have had the time to let God down!

"...like Eden...like the garden of the LORD. Joy and gladness will be found in her, thanksgiving and the sound of singing." Is.51:3.

Edgar

From Old English meaning 'a happy spear'. Popular for hundreds of years by kings and romantics.

This name is a compound of two old English words; 'ead' which means 'happy' or 'rich' and 'gar' which means 'a spear'. The name has been used from King Edgar ('The Peaceable') in the 10th century through the Norman Conquest until the present day. Shakespeare includes it in "King Lear" (Gloucester's virtuous son) and Sir Walter Scott includes it in his romantic novel "The Bride of Lammermuir".

"Is any one of you in trouble? He should pray. Is anyone happy? Let him sing songs of praise." Jas.5:13.

Edith

From Old English meaning 'Victory' (or 'a happy war'). The name of saints, queens and martyrs.

There were at least two saints in the 10th century called Edith.

The daughter of King Edgar also in the 10th century and the wives of Henry I and Harold II were called Edith (Eadgyth) - although Henry's wife preferred to be called Matilda or Mold.

Another wonderful Edith was Edith Cavell who was executed by the Germans in the First World War (1914-18) because she assisted allied soldiers to escape. Before she died she said; "I realise that patriotism is not enough, I must have no hatred or bitterness toward anyone." That would be a good definition of victory.

"You give me Your shield of victory; You stoop down to make me great." 2 Sam.22:36.

Edmond Edmund

Irish form: Eamon Eamonn

From the Old English meaning 'happy protection'. The name of an Archbishop, Kings and Saints. A name from antiquity.

St Edmond the Rich was Archbishop of Canterbury in the 13th century and Edmond the Magnificent and Edmund Ironside were Kings in the 10th and 11th centuries.

Another King Edmund came to the throne in AD855 when he was only fifteen years old. He ruled for fourteen years and was then martyred by the invading Danes because he refused to renounce his Christian faith. He is buried at 'Bury St Edmunds' which means 'Fortress of St Edmund'.

"...I will put you in a cleft in the rock and cover you with my hand..." Ex.33:22.

Edna

From Hebrew meaning 'delight', 'pleasure' or 'rejuvenation'. There may be a connection with the Garden of Eden.

The history of the name is unclear. It appears in ancient Jewish writings and it is thought that the origin may be the garden of Eden. Also the Hebrew word pronounced 'aid' (which means 'witness') could be the first part of the name. ('Aid' is an acrostic made up from the first and last letters of the Hebrew 'Shma' declaration of Deut.6:4).

"Hear, O Israel: The LORD our God, the LORD is one" (the Shma). "Love the LORD your God with all your heart and with all your soul and with all your strength." Deut.6:4.

Edward Eddie Eddy Ted Teddy Ned Neddy

The origin of this name is from an old English word meaning; 'lucky guardian'. There have been a number of famous 'Edwards' in English history.

Edward the Confessor who was so-called because of his piety. He was the son of Ethelred the Unready and he died in the year 1066. Because of his fame England had kings called Edward for one hundred years.

One of the most outstanding was Edward VI the boy king. He was crowned when he was nine and died when he was sixteen and so he only reigned six years. Many Grammar and Secondary Schools have been named after him. He was very intelligent and a devout Christian.

"See, I am sending an angel ahead of you to guard you along the way and to bring you to the place I have prepared." Ex.23:20.

Edwin Edwina

From Old English meaning 'a happy friend'. The name of an ancient King.

King Edwin of Northumbria (AD585-633) was a heathen king who had a strange dream one night. He vowed that he would become a Christian if the dream came true. It did, and he was baptised on Easter Day AD627 at York. He built a Church of wood and later laid the foundations for one of stone - which became York Minster.

Edwin means 'a happy friend', and everyone needs a friend like that.

"...there is a friend who sticks closer than a brother..." Prov.18:24.

Eileen - see Aileen

Eilis – see Margaret

Elaine Elaina - see also Helen

The old French form of 'Helen' which means 'the bright one'. There is also an identical Welsh word which means 'a fawn'.

A lovely name which Malory used in "Morte d'Arthur" and Tennyson used in "Lancelot and Elaine". The root of the name means 'a bright one' and refers to St Helena the mother of the first Christian Emperor Constantine. There is a legend that she was born in England the daughter of 'Old King Cole' the ruler of Colchester. She went to the Holy Land and located many of the sites where Jesus ministered, died and rose again. Some of these sites may not be the actual places - but that is not important. What is important is that the events happened.

"Jesus spoke again...'I am the light of the world'" John 8:12.

Eion – see John

Eira

A lovely Welsh word for 'white as snow'. A beautiful South-American mammal and an ancient middle-eastern town.

The name 'Eira' is a modern Welsh word for 'snow' and also an ancient word for a Spartan city of refuge about 600 years before Christ. The prophet Isaiah lived at about the same time as the Spartan war - his name means 'The Lord saves me'. Isaiah wrote about snow and revealed a wonderful truth that many people have still not yet realised.

He said: *"Come now, let us reason together," says the LORD. "Though your sins are like scarlet, they shall be as white as snow; though they are red as crimson, they shall be like wool." Isaiah 1:18.*

Eleanor

From Greek meaning 'a bright one' or 'light'. From the 12th century.

Eleanor originally came from 'Helen' which is 'bright shining one' in Greek. Today Eleanor is a name in its own right and late in the 20th century was listed in the "50 most popular names" recorded by the Registrar of Births.

It was the name of Henry II's Queen (Eleanor of Aquitaine) who was born in 1122.

John, the gospel writer portrays Jesus as the 'light of the world' and uses light in the sense of 'revelation'. In other parts of the Bible light is used as the opposite to darkness and also as a picture of the holiness and purity of God.

"Eternal light! Eternal light! how pure the soul must be, When, placed within Thy searching sight, It shrinks not, but with calm delight Can live, and look on Thee." Thomas Binney (1798-1874).

"I am the light of the world. Whoever follows me will never walk in darkness." John 8:12.

Elena - see Helen

Elias Elijah

From the Hebrew 'Eli' (my God) and 'Jah' (Short form of Yahweh - 'the Lord') so literally 'The LORD is my God'. A fearless Old Testament prophet who is held up as an example of believing prayer in Jas.5:17.

The stories of Elijah's exploits are contained in 1 Kings 17-21 and 2 Kings 1-2. These chapters record six major events in the prophet's life but he is mainly remembered for the confrontation with the prophets of Baal on Mount Carmel (1 Kings 18). The worship of Baal-melqart had been tolerated and as a result, there had been a severe famine. Elijah now feels that the time has come for God to demonstrate His supremacy over nature and idols.

"Answer me, O LORD, answer me, so these people will know that you, O LORD, are God, and that you are turning their hearts back again." 1 Kings 18:37.

Elizabeth Elisa Eliza Elisabeth Bess Bessie Bessy Betsy Betty Libbie Libby Lisa Liz Liza Lizzy Lizzie
Scottish form: Elspeth

The name means 'God is my oath'. It is only used once in the Bible for the mother of John the Baptist.

The story of this special lady and her God-fearing husband is told in the first chapter of the gospel of Luke verses 5-25 and verses 57-66. God chose her to be the mother of the person who would announce the arrival of the Messiah.

Elizabeth was a close relative of the Virgin Mary. The angel announced to Mary that, although she was a virgin, she would have a baby and His name would be JESUS, He would be great, the son of the Most High and an eternal ruler. The angel then told Mary that Elizabeth had conceived "...in her old age." Luke 1:36.

"...For nothing is impossible with God". Luke 1:37.

Ella

From Old German meaning 'all'. Once a pet form of Isabella but now a lovely name in its own right.

The word 'all' is mentioned nearly 5,000 times in the Bible and the Oxford Dictionary gives 10 different definitions for the word. Generally we would accept that it means 'the total number' or 'the complete quantity'. Here are some Bible 'alls': "God saw all that he had made, and it was very good." Gen.1:31. "All have turned aside, they have together become corrupt" Ps.14:3. "we are all witnesses" Acts 2:32. "This righteousness from God comes through faith in Jesus Christ to all who believe." Rom.3:22. "...in all things God works for the good of those who love him" Rom.8:28.

"O LORD, with all my heart; I will tell of all your wonders." Ps.9:1.

Elliot Eliott Eliot

From the prophet 'Elijah' (Elias) in the Old Testament. An Elliot Varmus helped to discover the source of cancer in 1989. Another Elliot died trying to reach the Auca Indians.

Any name containing 'El' has something to do with God - and 'Elliot' is no exception! The Anglo-Saxon version came through the Norman-French 'Elie' which was a form of 'Elias' or 'Elijah' - which means 'the LORD is God'.

On January 8th 1956 five young men were martyred whilst trying to reach a stone-age tribe in Ecuador. One of them seven years earlier he had written: "He is no Fool, who gives what he cannot keep, to gain what he cannot lose."

"Whoever finds his life will lose it, and whoever loses his life for my sake will find it."
Mt.10:39.

Ellen – see Helen

Elisha Elijah Ellisseuss Eijahu

From the Hebrew and meaning 'God is salvation'. He was a great prophet and miracle-worker whose ministry covered the lives of four kings of Israel. He was mentioned by Jesus.

Elisha means 'God (El) is salvation' and for many years he demonstrated this to the kings and people of Israel. He was the successor to Elijah and because he witnessed Elijah's translation into heaven he was given a double portion of Elijah's spirit. One of the great miracles of his lifetime was the cleansing of Naaman's leprosy recorded in 2 Kings 5. Many spiritual parallels can be drawn from this story and for years preachers have shown that leprosy is similar to sin and that the cleansing in the Jordan can be equated with the cleansing which Jesus can give.
"Elisha the man of God..."2 Kings 5:8.

Elma

A very old name from German and meaning 'seeking protection' (Originally a feminine form of 'William').

An occasional use of the name 'Elma' has been as an abbreviation of the names 'ELizabeth and MAry'. This dates from 1842 when the 8th Earl of Elgin's daughter was called Elma after her mother Elizabeth Mary. Although the name is becoming more popular it has, in the past, been restricted to parts of Scotland and when one remembers that the Shetland Isles were once ruled by Scandinavia this may explain the German word for 'seeking protection'.
"Let all who take refuge in you be glad...spread your protection over them." Ps.5:11.

Eloise

Old German meaning 'a protected head'. In the UK from the 12th century. (H)eloise was known for her beauty, intellect and faithfulness in love.

Abelard and (H)eloise were two famous 12th century lovers and (H)eloise was renowned for her beauty, cleverness and faithfulness to Abelard. There is also the possibility the name may have a French origin in 'Aloys' or 'Aloyse' - the origin of our 'Aloysius' (Al-O-Wish-Us), which in turn came from 'Louis'.
"Let love and faithfulness never leave you... write them on the tablet of your heart." Prov.3:3.

Eluned

Probably from the Welsh Celtic for 'to be worshipped'. Also Spanish for 'pretty' and a similar word in Old German means 'wise and supple'.

When Tennyson brought this name to public attention in his "Idylls of the King" (1834) he used a slightly adopted form of the original 'Eluned'. The name is shrouded in antiquity - although there are similar names in both Spanish and Old German. From these we now have Lynn, Lynnette, and many other names. It is interesting to note that the prefix 'El' in Hebrew always means 'God' so the Celtic meaning is very plausible!

"Your beauty should not come from outward adornment...instead it should be that of your inner self, the unfading beauty of a gentle and quiet spirit..." 1 Peter 3.3-4.

Elsa Elsie

Old German meaning 'noble-one'. The hero of a Wagner opera.

Everything about these names speak of royalty. The ancestry was either Alison (which means 'I am noble') or Elizabeth (which means 'God is my oath'). Today they are attractive names in their own right which mean 'noble-one'. It must have been this which inspired Wagner to call his heroine "Elsa" in his famous opera "Lohengrin". As a result many people chose the name in the 19th and 20th centuries.

"Finally, whatever is true, whatever is noble, whatever is right, whatever is pure, whatever is lovely, whatever is admirable - if anything is excellent or praiseworthy - think about such things." Phil.4:8.

Elspeth - see Elizabeth

Emily - see Amelia

Emlyn

From Latin 'Aemilius' (worker) the name of a Roman family. A Welsh town and a name used by Welsh Bards in the annual Eisteddfod.

This name has come down to us through centuries and civilisations. The name is more common in Wales than anywhere else and many 'bards' use it, together with other 'bardic' names, at the Royal National Eisteddfod. The Eisteddfod has been held each year since the first one at Cardigan Castle in 1176 and singing plays a major part - particularly hymns from the 18th century and early 20th century revivals. The town of Castell Newydd Emlyn is the place where the famous preacher Dr Martin Lloyd Jones is buried, for many years he was the Minister of the Westminster Chapel.

"Sing to God, sing praise to His name, extol Him who rides on the clouds...and rejoice before Him." Ps.68:4.

Emma

From Old German meaning; 'universal'. Popular since the 11th century now one of the top ten names in the western world. Featured by poets and novelists.

Famous people who have had the name Emma include: the wife of King Ethelred (the mother of King Edward the Confessor), Lady Emma Hamilton and the heroine of Jane Austen's novel "Emma". In the 18th century it was featured in Matthew Prior's poem "Henry and Emma" which was a paraphrase of Chaucer's "The Nut Brown Maid".

"From the rising of the sun unto the going down of the same the Lord's name is to be praised." Ps.113:3 KJV.

Emmanuel Emanuel Emanuelle Immanuel Manuel

From the Hebrew 'Immanuel' meaning 'God is with us'. Mentioned three times in the Bible.

The name 'Immanuel' is found in Is.7:14, 8:8 and the Greek transliteration 'Emmanuel' in Mt.1:23 (RSV and KJV). The prophecy in Isaiah is particularly important because of the time in which it was given. Assyria had become very powerful. Israel, Judah and Syria had proposed an alliance in opposition. Judah had hesitated and as a result Israel and Syria moved to punish her. This made King Ahaz worried and at that precise moment Isaiah delivered his prophecy.

It is at times of trial and stress that we really need to know that 'God is with us'.

"Devise your strategy, but it will be thwarted; propose your plan but it will not stand, for God is with us." Is.8:10.

Emmeline - see Amelia

Ena

From the Irish Gaelic word 'Eithne' which means the heart (central) part of the matter. One of St Patrick's first converts and also one of Queen Victoria's grandchildren!

What a lovely name and what a lovely heritage. St Patrick was a wonderful evangelical Christian but so many myths have grown up around him that this is now no longer recognised. His first convert would certainly have known the importance of loving God with all your heart. The heart is mentioned over 700 times in Scripture and at least a tenth of these are in the book of Proverbs. It is generally accepted to be the root of our emotions and our will.

"The king's heart is in the hand of the LORD; he directs it like a watercourse wherever he pleases." Proverbs 21:1.

Enid

This name means 'soul' or 'life' and originated in Wales in fairly recent years. Among the famous owners of the name is Enid Blyton, the author of many children's books.

Enid Blyton could see life through the eyes of a child - a rare gift. Jesus told His followers that they must enter the kingdom of God like children - with child-like trust (NOT child-ish!). When we do this He promises that we will become children of God - Christ will dwell in our hearts by faith and our souls will be saved eternally. This is His promise to those who will take that step of faith.

"You know with all your heart and soul that not one of all the good promises the LORD your God gave you has failed. Every promise has been fulfilled; not one has failed." Josh.23:14.

Enoch

From Hebrew meaning 'trained, disciplined or experienced'. A man who "walked with God". The oldest man who ever lived died before his father!

The original Enoch lived in the early days of creation when men survived for many more years than they do today - Enoch walked with God for over 300 years. He gave birth to many children and one of them was Methuselah the man who is reputed to have lived longer than any other man. Because of Enoch's walk with God it is said that he did not die becausej "God took him away" (Gen.5.24.). So the father of the oldest man who ever lived did not die!

"By faith Enoch was taken from this life, so that he did not experience death...For before he was taken, he was commended as one who pleased God." Heb.11;5.

Eoin - see John
Eric Erica Erik Erika

From a Scandinavian origin meaning 'always ruling'. In use since the 9th century. History is full of stories of good and bad rulers - God's people are no different except that we are enlightened people and we should know that God's way is the only way. God allows wicked men to rule and we must learn from their folly. If God chooses to give us a position of responsibility we must realise that, as the psalmist says, "...it is God who judges: He brings one down, He exalts another." Ps.75:6-7.

"Many seek an audience with a ruler, but it is from the LORD that man gets justice." Pr.29:26.

Erin

An ancient and romantic name for the country of Ireland from Irish gaelic. A

first-century famous theologian and the last stop on a steam train!
This name has some great associations - from the Christian theologian John
Scotus (810-877AD) called 'Erigena' meaning 'from the country of 'Erin' to
the last stop on the Isle of Man steam train - Port Erin! But its origin lies in
the lovely island of Ireland and its ancient Gaelic 'Eirinn' - the very
pronunciation of the name brings a vision of the beautiful green of Ireland
with its incredible scenery and lovely, warm-hearted people.
Among its many accomplishments Ireland has provided the world with
more Christian missionaries per capita than any other country.
"Sing to the LORD a new song...you islands, and all who live in them." Isaiah 42:10.

Ernest Ernie

*From Old German meaning 'to be vigorous'. Introduced in the 18th century it
became even more popular after Oscar Wilde's play "The Importance of Being
Earnest".*
This name became popular in the last few centuries - although its origins
have been traced to the 11th and 12th century. In 1895 Oscar Wilde wrote
his famous play "The Importance of Being Earnest" and from then the
name has become even more popular. The double meaning of the name
lends itself to additional uses. God loves 'Earnest' people - many of His
followers have been enthusiastic, sincere, warm, devoted, serious people -
EARNEST!
"Whatever your hand finds to do, do it with all your might." Eccl.9:10.

Errol

*From 'Eral' a medieval form of 'Harold' which means 'ruling soldier'. King
Harold, the last of the Saxon kings was killed at the battle of Hastings in 1066.*
The British Army has a fine tradition of Christian 'ruling soldiers'. From
Cromwell through to more modern examples such as General Havelock,
General Gordon, Brigadier Orde-Wingate, Field Marshall Montgomery,
General Allenby and very many others who were committed to the Lord
Jesus Christ. There were many 'ruling soldiers' in the Old Testament,
among them Barak, Joshua, Gideon, Saul and David.
"The battle is not yours - but God's." 2 Chron.20:15.

Esme Esma Esmee

*Possibly from the French for 'esteemed' or 'beloved'. A unique and enviable
combination of attributes.*
To be 'esteemed' means to be 'thought highly of' according to the
dictionary. To also be 'beloved' - 'loved and loving' means that these names
capture some of the rarest qualities that people strive all their lives to attain.
Only in God's family can one come anywhere near to such a standard.

"Do not be afraid, O man highly esteemed...Peace! Be strong now; be strong."
Dan.10:19.

Estelle

'A heavenly being'! From the Latin word for a 'star'. One of God's major creations on the fourth day "He also made the stars". Genesis 1:16.
When God promised Abraham that he would make his descendants"...as the stars of the heavens and as the sand which is on the seashore..."(Genesis 22:17) Abraham must have thought there was no real comparison - he could only see a few hundred stars and he could hold that number of grains of sand in one hand! Today scientists know that there are possibly more stars than grains of sand on all the sea shores of the world!
Like people, each star is different "...and star differs from star..."
(1 Corinthians 15:41)
"I Jesus, have sent My angel to testify to you... I am... the bright morning star."
Revelation 22:16.

Esther Hester

A Jewish Queen of the Persian Empire, whose Hebrew name means 'myrtle'.
Myrtle is an evergreen tree with fragrant leaves and scented flowers.
The book of Esther tells the story of a wicked plot against the Jews whilst they were in exile in Mesopotamia. The heroine of the story is Queen Esther who saves her people and sees the wicked Haman hanged on the gallows he had constructed for one of the leading Jews. The event is celebrated each year during February or March and is called the festival of Purim. The story illustrates that God has a plan for each life and His timing and justice cannot be thwarted.
"And who knows but that you have come...for such a time as this?" Est.4:14.

Ethan

The Hebrew word for 'firm' or 'enduring'. A wise man in the time of Solomon - who was reputed to be the wisest man who ever lived!
There are three people with this name in the Bible - 1 Kings 4:31. (Also in the title of Psalm 89), 1 Chronicles 6:42. and 1 Chronicles 6:44. "Solomon's wisdom was greater than the wisdom of all the men of the East, and greater than all the wisdom of Egypt. He was wiser than any other man, including Ethan the Ezrahite...." 1 Kings 4:30-31.
Solomon's wisdom was a gift from God - as is all wisdom. In James 1:5 we are told that we can ask God for wisdom because wisdom is the ability to practice knowledge.
"...he had wisdom from God...." 1 Kings 3:28.

Ethel

From the Old English word for 'noble strength' "Etheldreda". Also a Saint of that name in the 7th century who is reputed to have founded Ely Cathedral.

A number of churches are also dedicated to her so clearly she was a very popular saint.

As you approach the city of Ely the one feature which dominates the landscape is the beautiful cathedral. It was built in 1080 on the site of the old wooden building which preceded it. Parts of it are clearly Norman and there are some lovely carvings in the nave and choir. The west front is particularly imposing.

"The LORD is my strength and my song; He has become my salvation." Ex.15:2.

Euan - see John

Euan Ewen

From the Scottish and Irish Gaelic 'Eoghan' and probably meaning 'a young man born of the Yew tree'. The exact history may be lost in the mists of time!

A famous Scottish folk-singer, the architect who designed the National Gallery and a notorious judge on the Isle of Man all share this very ancient name. If there is an association with the Yew tree it should be noted that Yew wood is hard, fine grained, and heavy, it was once popular with cabinet workers. Its leaves hide a deadly secret - they are poisonous when left to ferment! Its historical and best-known use is for making bows because it is strong and flexible.

"I do not trust in my bow, my sword does not bring me victory; but you give us victory..." Psalm 44:6-7.

Eunice

Greek for 'good victory'. She was a Jewess and the mother of Timothy, Paul's companion (Acts 16:1). She was a woman of faith (2 Tim.1:5). She had taught Timothy the scriptures (2 Tim.3:15).

Although she was Jewish her husband was Greek - he may not have been alive when the letter to Timothy was written. Her home was at Derbe or Lystra - it is not clear. What is clear is that she exercised a strong and godly influence over Timothy. The mother of the great John Wesley was very similar. Although she had many children she tried to spend time with each one every day talking, praying and reading the scriptures.

"From infancy you have known the holy scriptures, which are able to make you wise for salvation." 2 Tim.3:15.

Euphemia

From the Greek 'Euphemizein' - meaning to speak words in a beautiful way.
The name of a number of Christian saints and a lost art!

Proverbs 25:11 says; "A word aptly spoken is like apples of gold in settings of silver." What a lovely way to describe the right word at the right time spoken in the right way. This seems to be a lost art today!

Such is the power of speech that Proverbs 18:21 says; "The tongue has the power of life and death..." Jesus said that we speak 'from the heart'.

"He who loves a pure heart and whose speech is gracious will have the king for his friend." Prov.22:11.

Evan - see John

Eve Evie Evita
Latin form: Eva

She was the first woman ever and her name means 'life', 'living' and 'enlivening'.

LIFE. She was the means whereby God would provide other men and women to inhabit and enjoy His world.

LIVING. Someone said that when God created Eve He didn't take her from Adam's head - to rule over him, nor did He take her from Adam's feet to be ruled by him but God took her from near Adam's heart to be equal and loved by him. ENLIVENING. One modern translation indicates that when Adam first saw Eve he said "Wow! This is it!"

" God said, 'it is not good for the man to be alone. I will make a helper (companion) suitable for him'". Gen.2:18.

Evelyn Aveline
Latin forms; Elvina Elevelina

From Old German in Norman times meaning 'a wished-for child'. An English name from the 17th century.

When the Normans first invaded Ireland they brought with them a whole host of new names. The girl's name 'Aveline' was one of them and this developed into the name 'Evelyn' that we know so well today.

Men have also used it - Evelyn Pierepont 1st Duke of Kingston and Sir Evelyn Alston are among them.

Isaac, Samuel and John the Baptist are among famous 'wished-for' children.

"Bring my sons from afar and my daughters from the ends of the earth everyone who is called by my name, whom I created for my glory, whom I formed and made." Is.43:6-7.

Ezekiel

From Hebrew meaning 'God will strengthen you'. A powerful prophet who witnessed both the captivity by the Babylonians and the fall of Jerusalem yet kept his faith in a supernatural God.

When you see the suffering of God's people and also experience it for yourself, it is easy to ask "Where is God?". Although Ezekiel refrained from public ministry for two years he never lost his faith and his message has been enshrined in the famous Negro spiritual based on the valley of dry bones. This is a picture of the spirit of God moving into a desolate place and breathing life into a hopeless situation.

"do not fear, I am with you; do not be dismayed, I am your God. I will strengthen you and help you;" Is.41.10.

Ezra

From Hebrew meaning 'help' - it may be an abbreviated form of 'Ezra-yah' which means 'the Lord God helps'. A fearless man who was concerned about the purity of God's chosen people!

Ezra was the writer of the book of his name, he and Nehemiah were contemporaries. He was a priest who, during the captivity, returned to Jerusalem to assist Nehemiah in the rebuilding of the walls of the city. When he arrived he was horrified to find that many of the other returning Jews had inter-married with the heathen tribes. With weeping and repentance he brought the people back to God.

"Ezra praised the LORD, the great God; and all the people lifted their hands and responded, "Amen! Amen!"" Nehemiah 8:6.

Faith

One of the great virtues of the Christian life - vital to its inception and continuance.

Faith as a name came into use after the Reformation (1500-1700) and was then given to both girls and boys. If you had girl triplets you were expected to call them "Faith, Hope and Charity"! (1 Cor.13:13. KJV).

Basically, 'faith' means 'to trust God' and it is a word which is used in the Bible many times. In the Old Testament it is used mainly in connection with 'breaking faith' but in the New Testament it is used in connection with healing and trust. A good acrostic is: Forsaking All I Trust Him.

"Trust in the LORD with all your heart..." Prov.3:5.

Fateh

From a Sanskrit word meaning 'to conquer, to achieve victory'. Used in the 17th century - also the name of a famous king in the 19th century.

Towards the end of the 17th century Fateh Sah was Rajah of Garhwal and later there is mention of King Fateh (of Sind) who was one of the first rulers of northeast India to establish contact with the British.

The Bible has many references to 'victory'. Prov.11:14. says: "For lack of guidance a nation (or person) falls, but many advisers make VICTORY sure."

"This is the VICTORY that has overcome the world...our faith." 1 John 5:4.

Felicity Fay Faye Felicia Felix

From Latin 'felicitas' meaning 'happiness' or 'good fortune'. Used in the 17th century and traced to the 3rd century.

There were two saints with the name Felicity, both were martyred. One of them died with her seven sons - she was identified with the mother of the famous Maccabees. The use of many similar abstract nouns as names followed a period of spiritual awakening in Europe and these names are among the most attractive. The apostle Paul appeared before Felix the Roman Governor and was 'remanded in custody' for two years - the story is told in Acts 24.

"To the man (or woman) who pleases Him - God gives...happiness..." Eccl.2:26.

Fenella Finola Nola

The Irish form of the Gaelic word for 'white-shouldered'. A character in a Sir Walter Scott novel.

Sir Walter Scott wrote his novel "Peveril of the Peak" in 1822 just ten years before he died and during a period of prolific work. It is the earliest reference to the name 'Fenella Finola'. The Gaelic word is made up of two parts; fionn which means 'white' and 'guala' which means 'shoulder'. In Deut.1:31. we read; "...the LORD your God carried you, as a father carries his son..." (on his shoulders). This is the place of safety and authority and it is amazing how different the world seems from this vantage point.

"...the one the LORD loves rests between His shoulders." Deut.33:12.

Fergal Fergus

From Irish Gaelic meaning 'a man of valour'. A comparatively recent name.

Gideon was described as "a...man of valour" Judg.6:12 whilst he was secretly threshing wheat for fear of the Midianites - the very people God would send him to conquer. Gideon had to learn being a man of valour meant putting your trust in God. All men like to be thought of as someone brave and fearless. The truth is that most of us are just ordinary people with the same measure of these qualities as everyone else. In a difficult situation one person was heard to say; "if you were as scared as I am - you would have been running by now!" That's valour!

"And the angel of the LORD appeared unto him, and said unto him, The LORD is with thee, thou mighty man of valour." Judg.6:12 KJV.

Finn

From Irish Gaelic meaning one who is 'fair' or 'white'. From Finn mac Cumaill the hero of Irish mythology.

Finn mac Cumaill or 'MacCool' was a legendary leader of the Fenians or Fianna who were warriors that defended Ireland against the Norse invaders. General Finn has a great reputation for bravery, strength, wisdom and above all, fairness. His world ends when his lovely princess Grainne is lured away by the wicked Diarmaid (Dermot) and Finn pursues them and kills Diarmaid. Finn is eventually taken to the land of eternal youth (Tir na nOg). In some of the ballads and poems he is implicated with St Patrick. The moral of the legends seems to be that however pure a man's motives - like Solomon of old he can be ensnared and brought down! The Psalmist found the answer;

"How can a young man keep his way pure?....by living according to your word". Ps.119;9.

Finola - see Fenella

Fiona

Originally from Gaelic and meaning 'white and fair'. A name which came to prominence late in the 19th century when it was used as a pen name for the Scottish writer William Sharp.

'White and fair' could be a good description of character or looks. "White as snow" is a Bible term for God's forgiveness and cleansing.

To be 'Fair' is a characteristic we all strive to achieve. God promises that we can acquire fairness if we will first of all trust Him and His word. See Proverbs 2:9.

"Come now, let us reason together, says the LORD. Though your sins are like scarlet, they shall be as white as snow; though they are red as crimson, they shall be like wool." Is.1:18.

Flora

From Latin meaning 'flower'. Well-liked in Scotland from the 18th century.

The name Flora has been very popular in Scotland because of Flora MacDonald. She was a Jacobite who played an important part in the escape of Bonnie Prince Charlie to France after the Battle of Culloden in 1746.

'Flora' is now used as a general name for all flowers and is usually linked to 'Fauna' to describe all God's beautiful creation. God has created a wonderful world with very many lovely things for our pleasure and enjoyment - we must learn to appreciate them and return thanks.

"See! The winter is past; the rains are over and gone. Flowers appear on the earth; the season of singing has come, the cooing of doves is heard in our land." S. of S.2:12.

Florence Florrie Flossie

From the Latin 'Florentius' which means 'flowering'. The name of an Italian city. Also the name of the founder of modern nursing.

The Italian City of Firenze (Florence) is one of the most beautiful cities in the world. It is situated in central northern Italy on the banks of the river Arno. It is rich in works of art and historic sites. One of its most famous children was born there in 1820 and named Florence Nightingale. She was the founder of modern nursing and she became known as "The Lady with the Lamp". Few people appreciate that her great work was the result of 'a call from God' in 1837 when she heard "the voice of God speaking". Did her story prompt the hymnwriter to write: "Lord speak to me that I may speak in living echos of Thy tone..." (Frances R Havergal c1860)

"...the grass withers and the flowers fall...but the word of the Lord stands forever." 1 Pet.1:24-25

Frances Francis Frank Frankie
Italian form: Francesca

Originally from the Italian 'Francesco' which means literally, 'a little Frenchman'.

St Francis of Assisi was founder of the Franciscan order of preaching friars which advocates a life of simplicity, poverty and service to others. The tradition is that when he, Giovanni (John) returned from France, his father nicknamed him 'Francesco' (little Frenchman). He was greatly influenced by reading Matthew 10:7-10. As a result he began to preach brotherly love and repentance. One of the most famous of his prayers (now a hymn) says: "Make me a channel of your peace. Where there is hatred let me bring your love; where there is injury your pardon Lord; and where there's doubt true faith in you."

"Blessed are the poor in spirit, for theirs is the kingdom of heaven." Matt.5:3.

Folu

This is a Yoruba Christian name – the full spelling is 'Fyinfoluwa' and it means 'Give glory to God!'

It is interesting to note that when the angels appeared to the shepherds and announced the birth of the Saviour of the world their chorus was; "Glory to God in the highest and on earth peace to men on whom His favour rests" Luke 2:14.

This verse was used by one town in their Christmas decorations – unfortunately the weather damaged the banner and it finished up reading "Glory to God in the high st" That's sounds like divine intervention to me!

"But grow in the grace and knowledge of our Lord and Saviour Jesus Christ. To him be glory both now and forever! Amen." 2 Peter 3:18.

Franklin

From Old English and meaning 'a free man' - honoured and free of taxation without noble birth. The name of at least two great American Presidents.

Franklin D Roosevelt (1882-1945) and Benjamin Franklin (1706-1790) were both American Presidents of distinction.

The title 'freeman' came from the Old English word 'frankelyn' which in turn came from the Latin word 'francalia' which was land owned by Franks (originally German warrior tribes) who were not subject to taxation. Today in Britain a Freeman is a recipient of an honour bestowed on him or her by their Borough. As such they are exempt from any tolls levied in that area.

"...if the Son sets you free, you will be free indeed." John 8:36.

Fraser Frazer

A Scottish surname with an obscure history now used as a Christian name. A pioneer who left his mark on China.

J.O.Fraser (1886-1938) felt his heart "strangely warmed" when, as a young student at Imperial College London, he heard the gospel message. He completed his degree and by the age of 22 was working as a missionary in China. His father had been President of the Royal College of Veterinary Surgeons and a similar career could have been his, or he might have chosen music - he had given his first piano recital in London at the age of 20. Instead, he spent his life travelling on horseback in the rugged mountains of inland China telling people the good news of Jesus Christ.

"I will not sacrifice...to the LORD my God...that costs me nothing." 2 Sam.24:24.

Fred Freda Freddie Freddy Frederick - see also Alfred

From Old German meaning 'a peaceful ruler'. Popular in the 17th and 18th centuries.

These names date mainly from the 16th century and the French form of 'Frery' although they have been traced back to the 12th century in the case of the Holy Roman Emperor Frederick Barbarossa (1123-1190).

From Frederick, Prince of Wales and son of George II, they became more popular and today are used in various forms.

"Peacemakers who sow in peace raise a harvest of righteousness". Jas.3:18.

Freya

From 'Freyia' the name of the ancient Norse goddess of love, beauty and fertility. Possibly also Old English for 'Friday'.

The conversion of Britain to Christianity began in AD597 and was completed within 100 years - the process among the Teutonic peoples took almost seven centuries. Frey was the chief god of the north together with his sister Freyia and Uppsala in Sweden was the centre of their worship. This group of cult worshippers were enemies of the southern worshippers of Odin - whose wife was called Frigg - the origin of our Friday. Frigg was the god of peace and plenty.

"Your beauty should not come from outward adornment...it should be that of your inner self, the unfading beauty of a gentle and quiet spirit..." 1 Pet.3;3-4.

Gabriel Gabriell Gabrielli

From Hebrew, one of the archangels of Scripture. The word means 'a person who prevails with God'.

The Hebrew word is mentioned four times in the Bible. On each occasion he brings a momentous message. In the first chapter of Luke's gospel it is the greatest message ever entrusted to any messenger; "You will be with child and give birth to a son, and you are to give him the name Jesus." Luke 1:31. As one of four archangels he stands in the very presence of God (Luke 1:19). An alternative translation of the name would be 'the strength of God'.

"The angel (Gabriel) went to her and said, "Shalom, you who are highly favoured! The Lord is with you."" Luke 1:28.

Gaenor Gaynor - see also Gwyneth

The Old Cornish/Welsh form of the name of King Arthur's wife 'Guenevere'. It means 'white spirit'. A woman of mystery and intrigue!

Some say that she was Cornish - others that she was Roman - but these are nothing compared with the other fables that surround the lovely Guenevere. One story says that became a Christian at the end of her life and lived in poverty in order to help the poor - but like many of the Arthurian legends there is little evidence to support it.

Because Old Cornish and Welsh have so much in common the name has become popular in Wales and now has very many different spellings. The name Gaenor is one of the loveliest of these.

"Many women do noble things...but a woman who fears the Lord is to be praised." Prov.31:29-30.

Gail - see Abigail

Gaius Caius

Latin meaning 'bridegroom' (from 'gavisus' meaning 'rejoiced'). Both are usually pronounced 'guy-us' with the exception of the Cambridge College which is pronounced 'Keys'.

Rejoicing is not a common concept today. People speak about 'being happy' or 'very glad' or even 'elated' but seldom 'joyful'. I wonder why that is? 'Joy' and 'rejoicing' are mentioned at least 250 times in the Bible - as many times in the Old Testament as in the new. Philippians has been called "The life of continual rejoicing".

"...my soul will rejoice in the LORD and delight in His salvation." Ps.35:9.

Gareth Garth - see also Gary

From Welsh meaning 'gentle'. Both Malory and Tennyson used the name 'Gareth'.

'Gentleness' is not always thought to be a male attribute - but even huge strong elephants are 'gentle' creatures.

The Greek origin of the word 'gentle' in Gal.5:23 suggests the picture of a judge who instead of demanding the full penalty required by law gives way to mercy and makes a less strict but suitable and appropriate sentence. In this way, a 'correct' judgement yields to a 'gentle' one because the wrong-doer may be more inclined to amend his ways.

"But the fruit of the Spirit is love, joy, peace, patience, kindness, goodness, faithfulness, gentleness and self-control. Against such things there is no law." Gal.5:22-23.

Garfield - see also Gary

From Old English and meaning 'spear-field'. Made famous by the American President James A. Garfield in the 19th century and the cricketer Sir Garfield Sobers who used the short form 'Gary'.

'Spear-field' has an uncertain history but 'spears' in one form or another have been used since time began.

David said to Goliath the Philistine, "You come against me with sword and spear and javelin, but I come against you in the name of the LORD Almighty" 1 Sam.17:45 (it is said Goliath's spear weighed 7 kilos).

"...the battle is the LORD's" 1 Sam.17:47.

Gary Garry

American origin but sometimes used as a short form of either Garfield (old English) or Gareth (Welsh).

Elbert Henry Gary lived in the 19th century in Wheaton USA. He became one of the most successful American businessmen. His vast empire included steel, banking, law, building and education. His steel interests alone were valued at one thousand million dollars at the beginning of the 20th century. Four American towns were built and named in his honour. The great film star Gary Cooper (born Frank James Cooper) chose his name as a result of the fame of E.H.Gary.

"Wealth and honour come from you; you are the ruler of all things. In your hands are strength and power to exalt and give strength to all." 1 Chron.29:12.

Gavin
From Celtic 'Gawain' and meaning 'white hawk'. One of the Knights of the Round Table.
Sir Gawain was King Arthur's famous nephew and a Knight of the Round Table according to the legend. The name fell into disuse until it was revived around the 16th century in Scotland.
Hawks are birds of prey and in the UK the only 'white hawk' is the male Hen Harrier, known as the 'Marsh Hawk' in North America, and it is only partially white. In North America there is also the 'Coopers Hawk' which is one of 48 species. It is white underneath when it is young and grows to a length of 50cm when fully grown.
"Does the hawk take flight by your wisdom...?" Job 39:26.

Gay Gaye
A traditional old English word meaning; 'happy, bright and lively'.
Cheerfulness is a constant theme in Scripture. The writer of Ecclesiastes even tried hard drink to achieve it (Eccl.2:3). The book of Proverbs has the answer when it says: "A happy heart makes the face cheerful" Prov.15:13. A 'happy heart' is a cleansed heart and a heart which is obedient to the Saviour's will.
"When times are good, be happy; but when times are bad, consider: God made the one as well as the other." Eccl.7:14.

Gayle – Abigal

Gaynor Gaenor – see Gwyneth

Gemma Jemma
From the Italian word for 'gem' or 'jewel'. Used from the 13th century. Originally an Italian name.
Now ranked as one of the most popular names, this name has grown in popularity from the 12th century. The Medieval Italian word for jewel is 'gemma'.
In Exodus 25 we are told about the 'other gems' that would be added to the breastplate of the High Priest, then in chapter 39:8-14 we are given the complete list. There are many other 'gems' listed in scripture and clearly they play an important part in the eternal city (Rev.21:18-21).
"Engrave the names...the way a gem cutter engraves a seal...as a memorial before the LORD." Ex.28:11-12.

Geoffrey Geoff

Means 'peace' from an Old German word. A surname as well as a Christian name for many years.

Not everyone realises that 'peace' is one of God's names. In Judg.6:24. we read; "So Gideon built an altar to the LORD there and called it: 'The LORD is Peace' (Yahweh-Shalom)". Today the word 'peace' is a common greeting in Israel and among Hebrew and Arabic speaking people everywhere. Real peace is not the absence of conflict - it is the presence of God in your life.

"the peace of God...will guard your hearts and your minds in Christ Jesus." Phil.4:7.

George Georgia Georgina Gina
Swedish form: Joran

Greek meaning 'farmer'. From the 3rd century St George - who slew the dragon.

The story of St George revolves around a real person who was born and died at Lydda in Israel (close to Ben Gurion Airport). The legend of Perseus' killing of the sea monster Andromeda which is supposed to have occurred in the same area, became inherited by St George and so we have the legend of "St George and the dragon". Whilst some legends lack any semblance of reality, the truth that medieval writers wanted to convey is that of a spiritual battle.

"For our struggle is not against flesh and blood...therefore put on the full armour of God..." Eph.6:12-13.

Gerald Geraldine Gerard Gerry Jerry

Old German meaning 'spear brave'. Popular from the 11th century. The old German word for 'spear' was 'ger' and the word for 'rule' was 'vald' and these names developed from this.

Original names were brought by the Normans and survived in Ireland through the Fitzgeralds (sons of Gerald).

One of the most famous spears of the Bible is the one which Goliath carried when he met the shepherd-boy David. It is said that it weighed 7 kilos (around 15 lbs.).

"He makes wars cease to the ends of the earth; He breaks the bow and shatters the spear...Be still, and know that I am God." Ps.46:9-10.

Gertrude Gert Gertie Trudi Trudie Trudy

Old German meaning 'a strong spear'. The original name Gertrude was brought to Britain in the Middle Ages from Scandinavia.

The old German word for 'spear' was 'ger' and the word for 'strength' was 'drudi'.

There were two saints with this name; Gertrude Abbess of Nivelles and Gertrude the Great.

In a remarkable prophecy concerning the Lord Jesus Christ, Simeon said to Mary, His mother, in Luke 2:34-35. "This child is destined to cause the falling and rising of many in Israel...And a sword will pierce your own soul too."

"Put on the...armour of God so that you can take your stand against the devil's schemes." Eph.6:11.

Gervase Jarvis
French form: Gervais

Old German meaning 'an armour-bearer'. A 1st century martyr. The origin of 'Jarvis'.

'Ger' is the Old German word for spear and 'vass' (vassal) is the Celtic word for 'servant'. This name was introduced to England by the Normans. From 'Gervase' came the name 'Jarvis'.

The body of St Gervase was discovered with that of his brother in AD386 when Ambrose wanted to build a new church in Milan. They had been martyred for their faith in the first century.

The Bible encourages us to "put on the full armour of God" - to be an 'armour-bearer'.

"Do all that you have in mind,' his armour bearer said...'I am with you heart and soul.'" 1 Sam.14:7.

Gianna Giovanna Giovanni - see John

Gideon

From Hebrew meaning 'he who bruises, breaks or smites'. From threshing wheat to thrashing the Midianites. A man on the roll-call of faith.

When the writer to the Hebrews wanted to select less than 20 people of faith from the last 4,000 years of history, GIDEON is one of the names he decided to include (Heb.11:32). Gideon was a farmer in the times of the Judges and you can read his story in Judges chapters 6 to 8.

The thrilling story of his defeat of the Midianites is told in chapter 7. It is a classic case of fine military strategy. He reduces his army from 32,000 to 300 and once again demonstrates that God and one man are always a majority.

"The LORD is with you, mighty warrior." Judg.6:12

Gilbert

An 11th century name from Old German meaning 'a bright pledge'. The name of an Opera librettist - ludicrous and paradoxical.

The name Gilbert began with a strong and positive meaning (a bright pledge) in the 11th century or before. The name became the basis for many surnames such as; Gilbertson, Gilbart, Gilson, Gibson, Gibbons etc. The 20 year partnership of Gilbert and Sullivan, during which both were knighted, lasted until 1911. Gilbert's wit and the way he dealt with paradoxes and ludicrous dilemmas caused a new word to be coined: 'Gilbertian'.

"If you take your neighbour's cloak as a pledge, return it to him by sunset...What else will he sleep in? When he cries out to me, I will hear, for I am compassionate." Ex.22:26-27.

Giles

From the Latin word 'Aegidius' originally meaning 'a kid'. According to legend St Giles was from Athens and was so named because of the goatskin which he wore. In France the name 'Aegidius' soon became 'Gilles'.

Apparently St Giles fled to France for some peace and quiet because his 'miracles' were attracting so much attention. All this was supposed to have happened in the 12th century and even though it is legend there are at least 162 Churches named after him in England alone. Because of his 'miracles' he is the patron saint of beggars and cripples.

It was the Lord Jesus who called "the poor, the crippled, the lame, the blind" (Luke 14:13) to come to His great feast.

"Come to me, all you who are weary and burdened, and I will give you rest." Matt.11:28.

Gillian Gill Jillian

From Juliana - it means 'gentle and sensitive'. It was originally a Roman family name and it was the name of the man who escorted the Apostle Paul on his journey to Rome (Acts 27).

Julius was the name of an old Roman family connected with the Caesars and in his letter to the Philippians (written from prison in Rome), Paul mentions that there were believers in "Caesar's household" Phil.4:22. So it seems that somewhere on his journey or in Rome, Paul had led members of the family to the Lord Jesus Christ. I wonder if this Julius was the first? They were clearly good friends - see Acts 27:3. Perhaps this was one Roman soldier who lived up to his name?

"A gentle answer turns away wrath, but a harsh word stirs up anger." Prov.15:1.

Gina – see George

Ginni Ginny - see Virginia

Gisella Giselle

From Old German meaning 'a pledge'. The daughter of Charles the Simple who married Rollo 1st Duke of Normandy.

To make or give 'a pledge' in Old Testament times was a very serious business and certain rules were laid down to ensure that unreasonable pledges were not made or accepted. For example: "If you take your neighbour's cloak as a pledge, return it to him by sunset, because his cloak is the only covering he has for his body. What else will he sleep in? When he cries out to me, I will hear, for I am compassionate." Ex.22:26-27.

In the New Testament, the concept is of an engagement pledge when Paul uses the word "seal" or "deposit".

"Having believed, you were marked in Him with a seal, the promised Holy Spirit, who is a deposit guaranteeing our inheritance." Eph.1:13-14.

Gladys

From 5th century Welsh meaning 'a ruler'. Was this the 'Claudia' of 2 Tim.4:21?

The Welsh history of this name dates back to the 5th century. The earliest date it is recorded in England is the 13th century when the name 'Gladusa' is found in Cumberland.

There is a suggestion that the 'Claudia' of 2 Tim.4:21 was a Welsh lady and that her name equated to 'Gwladys', when translated into Welsh. This may be so - even though translators of Welsh Bibles have declined to use it.

It is often shortened to 'Glad' which is another of those words with a delightful double-meaning.

"I will be glad and rejoice in your love..." Ps.31:7.

Glen Glenn Glenna Glyn Glynn

Celtic and Welsh for 'valley'. Included in place-names in the UK. A place that can be a 'door of hope'.

If you travel north from Ben-Gurion Airport in Israel you will soon come to one of the first settlements of the new state - the city of Petach-Tikvah. In Hebrew this means 'door of hope' and is a quotation from Hos.2:15 where the prophet says that God will make 'the valley of Achor a door of hope'. God is able to transform our lowest moments or 'valley' experiences into blessings. He can make the place of our defeat a 'door of hope' and blessing.

"...they assembled in the Valley of Beracah (blessing), where they praised the LORD. This is why it is called the Valley of Beracah to this day." 2 Chron.20:26.

Glenda Glenys Glennis

From Welsh meaning 'holy and good'. Set apart for a special or unique purpose.

A sacred and high calling.
Every religion in the world has a line between 'holy' and 'profane'. Those who seek to live in the 'holy' domain are usually described in one way or another as 'holy people'. But what does 'holy' really mean?
As far as the Bible is concerned 'holiness' means 'to be separate' or 'set apart'. So we have "holy land", "holy Sabbaths", a "holy nation", a "holy place" etc. So 'holiness' is belonging to, or being part of something that is chosen by God and is part of His nature or character.
"Great is the LORD, and most worthy of praise, in the city of our God, His holy mountain." Ps.48:1.

Glenn Glenna - see Glen

Glenys - see Glenda

Glinys Glynis
From the Welsh 'Glyn' for 'a valley'. A picturesque name from the land of song.
Similar to some Old-English words 'Glinys' means a valley or a small recess. In the Bible valleys or glens have an additional significance - they speak of human experiences. As a result of this we sometimes say "that was a mountain-top experience" or "you seem down today".
One of the features of Jerusalem is the mountains and the valleys that surround it - perhaps that is why the psalmist could say; "Though I walk through the valley of the shadow of death I will fear no evil - for you are with me" Ps.23:4. We can trust God in the valleys or on the mountains - after all, He made them!
"As the mountains surround Jerusalem, so the LORD surrounds His people both now and for evermore." Ps.125:2.

Gloria
Latin for 'glory' or 'fame'. First used by George Bernard Shaw. A word which describes a characteristic of the presence of God.
As far as can be ascertained the first use of this Latin name in English was by George Bernard Shaw in his play "You Never Can Tell" (1898) - it has been popular since.
The 'Glory of God' is a regular expression in the Old Testament. When Israel came out of Egypt, God's glory was revealed in the cloud during the day and in the pillar of fire at night. When the Temple was built we are told that the "...glory of God filled the place." 1 Kings 8:11. In the New Testament the Transfiguration, Resurrection and Ascension all display the glory of God in Jesus Christ.
"Glory in His holy name; let the hearts of those who seek the LORD rejoice." 1 Chron.16:10.

Glyn - see Glen

Glynis - see Glinys

Glynn - see Glen

Godfrey

From Old German and meaning 'God's peace'. In use from the 11th century. A French Crusader.

The name Godfrey became a surname and also initiated other surnames such as; Godfry, Godfree, Godfreed and Godefray. A French Crusader by the name of Godfrey led the first German crusade and captured Jerusalem in 1099. He was made 'Protector of the Holy Sepulchre'.

The meaning 'God's peace' is possibly the best meaning of any name. The Hebrew equivalent is 'Shalom' but it is more than just 'peace'. We would classify 'peace' as a cessation of conflict but the Hebrew word is far more descriptive - it means 'God's wholeness' and has the sense of being an endowed blessing rather than wishful thinking.

"...the LORD turn His face towards you and give you peace." (Shalom) Num.6:26.

Gordon

From Celtic meaning 'spacious fort'. An old Scottish surname and place-name. A famous General in the 19th century.

'Gordon' was originally used as a place-name before it was adopted as a surname of some Scottish Lords - or 'Lairds'. It became very popular after the death of the famous General Gordon in 1885 defending the city after which he is now named - Gordon of Khartoum. It is not widely known that General Gordon was a born-again Christian and he used to spend hours reading his Bible and praying. One day he was doing this on the roof of a friend's house in Jerusalem. He glanced to the north and saw what he thought was the shape of a skull ("Golgotha...The Place of the Skull" Mt.27:33) in the rocks. This area is now known as 'The Garden Tomb' and 'Gordon's Calvary'. He had discovered a place where Jesus could have died and risen again.

"If anyone would come after me, he must...take up his cross daily and follow me." Luke 9:23.

Grace Gracie Caris Charis - see also Grainne Grania

From Latin 'gratia' meaning 'a religious virtue'. Thankfulness at meal-times. A thing of beauty and elegance...

The word 'grace' occurs some 124 times in most English translations of the

Bible and of these only 8 are in the Old Testament - usually the word meaning grace there is translated "mercy", "loving-kindness", "goodness" etc. One of the most descriptive verses in the New Testament is John 1:14. "We have seen His glory...full of grace and truth". There was virtue in Christ which meant that He could be described as 'grace'. We also use the word to portray someone as 'graceful' and this means that their deportment is poised, charming and balanced. Many Christian families like to say 'grace' before meals.

"...grow in the grace and knowledge of our Lord and Saviour Jesus Christ." 2 Pet.3:18.

Graham Graeme

This name like very many others developed from a place name - Grantham (home of a man called 'Grant'). Many famous people have used it as a Christian and a surname.

Perhaps one of the most famous of the 20th century has been Dr Billy Graham the great evangelist. He was converted through a man called Mordecai Ham. Other well-known Grahams have been; Graham Hill the racing driver, Graham Greene the novelist, Kenneth Grahame the author of "Wind in the Willows", Sir Gerald Graham - one of the most decorated men in history, Sir James Graham the 18th century politician and even a town called Graham in Texas.

"the God who has been my shepherd...may he bless these boys." Gen.48:15-16.

Grainne Grania

From Irish Gaelic meaning 'she who inspires fear'. 'Grace' is often substituted. Scottish and Irish legends abound.

Few ladies realise that one of the chief emotions that they inspire in men is that of fear and this name brings that to the surface - but 'Grace' is not far away! The legends that surround the name come from around AD250 when a certain Finn MacCumhail was the General to whom the king gave the task of organising the Irish army. Finn tried to usurp the king and in the process fell in love with the king's daughter - Grainne. One of his lieutenants eloped with his destined bride and Finn pursued him and killed him. There are many variations to the legend - but like all legends there may be some truth in the original.

"...perfect love drives out fear, because fear has to do with punishment." 1 John 4:18.

Grant

From Norman French 'le grand' meaning 'tall' or 'large'. A Scots surname. A famous American President in the 19th century.

'Grant' was originally a surname which was very popular in Scotland and North America. It came into use as a Christian name in the 19th century following the popularity of General Ulysses Grant the 18th President of the USA. His father was from Scotland and he came to prominence during the American Civil War. He was a man of many talents and some faults. There is no doubt that he saved the Union and his greatest battle for this was at 'Shiloh' - like Joshua of old (Josh.22). 'Grant' is also a verb - usually used as the preface for a request or prayer.

"May the LORD grant all your requests." Ps.20:5.

Gregory

From Greek meaning 'a watchman'. The Pope who sent St Augustine to England.

When Pope Gregory the Great sent Augustine to England in AD596 he knew that the time was ripe for the conversion of the pagan Anglo-Saxons. Augustine on the other hand was a little fearful of these fierce islanders and asked for permission to turn back. He finally crossed the channel and established himself at Canterbury.

Watchmen had vital roles in Old Testament days. Their first task was to watch out for enemies, this was even more important at night. Secondly, they were to guard the animals whilst they were feeding. Thirdly, they were responsible for internal security and care of the inhabitants.

"Son of man, I have made you a watchman...so hear the word I speak..." Ez.33:7.

Greta - see Margaret

Gustav Gustave

From Old Norse 'Gautr's staff'. The name of several Swedish kings and the name of a great Austrian composer. An essential part of God's protective care.

'Gautr' was a the name of an ancient tribal group of Scandinavian or Slavonic origin. The earliest Swedish king with this name was Gustav Vasa who lived in the 15th century.

The Austrian composer Gustav Mahler earned the nickname of "the tyrant" because he was so tireless in his writing and promoting opera.

"Even though I walk through the valley of the shadow of death, I will fear no evil, for you are with me; your rod and your staff, they comfort me." Ps.23:4.

Guy

From Old German meaning 'wide' or 'wood'. The Old German 'Wido' in Latin became 'Guido'. Remember, remember the 5th of November.

This name like many others has arrived by a tortuous route. In Latin it means 'lively'.

'Guy Fawkes' Day' is the name given to the 5th of November each year when the infamous 'Gunpowder Plot' is remembered. A group led by Guy planted a large quantity of gunpowder beneath Parliament and planned to ignite it when King James 1st was there. Someone wrote to Lord Monteagle warning him not to go and he showed the letter to fellow members of the House of Lords. The cellars were searched a week later and all was discovered. As a result Guy Fawkes and 7 others including two named 'Winter' (the writer's name) were executed.

"O LORD... other lords beside you have ruled over us but your name alone do we honour." Is.26:13.

Gwen Gwendolen Gwendolyn - see Guendolen

Gwyneth Gwenneth Gwyn Gwynneth

A Welsh name which means 'fair maiden' (it can also mean 'happy' or 'blessed'). The name has been famous since King Arthur.

'Fair maiden' is a good description of a person - particularly when 'fair' is a description of inner character and beauty. If this is true then she certainly will be 'blessed' or 'happy'.

"Fair" is a characteristic we all strive to achieve and God promises that we can acquire it if we will first of all trust Him and His word (Proverbs 2:9). As far as external 'fairness' is concerned - there is another proverb which says: "Charm is deceptive and beauty is fleeting; but a woman who fears the LORD is to be praised." Prov.31:30.

"...provide...what is right and fair...you also have a Master in heaven." Col.4:1.

Hamish - see James

Hannah

Hebrew for 'God has graciously favoured me'. Hannah was the mother of the great prophet Samuel.

Hannah was a woman of prayer and one day after she had been praying and weeping in the Temple she promised God that if He gave her a son she would dedicate him to God. He granted her wish - see 1 Samuel chapter 1.

Her husband was very fond of her and it says: "he gave her a double portion - because he loved her" 1 Sam.1:5. *"Then Hannah prayed and said: My heart rejoices in the LORD." 1 Sam.2:1.*

Harold

From Old Norse meaning 'ruling soldier'. King Harold, the last of the Saxon kings' was killed at the battle of Hastings in 1066. Since then many famous people have been called Harold.

In the 20th century two British Prime Ministers were 'Harolds'; Harold MacMillan and Harold Wilson but neither were 'ruling soldiers'. There were 'ruling soldiers' in the Bible, such as; Joshua, Gideon, Saul, David and Nehemiah.

"The LORD is a warrior - the LORD is His name." Ex.15:3.

Harriet - see also Henrietta

French 'Henrietta' meaning 'power'. Popular in the 18th and 19th centuries. The wife of Charles 1st.

The wife of Charles 1st Henrietta Maria joined Charles from France during a very turbulent period in his reign.

On a happier note, if you would like a long walk you could try the Pilgrim's Way which leads from Winchester to Canterbury and used to be a pilgrimage route to Canterbury. Should you follow the parallel North Downs Way you could enjoy 225 km (140 miles) of footpath and between Maidstone and Ashford you will pass HARRIETsham.

"Not by might nor by power, but by my Spirit,' says the LORD Almighty." Zec.4:6.

Harrison Harry - see Henry

Harvey

From French Old Breton (Celtic) origin meaning 'battle-worthy'. In England from the 12th century.

Harveys have 'battled' for hundreds of years and we should be thankful that they have!

Your car wouldn't run so well if Harvey Firestone had not set up the "Firestone Tire Company" in 1900 with just 17 workers. Firestone became one of the largest rubber companies and developed rubber estates in South America and the Philippines. William Harvey was a doctor and lived from 1578 to 1657. He pioneered work that Harvey Williams built on at the turn of the 19th century when he developed Blood Pressure monitoring and used X-rays in his work as a brain surgeon.

"I praise you because I am fearfully and wonderfully made...I know that full well." Ps.139:14.

Hattie – see Henrietta

Havana

Possibly inspired by the Hebrew folk-song 'Hava nagila' (rejoice and be glad!). The capital city of Cuba and a very fine cigar!

The popular Jewish folk-song 'Hava nagila' was the work of composer and cantor Abraham Zevi Idelsohn who was born in Latvia in 1882. He took the melody from an ancient Hasidic tune. There was little to 'rejoice and be glad' about in his day but he emigrated to Israel in 1905 and set up the Institute for Jewish Music in Jerusalem. He also composed other operas and was a distinguished ethnomusicologist.

Havana is a beautiful city of some 2 million people and was named by Spanish colonialists 'La Habana'.

"This is the day the LORD has made; let us rejoice and be glad in it." Ps.118:24.

Haydn Hayden

Names in honour of the famous Austrian music composer Franz Joseph Haydn who lived in the 18th century. Some similarity to a Welsh word 'Rhedyn' meaning 'bracken'.

The composer Haydn was from a deeply religious family and his major works reflect this. One of the best of his Oratorios "The Creation" is still regularly performed and greatly appreciated.

Have you noticed the power of music to release emotions? "David sang to the LORD...when the LORD delivered him from the hand of all his enemies and from the hand of Saul. He said: 'The LORD is my rock, my fortress and my deliverer; my God is my rock, in whom I take refuge, my shield and the horn of my salvation.'" 2 Sam.22:1-3.

"He is my stronghold, my refuge and my Saviour." 2 Sam.22:3.

Hayley

Old English word which means 'a hay-clearing' that is, a field (lea) set apart for the purpose of hay production. Made popular by the film star Hayley Mills.

The cultivation, harvesting, storage and wise use of hay is a theme of scripture which is best summed-up by the writer of Proverbs: "... riches do not endure forever, and a crown is not secure for all generations. When the hay is removed and new growth appears and the grass from the hills is gathered in, the lambs will provide you with clothing, and the goats with the price of a field. You will have plenty of goats' milk to feed you and your family..." Prov.27:23-27.

"...do good...be rich in good deeds...be generous and willing to share." 1 Tim.6:18.

Hazel

An attractive name from the world God created for our pleasure.

The name Hazel has been very popular in the last century. The tree from which we get the name grows all over the northern hemisphere. There are two common species and both have tasty, edible nuts. Several varieties are used as ornamental trees because they are so beautiful. "For the beauty of the earth, for the beauty of the skies. For the love which from our birth over and around and around us lies; Christ our Lord to you we raise this our hymn of grateful praise." F.S.Pierpoint (1835-1917).

"The fruit of the righteous is a tree of life, and he who wins souls is wise." Prov.11:30.

Heather Hedley

'Hedley' means 'a field of heather'. A beautiful 'clothing' for the hills of the north of England and Scotland. One of the prettiest names chosen from plants. The Latin name for heather is 'Erica'.

These names have been very popular in Scotland and there are very many songs written mentioning heather. For the Romany it has taken on a mystical significance, but it has no magical qualities, it is simply one of the most beautiful sights on the hillsides of the north, and occasionally, other areas. *"You will go out in joy...and all the trees of the field will clap their hands." Is.55:12.*

Hector

From Greek meaning 'hold fast'. A Trojan hero. A name popular in Scotland.

In Greek mythology Hector was the chief Trojan warrior-son of Priam and Hecuba and the husband of Andromache. He was killed during the battle for Troy and buried with great pomp and honour.

The name became popular in Scotland because it is similar to the Gaelic name 'eachan' meaning 'brown horse'. The meaning is 'hold tight' or 'hold fast'. This is an injunction to all who know and love the Lord Jesus Christ.

"You are to hold fast to the LORD your God," Josh.23:8.

Heidi - see also Adelaide

From German 'adelheit' which means 'nobility'. The name of a favourite story.

Heidi comes from 'adelheit' which is the German for 'nobility'. This was the name of King William IV's wife in the nineteenth century and from her, the town of Adelaide in Australia was named.

One of the most fascinating children's books is the story of "Heidi" by Johanna Spryri.

There is a link (through Adelaide) with 'Adah' in the book of Genesis ('Adah' means 'an ornament' or 'adorned').

"All...know...you are a woman of noble character." Ruth 3:11.

Helen Helene Elena Helena Ellen Leonora Lena

Greek meaning 'a bright one' or 'light'. Some 135 churches are dedicated to 'St Helena' in England.

St Helena was the mother of the first Christian Emperor Constantine. There is a legend that she was born in England the daughter of 'Old King Cole' the ruler of Colchester. It was Helena that went to the Holy Land and located many of the sites where Jesus ministered, died and rose again. Some of these sites may not be the actual places - but that is not important, what is important is the fact that the events actually happened.

"And God said; 'Let there be light,' and there was light." Gen.1:3.

Helga

Norse meaning 'holy' or 'prosperous'. Set apart for a unique purpose. A sacred, high calling.

Every religion in the world has a line between 'holy' and 'profane'. Those who seek to live in the 'holy' realm are usually described in one way or another as 'holy people'. What does 'holy' really mean? As far as the Bible is concerned 'holiness' means 'to be separate' or 'set apart'. So we have "holy land", "holy Sabbaths", "holy nation", "holy place" etc. So 'holiness' is belonging to and being part of something that is chosen by God.

"Holy, holy, holy is the LORD Almighty; the whole earth is full of his glory." Is.6:3.

Henderson

Originally Scottish and from the surname 'Hendry' which then became 'Henry' - his son was called 'Henry's son' and then 'Henderson'.

There have been many famous 'Henrys', 'Henrysons' and 'Hendersons' and among them were two of note:

In the 17th century Alexander Henderson was an ordained Minister and approved by the Bishop. He arrived at his appointed Church only to find that the parishioners had barred the door of the building because they knew that he was unconverted. Later he heard Robert Bruce and became a

Christian and an outstanding leader as a result.

Matthew Henry was a famous bible expositor - he used to rise at 4 am to work on his Bible Passages. Friends completed his commentary after he died. He wrote a 190-word comment and a three-part sermon on Gen.26:34.

"A wise son brings joy to his father." Prov.10:1.

Henrietta Hattie - see also Harriet

From the French meaning 'power'. The wife of Charles 1st. Popular in the 18th and 19th centuries.

The wife of Charles 1st was called Henrietta Maria and she joined Charles from France during a very turbulent period in his reign. She was married to Charles by proxy in Paris in 1625. The name 'Harriet' developed from it.

'Will-power' can be a force for good or evil because God has given us the ability to 'make up our minds' about almost every issue. That is why the hymn writer says in the famous consecration hymn;" Take my will and make it thine, it shall be no longer mine: "Take my heart - it is thine own; it shall be thy royal throne." Francis Ridley Havergal (1836-79).

"...I know that the LORD saves his anointed...with the saving power of his right hand." Ps.20:6.

Henry Harry Harrison

'Henry' or 'Harry' is from French and means 'power'. 'Harrison' is literally: 'Harry's-son' The name of many English Kings.

These names have been very popular in the USA - including the 9th and 23rd presidents. They are now being used more in the UK by royalty. Being 'Harry's-son' is similar to being 'Bar-abbas'. ('Bar' means 'son of' and 'abba' means 'father' - so like you and I he was the son of his father! He is the man in whose place Jesus died).

"...They will see the Son of Man coming...with power and great glory." Mt.24:30.

Herbert Bert

From Old German and meaning 'bright army'. Mentioned in the Doomsday Book.

'Herbertus' and the corresponding Old English word 'Herebeorht' or a very similar name is recorded long before the Norman Conquest but it was then that it became prominent in its present form.

The Hymn writer George Herbert lived from 1593 to 1633 and is responsible for such hymns as "Let all the world in every corner sing", "The God of love my Shepherd is", "Teach me my God and King" and many more. He was a brilliant man and wrote poetry as well as hymns. He died at the age of forty just four years after his marriage.

"Speak to one another with psalms, hymns and spiritual songs. Sing...to the Lord..."
Eph.5:19.

Herman – see also Armin

From Old German meaning 'a soldier'. Brought to Britain by the Normans.
A man named Hermann of Reichenau who lived early in the 11th century was terribly deformed but he loved God and promised to serve Him when he was only seven years old. He was the most scholarly man in the country proficient in Theology, Latin, Greek and Arabic and an outstanding poet, mathematician, astronomer and musician. His students loved him. He wrote one of the most amazing chronicles covering the period from the life of Christ to his own death at the age of 41.
"...my brother, fellow worker and fellow soldier..." Phil.2:25.

Hester - see Esther

Hilary

From Greek meaning 'cheerful'. Also the name given to two saints in the 4th and 5th Century.
Hilary of Arles became Bishop in AD428. He was an ascetic, born of a noble family and an admirer of St Augustine of Hippo. The other Hilary was Bishop of Poitiers. He was converted to Christianity in AD350.
Cheerfulness is a constant theme in Scripture. The writer of Ecclesiastes even tried hard drink to achieve it! (Eccl.2:3.)
"A happy heart makes the face cheerful." Prov.15:13.

Hilda

An Old English word for 'battle'. There have been a number of famous Hildas in history.
Hilda the Abbess of Whitby was the nephew of King Edwin of Northumbria and was converted to Christ and baptised in the year AD627. She was later appointed Abbess of Whitby by Aidan the 'Apostle of England' in AD649. Her school became famous as a place of learning and produced at least five Bishops.
Hildegard of Bingen was a visionary who wrote many apocalyptic books as well as poems, hymns and even her own alphabet. The Bible has a lot to say about 'battle'.
"The horse is made ready for the day of battle, but victory rests with the LORD"
Prov.21:31.

Holly

From Old English 'Holegn'. A name from the natural world.

There are at least 180 different types of holly in the world - most of them survive in the northern hemisphere and in particular in northern Europe. Botanists tell us that Holly will not grow in the shade but will flourish in any type of soil or weather. Neither Holly nor Ivy are mentioned in Scripture. "The holly bears a berry as red as any blood, and Mary bore sweet Jesus Christ for to do poor sinners good." (Traditional Carol).

"Whoever trusts in his riches will fall, but the righteous will thrive like a green leaf." Prov.11:28.

Honour Honoria Honor Nora Norah
Irish Gaelic: Noreen

From Latin 'honoria' which means 'honour'. First recorded in the 12th century.

This was a common Norman name. There are some Latin records of saints called 'Honor' - or a similar name. It was very popular among the Puritans in the 17th century and is currently enjoying a revival.

'Honour' is an important principle in Scripture. Among others we are told to honour our father and mother (Ex.20:12) and most of all, to honour God (Num.20:12).

"Those who honour Me I will honour..." 1 Sam.2:30.

Hope

One of the three great Christian virtues from 1 Cor.13. "...faith, hope and love..."

If you had female triplets after the Reformation you were expected to call them "Faith, Hope and Charity"!

The dictionary definition is: "look forward to with expectation and desire". The Christian hope is all of this and more. All people, because we are made by God, have a basic necessity to hope - it is something which has been planted in our very nature and character. Even when there is little prospect we will still hope.

"And hope does not disappoint us, because God has poured out His love into our hearts.." Rom.5:5.

Horace Horatio

From the Latin name 'Horatius' which was the name of the well-known Roman lyric poet known in English as 'Horace'. The first name of Admiral Lord Nelson and other aristocrats.

The names 'Horace' and 'Horatio' are identical in meaning and history so they are often interchanged. The Roman family was very distinguished and perhaps the most famous of them all was Horatius Cocles who was the man who defended the bridge across the Tiber single-handed. Its general use on the Continent started in the 16th century in Italy and is used by Shakespeare in "Hamlet".

Admiral Horatio Lord Nelson died in 1805 and the last words of the most famous seaman ever were: "Thank God I have done my duty".

"Now...here is the conclusion : Fear God and keep His commandments, this is the whole duty of man." Eccl.12:13.

Hortense

'Hortense' means 'a garden'- it is a French form of the old Latin family name 'Hortensius' used by the Romans also used in Britain during the 19th century but not common today.

Scripture opens and closes in a garden! The story of creation began in the garden of Eden and the final chapter of the book of Revelation says: "...On each side of the river stood the tree of life, bearing twelve crops of fruit, yielding its fruit every month." Rev.22.2. In the place where Jesus was crucified and buried there was a garden (John 19.41.).

"...like the garden of the LORD. Joy and gladness - thanksgiving and the sound of singing." Is.51.3.

Howard

Old German meaning 'heart - protection'. Family name of the Dukes of Norfolk. From the 11th century.

The origin of the name Howard is not clear but it was certainly used from the 11th century as a surname for several aristocratic families including the Dukes of Norfolk whose ancestral home is Arundel Castle in Sussex. The Duke is responsible for the ceremonial arrangements on State occasions for the Royal Family.

The Old German meaning is in two parts: 'hugu' which means 'heart' and 'vardu' which means 'ward' or 'protection'.

"Lord, you know everyone's heart." Acts 1:24.

Howell

From the Welsh 'Hywel' which means to be 'celebrated' or 'prominent'. There is an Old English word 'Hugol' which means 'a small hill'.

This name is mentioned in the Doomsday Book of 1086 where it is listed as a village in Lincolnshire called 'Huuelle' and for some time has also been used as a surname - in common with very many other Christian names. Both the Welsh and Old English concur in the meaning - someone who was (or is) 'conspicuous'. How wonderful to know that in God's eyes we are all 'conspicuous'!

"What is man that you make so much of him, that you give him so much attention...?"
Job 7.17. "...the Son of God, who loved me and gave himself for me".Gal.2.20.

Hubert

From Old German meaning 'a bright heart'. Cult name in the Middle Ages because of the 8th century Saint Hubert - patron saint of huntsmen.

The Old German meaning is a compound of 'hugu' which means 'heart' and 'berhta' which means 'bright'.

St Hubert is the patron saint of hunters because it is said that his conversion was brought about through a vision he received whilst out hunting on Good Friday. St Hubert's day is celebrated on the 3rd November.

"My words come from an upright heart; my lips sincerely speak what I know." Job 33:3.

Hugh Huw
Latin form: Hugo

From the Old German meaning 'heart'. In the Doomsday Book many times. A Bishop who loved Jews.

St Hugh was Bishop of Lincoln in the 12th century and he was a godly man who introduced many reforms into the church of his day. He was a tireless campaigner for justice and began the rebuilding of the cathedral - even doing some of the labouring jobs himself at times. There was violent anti-Semitism in England at that time and St Hugh did all he could to protect and defend the Jewish population.

Jesus taught that evil comes from our hearts but we can also love God with "all our heart" Deut.6:5.

"I saw the Lord always before me. Because He is at my right hand, I will not be shaken. Therefore my heart is glad and my tongue rejoices." Acts 2:25-26.

Huldah

From Hebrew and meaning 'a small furry mammal'. She was only a wardrobe attendant's wife but became a vital link in a revival.

Huldah lived six hundred years before the birth of Christ when Josiah was the 17th King of Judah. He had been crowned at the tender age of eight and in his early twenties began to earnestly seek God. He began by putting things right in the Temple and in the process they found the 'Book of the Law' (probably Deuteronomy). He sent the book to Huldah because she was a prophetess and she confirmed that it was the word of God. She also prophesied that righteous Josiah would die in peace because he had repented.

"Because your heart was responsive and you humbled yourself before the LORD...I have heard you, declares the LORD." 2 Kings 22:19.

Humphrey

From Old German meaning 'a peace warrior'. An original is in the Doomsday Book many times. Was there a 'great fall'?

There are a number of possible origins to this unique name - some of them Old English, others Norman, French or Old German. The translation 'peace warrior' is a 'liberal' translation from the Old German 'huni' meaning 'warrior' and 'frith' meaning 'peace'.

'Dumfrey' was a pet form of the name and from this developed 'Humfrey-Dumfrey' and the nursery rhyme of a similar name.

"Watch and pray so that you will not fall into temptation." Mt.26:41.

Hyacinth

From the Latin 'Hyacinthus'. A flower, a lovely colour and a precious stone! The name of a 3rd century Christian martyr.

According to Greek legend, Hyacinthus was killed by accident whilst learning to throw the discus. From his blood a beautiful flower emerged which had leaves which mourned him with cries of "ai, ai" (alas, alas). Because of this the Romans had a Spartan Spring festival in his honour. The festival celebrated the change from Winter to Spring-time and Summer.

"See! The winter is past; the rains are over and gone. Flowers appear on the earth; the season of singing has come, the cooing of doves is heard in our land." Song of Songs 2:11-12.

Hywell – see Howell

114

Ian Iaian Iain Iainn Ieuan - see also John

Means 'grace or mercy of the Lord'. When the name 'John' was introduced to Europe the French rendering was 'Jean' and resulted in diverse 'streams' one John and another Iain or Sean.

'Grace' is from the Latin 'gratia' meaning 'a religious virtue' also thankfulness at meal-times and a thing of elegance. Because we have no equivalent to the Hebrew word 'hesed', translators have used the words "grace and mercy" in the New Testament and "lovingkindness" in the Old Testament. One of the most descriptive verses in the New Testament is John 1:14. "We have seen His glory...full of grace and truth".

"...grow in the grace and knowledge of our Lord and Saviour Jesus Christ." 2 Pet.3:18.

Ibrahim - see Abraham

Ida

Old German meaning 'a hard worker'. Crowned by Tennyson and set to music by Gilbert and Sullivan.

The name Ida has a long and noble history. It was popular in the Middle Ages and was revived by Tennyson for his poem "The Princess Ida". It was set to music by Gilbert and Sullivan's "Princess Ida" in 1884. Scripture is full of exhortation to hard work - particularly in the book of Proverbs. Here is one example: "He who works his land will have abundant food, but the one who chases fantasies will have his fill of poverty." Prov.28:19.

"...and God's fellow worker in spreading the gospel of Christ..." 1 Thes.3:2.

Idris

A Welsh name meaning 'fiery lord'. A legendary figure whose observatory was from the top of Cadair Idris which is in southern Snowdonia between the towns of Dolgellau and Machynlleth.

In Welsh legend Idris was a giant of a man who was an astronomer and a magician. He surveyed his realm from the top of Cadair Idris which is Wales' second largest mountain rising to a height of 2,927ft. The name means 'the throne of Idris'. On its south flank it has a rock-bound hidden lake called Llyn Cau. The whole of southern Snowdonia is a very beautiful area. *"Your righteousness is like the mighty mountains, your justice like the great deep..." Ps.36:6.*

Ieasha Ieesha Iesha Isha - see also Aiesha
Arabic meaning 'prospering' or 'alive, fit and well'. H Ryder Haggard used the name in his novel "She" and there the inference was 'she who must be obeyed'.
The ancient peoples placed great emphasis on physical health and fitness - as the Greek Olympic Games demonstrate. Physical prowess was worshipped like a god and those who proved themselves as athletes were greatly honoured. In comparison, the Bible has little to say about physical attributes but a great deal to say about the health of the spirit.
"For physical training is of some value, but godliness has value for all things..."
1 Tim.4:8.

Ieuan - see Ian

Ilene - see Aileen

Imogen
From the Greek meaning 'a beloved child'. 'Beloved' means one who is loved and one who is loving.
To receive love is very easy and it is something which we all crave because God made us that way. To give love is not always as easy. Some people are not really loveable or reject our admiration or esteem.
Doesn't this make it so much more wonderful that God loved US when we were so unlovely - and He still does!
"For I am convinced that neither death nor life...nor anything else in all creation, will be able to separate us from the love of God that is in Christ Jesus our Lord." Rom.8:38-39.

Ingrid
From Old Norse meaning 'fair and beautiful'. A mythological hero. A popular Scandinavian name. It may also mean 'ride'.
In Norse mythology the god Ingvi was the god of fertility for crops and he rode a golden-bristled boar. The name is very popular in the Scandinavian countries and was made even more popular by famous film stars such as Ingrid Bergman (1915-1982). There is also a possibility that the second part of the name was from 'rida' which means 'ride'. (The fact that the name is an anagram of 'riding' is a coincidence!)
"...His name is the Word of God. The armies of heaven were following Him, riding on white horses..." Rev.19:13-14.

Iona
Name of a beautiful island off the west coast of Scotland among the Inner Hebrides. An ancient religious site of great interest.

Often called the 'Holy Isle' the fascinating island of Iona is the place where St Columba landed in AD563. From here he brought Christianity to the whole of Scotland and beyond. In 1900 the Church of Scotland assumed responsibility for the monastic ruins built over Columba's original wattle chapel. It is said that over 60 monarchs are buried in the grounds. There is a thriving Christian community run from the island called the "Iona Community". Members have a three-fold commitment to prayer, Bible-study and tithing.

"...exalt the name of the LORD, the God of Israel, in the islands of the sea." Is.24:15.

Ira

From Hebrew and meaning 'watchful'. One of King David's 'mighty men' also a priest. A hymn- writer in the 19th century.

The name Ira features three times in the Bible and all of them are in the last few chapters of 2 Samuel. From these references it is clear that as far as David was concerned Ira was a hero.

More recently Ira D.Sankey was the musician who teamed up with D.L.Moody in 1870 and began a great revival in the UK in 1873. It was at that time that they published the very popular "Sankey and Moody Hymnbook" more generally known as 'Sankeys'. One of the themes of some of Sankey's songs was 'watchfulness' because there was a genuine expectation that the Lord would be returning in the near future.

"Devote yourselves to prayer, being watchful and thankful." Col.4:2.

Irene

From Greek meaning 'peace'. Two pronunciations. An early Christian name.

Irene was a common name in the first century among Christians because it was the Greek equivalent of 'Shalom' in Hebrew. It disappeared for a while but has recently re-emerged as a popular and meaningful name. There are two pronunciations; 'eye-reen' and 'eye-reen-ee'.

Not everyone realises that 'peace' is one of God's names. Judg.6:24 says: "So Gideon built an altar to the LORD there and called it: 'The LORD is Peace' (Yahweh-Shalom)". Today the word 'peace' is a common greeting in Israel and among Hebrew and Arabic speaking people everywhere.

"I will lie down and sleep in peace, for you alone, O LORD, make me dwell in safety." Ps.4:8.

Iris

The name of a flower but from the Greek word for 'rainbow'. A messenger from gods to men.

In Greek mythology Iris was the person who carried the messages to men using the rainbow as her bridge.

We learn from the story of the rainbow in Genesis chapter 9 that it is a sign of the covenant between God and man that God will never again judge the world by flooding it. This is part of God's covenant with Noah and demonstrates His faithfulness.

'Iris' is also the coloured part of the eye - and from this we get the 'iris' of the camera.

"I have set my rainbow in the clouds, and it will be the sign of the covenant between me and the earth." Gen.9:13.

Irvine Irving

This name was originally a Scottish place-name and it then became a surname. An anglicized form of Israel.

Irvine is a town on the west coast of Scotland some 32 km (20 miles) southwest of Glasgow. It is a royal burgh and seaport. Alexander II granted it a charter and this was confirmed by Robert the Bruce. In the 17th century it was a popular seaport but shipping and shipbuilding has declined in recent years.

The songwriter Irving Berlin was born Israel Baline and it is not uncommon for Jewish families to use the word 'Irving' or 'Irvine' as a substitute form for 'Israel'.

"Praise be to the LORD, the God of Israel." 1 Kings 1:48.

Isa - see Isabel

Isaac

Hebrew, meaning 'laughter'. The son of promise is almost sacrificed. One of the world's oldest names still in use today.

Isaac the 'son of promise' - God had said to Abraham; "I will make you into a great nation." Gen.12:2. When this news was broken to Abraham he laughed (Gen.17:17). Then, when he told Sarah, she laughed (Gen.18:12-15). On the day of Isaac's weaning even Ishmael laughed! (Gen.21:9). The laughter was not derisory - it was an expression of joyous relief. So when Abraham was instructed to sacrifice Isaac this was a test of his faith. The story is in Gen.22.

Sir Isaac Newton the great scientist was also a committed Christian.

"By faith Abraham...offered Isaac as a sacrifice...Abraham reasoned that God could raise the dead..." Heb.11:17-19.

Isabel Isa Isabella Isabelle Isobel

Means 'God is my oath'. (The name originally came from the Spanish for 'Elizabeth', which in the Bible is the name of the mother of John the Baptist).

'God is my oath' is the fascinating meaning behind these names. According to Moses making an oath is a very serious business and the Lord Jesus reinforces this when He says " let your 'yes' be 'yes' and your 'no' be 'no'" (Mt.5:37). "When God made His promise to Abraham, since there was no-one greater for Him to swear by, He swore by Himself ...Men swear by someone greater than themselves, and the oath confirms what is said and puts an end to all argument ...we have this hope as an anchor for the soul, firm and secure." Heb.6:13-19.

"But it was because the LORD loved you and kept the oath he swore to your forefathers that he brought you out with a mighty hand and redeemed you from the land of slavery..." Deut.7:8.

Ishmael

From Hebrew meaning 'the God who hears'. Abraham's son by Hagar. God's special promise to him. The father of one of the largest people groups on earth.

Ishmael the son of Abraham is one of 6 different people with that name in the Old Testament but he is the most important one. "God heard the boy" Gen.21:17 and made him several very specific promises; "I...will greatly increase his numbers. He will be the father of twelve rulers, and I will make him into a great nation." Gen.17:20. Although Ishmael and Isaac fell out because of jealousy they were united when their father died (Gen.25:9). Ishmael lived to be 137. God keeps His promises, He is 'the God who hears'. *"I will surely bless him; I will make him fruitful and will greatly increase his numbers." Gen.17:20.*

Ivan - see John

Ivor

English form of the Welsh name 'Ifor' meaning 'lord'. With French, Irish and Scottish connections.

This name could have several origins: there was an Old Norse name 'Ivarr' which was borne by several Danish Kings, alternatively there are traces in Ireland, Scotland and Wales. The welsh 'Yfore' comes from the 13th century.

'Lord' is a title which is given to various people and ranks - the Concise Oxford Dictionary lists 16 different definitions! Perhaps this is why we in the west find it hard to understand the concept of the Lordship of the Lord Jesus Christ.

"...every knee shall bow...and every tongue confess that JESUS CHRIST is LORD" Phil.2:10-11.

Ivy

'Ivy' is Old English for 'faithful'. A beautiful and harmless addition to any

structure. 50 different species but only 3 types - the 'English', the 'Irish' and the 'Boston' (poisonous).

There are 50 different species of Ivy - the horticultural sort (many more of the human type!). Ivy needs a strong support. As long as there is somewhere to go ivy will continue to grow but once it reaches the zenith of a structure it will cease to grow having attained its maximum potential. It is completely harmless to the construction on which it grows but will beautify, protect and keep it dry and warm. In addition, it will reduce the corrosive effect of the atmosphere. How many of these characteristics could we apply to ourselves?

"...cleave unto Him, and to serve Him with all your heart and with all your soul." *Josh.22:5 KJV.*

Jacaline - see Jacqueline

Jack Jackson Jak Jake Jock

Means 'the grace or mercy of the Lord'. It evolved from 'John' in the middle ages.
The 'grace or mercy of God' is translated in different ways - sometimes the Hebrew word 'hesed' is translated as "lovingkindness" in the Old Testament. In the New Testament the same word is invariably translated "grace". (From the Greek 'charis'). We also use the word for 'thanksgiving' before meals. (The Jewish people have the delightful practice of saying grace before, during and after the meal). God is "the father of mercies". Ex.34:6. & 2 Cor.1:3.
"For the LORD your God is a merciful God; He will not abandon or destroy you or forget the covenant with your forefathers..." Deut.4:31.

Jackaline Jackalyn Jackie Jacky - see Jacqueline Jacob

'Jacob' is Hebrew (rendered 'James' in the New Testament). Almost a quarter of the first book of the Bible is devoted to him. He was the father of God's chosen people and God gave him the name 'Israel' which means 'one who strives with God'.
The meaning is 'one who supplants' and the picture is of a racer who 'trips' his opponent in order to gain advantage over him in the race. In the Old Testament the most famous person with this name is found in Gen.25:23 to 49:33. God changed his name to 'Israel' and his birth, life and death are all significant. He has a revered place in Judeo-Christian history with Abraham and Isaac. The Jewish people who have inherited his name have also inherited its meaning!
"...Your name will no longer be Jacob, but Israel, because you have struggled with God and with men and have overcome." Gen.32:28.

Jacqueline Jacqui Jacaline Jackaline Jackalyn Jackie Jacky Jaqueline

These names are from the French feminine for 'Jacob' (whose name was changed to 'Israel' which is Hebrew and means 'one who wrestles or struggles with God').
These names come from the French 'Jacques' which in turn came from the ancient 'Jacob' of the closing quarter of the book of Genesis. His name

meant 'supplanter'. He had two great encounters with God, the first at Bethel and the second at Peniel. As a result of the second encounter at Peniel he was left with a limp and a new name. His priorities were now right and it is interesting to note that one of the brothers of Jesus was called 'James' (which is the English equivalent of 'Jacob') and James had a reputation for piety - it seems that the story of Jacob has completed its circle.

"...Your name will no longer be Jacob, but Israel, because you have struggled with God and with men and have overcome." Gen.32:28.

Jade

A precious and valuable stone, a thing of great beauty, elegance and attraction. Thought to come from a word sounding very like the Spanish for 'daughter' - a mother's most precious jewel.

This precious metallic stone has been a thing of value for thousands of years, particularly in China. The queen of Sheba presented Solomon with "...spices...gold...and precious stones..." 2 Chron.9:1. The Temple which Solomon built was also "...adorned with precious stones..." 1 Chron.29:8. In the New Testament we are warned to ensure that we build with "...gold...silver and precious stones..." because every man's work will be "...tried by fire..." 1 Cor.3:12-14.

"See, I lay in Zion, a chosen and precious cornerstone, and the one who trusts in Him will never be put to shame." 1 Pet.2:6.

Jake Jak - see Jack

James Jamie Jim Jimmy Jym
Cornish form: Jago
Irish Gaelic form: Seamas Seamus Shey
Scottish Gaelic form: Seumas Hamish

'James' of the New Testament is the English translation of the Hebrew name 'Jacob'.

James the son of Zebedee was present at some of the significant events in the life of Jesus such as the transfiguration and Gethsemane. His death is recorded in Acts 12 - a fulfilment of prophecy by Jesus (Mt.20:23).

James the brother of Jesus had a personal visit from the risen Christ (see 1 Cor.15:7), he was also leader of the Church at Jerusalem, presided at the Council of Jerusalem (Acts 15), wrote the epistle and suffered Martyrdom. Tradition claims that he was also known as 'James the Just' because of his holiness.

"James - a servant of God and of the Lord Jesus Christ." Jas.1:1.

Jane Jan Janene Janet Janette Janice Janina Janine Janis Janyce Jayne Netta
Gaelic form: Shona Sheena Sian Sine Siobhan
Means 'the grace or mercy of the Lord'. An illustrious record. Used from medieval times.

'Janeta' is a name common in medieval records and in 1660 the name Jennet is recorded by Edward Lydford. It is thought to have been a feminine equivalent of the New Testament 'John'.

'John the Apostle' wrote the fourth gospel and in the early part of chapter 1. there is an interesting word-play when John says that Jesus was full of 'grace' - knowing that his own name means 'grace'. The dictionary defines 'grace' as "the unmerited favour of God".

"For God so loved the world that He gave His one and only Son..." John 3:16.

Jaqueline - see Jacqueline

Jarvis – see Gervase

Jasmine
One of the popular names chosen from flowers.

The botanical name for Jasmine is 'Jasminum' and there are about 100 different species of which there are some 40 or more in the UK. The White Jasmine blooms from June to October and has single leaves. The Winter Jasmine has lovely sprays of dark green leaves and beautiful yellow flowers which brighten the days when little else is blooming.

"O LORD, how majestic is your name in all the earth!" Ps.8:1.

Jason
In Greek the name means someone who 'cures' or 'gives healing'.

There are no 'Jasons' in the Old Testament but those in the New Testament were clearly very good people.

Rom.16:21. This Jason, a relative of Paul, wanted to be included in Paul's greeting to the Christians in Rome and his name comes immediately after the warning about 'false teachers', so clearly he was not one.

Acts 17:5-9. This was the Jason of Thessalonica who was obviously very hospitable. When the opposing Jews couldn't find Paul and Silas they grabbed him and some other brothers and brought them before the magistrates with the accusation: "These men who have caused trouble all over the world (literally; 'turned the world upside down') have now come here". The charge against them was that they were declaring that "...there is another King - one called JESUS..." Acts 17:7.

Oh for many more 'Jasons' who will also 'turn the world upside down' by proclaiming that JESUS IS KING. This is the 'healing' that the world needs.

"...a trustworthy envoy brings healing." Prov.13:17.

Jasper

From old Persian and meaning 'to bring (or to keep) treasure'. From the 8th century. The name of one of the Magi at the birth of Christ? A quartz gemstone.

The name 'Jasper' has several origins. It is a quartz opaque stone of many colours which is hard but can be polished.

Its most common origin is from an 8th century chronicle (Excerpta latina barbari) where 'Gathaspa' or 'Gaspar', which became 'Jasper' in English, is the name of one of the Magi who visited the Lord Jesus at His birth (The Bible does not mention their number or their names).

"It shone with the glory of God, and its brilliance was like that of a very precious jewel, like jasper..." Rev.21:11.

Jay Jaye - see also Ajay

From Sanskrit and meaning 'victory'.

'Victory' in the Bible is always God's - although He often uses men to achieve it. Sometimes He brings victory in so-called impossible situations such as the time when David met Goliath. On that occasion David's proclamation was: "...the battle is the LORD's..." 1 Sam.17:47. This was to demonstrate God's glory.

In the New Testament the people of God enter into His victory through faith. Even though they may appear to be in the minority today, there is a day coming when all creation will be subject to Him.

"You give me your shield of victory, and your right hand sustains me." Ps.18:35.

Jayne - see Jane

Jean Jeanette Jeanie Jeannie Jenifer Jennifer Jennie Jennifer Jenny Jenna

These names are Scottish feminine forms of 'John' and mean 'the grace or mercy of the LORD'.

The 'grace or mercy of God' is translated in various ways - sometimes the Hebrew word 'hesed' is translated "lovingkindness" in the Old Testament. In the New Testament the same word is invariably translated "grace" (from the Greek 'charis'). We also use the word for 'thanksgiving' before meals. (The Jews have a delightful habit of saying 'grace' before, during and after the meal). God is "the father of mercies". Ex.34:6. & 1 Cor.1:3. 'Grace' is also a word which we use to describe elegance and poise.

"...the child grew and became strong...and the grace of God was upon him." Luke 2:40.

Jed

'Jed' is a short form of one of several Biblical names. All the meanings are complimentary.

2 Sam.12:25. King David had a son whose name was Jed. (which means 'loved by God'). His first name was Solomon ...the wisest man who ever lived.

1 Chron.12:20. This Jed. (which means 'known by God') decided that it would be good to be on the winning side and defected to join David in his impending victory against Saul.

1 Chron.16:41. This musical Jed. (which means 'giving thanks') was appointed to help lead the worship and held a conspicuous position. He must have been good because David dedicated Psalm 62 to him.

"My soul finds rest in God alone; my salvation comes from Him." Ps.62:1.

Jeffrey Jeff

From Old German meaning 'peace'. It has been a surname and a Christian name for many years.

Not everyone realises that 'peace' is one of God's names. In Judg.6:24 we read; "So Gideon built an altar to the LORD there and called it: 'The LORD is Peace' (Yahweh-Shalom)". Today the word 'peace' is a common greeting in Israel and among Hebrew and Arabic speaking people everywhere.

Real peace is not just the absence of conflict - it is the presence of God IN the conflict. The hymn "When peace like a river..." was written when the author was at the place in mid-Atlantic where his four daughters had drowned a few days before.

"...the peace of God, which transcends all understanding, will guard your hearts and your minds in Christ Jesus." Phil.4:7.

Jermaine – see Gemaine

Jemima Jemimah

Jemima or Jemimah is only recorded once in the Bible - it was the name of Job's first daughter born to him after his troubles ended (Job 42:12-14). It means 'as beautiful as the day' or 'a dove'.

A few verses later we read: "Nowhere in all the land were there found women as beautiful as Job's daughters and their father granted them an inheritance along with their brothers." Job 42:15. The story of Job is in the Bible to remind us that loving God and living an upright life is no guarantee that you will avoid problems or pitfalls. It does illustrate that, in the end, God will raise up those who have been cast down and vindicate His name.

"...the wings of my dove are sheathed with silver, its feathers with shining gold." Ps.68:13.

Jemma - see Gemma

Jenna Jennie Jennifer Jenifer Jenny - see Jean

Jeremy Jeremiah

Jeremy or Jeremiah means: 'May God be exalted'. The prophet of that name is the author of at least two books in the Old Testament and Jesus quoted him on a number of occasions.

Jeremiah is the prophet of the heart, he lived at a critical time in the history of Judah and warned the nation many times to turn from idolatry to serve God. They did not turn and Jeremiah lived to see his prophecy fulfilled. Some of his better-known quotations are: "The heart is deceitful above all things" Jer.17:9. "I the LORD search the heart" Jer.17:10. "You will seek me and find me when you seek me with all your heart." Jer.29:13.

"But may all who seek you rejoice and be glad in you; may those who love your salvation always say, 'Let God be exalted!'" Ps.70:4.

Jerome

From Greek and meaning 'holy name'. The first of the Bible translators. He made his home in Bethlehem.

Saint Jerome (AD345-419) was a great scholar and translated the Bible into the language of his day (Latin Vulgate). His methods of translation and working from the original languages set a high standard and have been followed by most translators since. In AD386 he moved from Rome and made his home in the Church of the Nativity in Bethlehem.

There have been other famous 'Jerome's' but this one brought the word of God to the common people. He was a brilliant scholar but a deeply humble man who enjoyed a simple lifestyle.

Glory in HIS holy name; let the hearts of those who seek the LORD rejoice."
1 Chronicles 16:10.

Jerry - see Gerald

Jeshurun

Hebrew for 'the upright' or 'beloved one'. This was the poetic name that God used for Israel - except for one instance it is always a title of loving honour.

Jeshurun is mentioned four times in Scripture: Deut.32:15, Deut.33:5, Deut.33:26 and Is.44:2. In the last reference it is used of 'the chosen servant' and the same Greek word is used in the Septuagint (Greek translation of the OT) as is used of Jesus in Eph.1:6, "the One He loves". It is also used of the Church "holy and dearly loved" Col.3:12, "loved by God...chosen" 1 Thes.1:4, and "loved by God" Jude 1.

"This is what the LORD says - He who made you, who formed you in the womb, and who will help you; Do not be afraid...my servant Jeshurun, whom I have chosen." Is.44:2.

Jesse

In Hebrew 'Jesse' means 'God is there now'. Jesse was a native of Bethlehem (which means: 'the house of bread').

Three important people are associated with Bethlehem and Jesse provides a link with each one of them.

RUTH was the great-grandmother of David and the grandmother of Jesse. KING DAVID was Jesse's youngest son and Israel's finest ruler who took the nation to the height of its glory and fame. THE LORD JESUS CHRIST was also born in Bethlehem and Jesse is included in His lineage (Mt.1:5&6 and Luke 3:32). Paul acknowledges him as a forerunner of the one who "...will arise to rule over the nations". Rom.15:12.

"In that day the Root of Jesse will stand as a banner for the peoples; the nations will rally to Him, and His place of rest will be glorious." Is.11:10.

Jessica Jessie Jess

From Hebrew meaning 'one who protects' or invented by Shakespeare? Recently one of the top seven most popular names.

The origin of this name has been the subject of debate. It could have been 'invented' by Shakespeare for his play "The Merchant of Venice" or it could be the daughter of Haran in Gen.11:29. If it is the latter then it means 'one who protects'. The task of protection is God's and we can only protect others as we allow Him to protect us.

"O LORD you will keep us safe and protect us..." Ps.12:7.

Jesusa - see Joshua

Jethro

The name means; 'abundance', 'excellence' or 'pre-eminence'. The only 'Jethro' in the Bible is a wise administrator who was the father-in-law of Moses.

In Exodus chapter 18 Jethro came to see Moses and he was alarmed at the way the people were judged. Jethro taught Moses the basic skill of delegation and 'minor' judges were then appointed, "capable men from all the people men who fear God, trustworthy men who hate dishonest gain" Ex.18:21. Jethro had already declared his allegiance to God by offering sacrifices - he now allowed Moses to submit his judgement to God for approval. Jethro teaches us that so-called 'worldly' advice CAN be the product of a sanctified mind....

"Jethro was delighted to hear about all the good things the LORD had done..." Ex.18:9.

Jill - see Juliana

Jim Jimmy - see James

Joachim

From Hebrew(MyqyOy)meaning 'Yahweh will establish' or, 'will lift up'. He was the father of Eliashib and his name means 'God will restore'. (Neh 12.)
When God begins a work He will always complete it and the story of Nehemiah restoring the walls of Jerusalem is a lovely picture of this truth. Joachim was the father of the High Priest Eliashib whose very name means 'God will restore'. So it is with us, the Apostle Paul says; "...he who began a good work in you will carry it on to completion until the day of Christ Jesus." Phil.1:6. So it doesn't matter how often or how deeply you fall - God is in the business of restoration! He will always lift you up - if you will allow Him to!
"Restore us, O God; make your face shine upon us, that we may be saved." Psalm 80:3.

Jo - see Joan Joseph Josephine

Joan Joanna Jo Joanne Johanna Johanne
Spanish form: Juanita Nita

These names mean 'the grace', 'the gift' or 'the mercy of the LORD'. Joanna was one of a number of women whom Jesus healed and, in return, she ministered to Him.
Luke tells us that she was the wife of the manager of Herod's household (Luke 8:1-3).
Joanna knew the healing and cleansing that Jesus could give because she had experienced it in her own life - now she could help others into that experience. Because she had been so helpful and a blessing in small ways, she was given the great task of announcing the fact that He had risen from the dead! (Luke 24:9-10). Joanna teaches us an important lesson: Someone who ministers must first receive ministry. Our prayer should always be: 'Lord, help me to teach others the things you first teach me'.
"I will heal their waywardness and love them freely, for my anger has turned away from them." Hos.14:4.

Jocelyn Jos

From Latin meaning 'cheerful' or Old German or even Breton.
This name is one of those names which could have several possible sources. The most likely is the Latin but there is also a chance that it came from Old German. A further derivation could be a 7th century Breton 'saint Jodoc' from which we get 'Joyce'. It has also been a boy's name.
Cheerfulness is a constant theme in Scripture. The writer of Ecclesiastes

even tried hard drink to achieve it! (Eccl.2:3). The book of Proverbs has the answer when it says; "A happy heart makes the face cheerful" Prov.15:13. A 'happy heart' is a cleansed heart and a heart which is obedient to the Saviour's will.

"...the days of the oppressed are wretched, but the cheerful heart has a continual feast." Prov.15:15.

Jock - see Jack

Jodie Jody - see Judith

Joe - see Joseph

Joel

Means 'the LORD is God'. It is mentioned twenty times in the Old Testament and once in the New.

'Joel' was the name of Samuel's first son. 1.Sam.8:2. Another Joel was one of the 'minor' prophets. His book is two thirds of the way through the Old Testament and is one of the shortest in the Bible - however, it was the one which Peter quoted on the day of Pentecost (Acts 2:16-21). He lived in a difficult time of impending judgement on the Kingdom of Judah but he was faithful in declaring all that God revealed to him. Some of the things which he prophesied have already come to pass, others are still to be fulfilled.

"And everyone who calls on the name of the LORD will be saved." Joel 2:32.

Johanna Johanne - see Joan

John Johnny Johnnie
Gaelic form: Eoin Euan Iain Sean Shane Shaun
Italian form: Gianna Giovanna Giovanni
Russian form: Ivan
Welsh form: Evan Sian Sion
Female form: Jenna Josann Josanna Josannah

'John' is from the Hebrew 'Johannes' meaning 'the grace' or 'mercy' of the LORD'.

There are two people in the New Testament with this name:

'John the Baptist' was a fiery preacher announcing the Kingdom of Heaven and demanding that all men repent and believe the gospel. He came to a sad end in prison where he was beheaded by the wicked King Herod whom he had denounced (Mk.6:14-29).

'John the Apostle' was different in character, he could be high-spirited (see Mk.3:17 & Luke 9:49 & 54) but he could also be loving and it was to his care that Jesus committed His mother when He was on the cross. (John 19:26-27.). He wrote the Fourth Gospel, the Epistles of John and the book of Revelation.

"For God so loved the world that He gave His one and only Son, that whoever believes in him shall not perish but have eternal life." John 3:16.

Jolyon - see Julian

Jonah

Hebrew for 'a dove' which is the symbol of the Holy Spirit and for peace. Jesus used it at Caesarea Philippi to show that Peter's statement was by divine revelation (Mt.16:13-20).

The dove has always been the symbol of peace and the symbol of the Holy Spirit. It was a dove that Noah sent out from the ark in order to find out if the waters had receded (Gen.8). It was a dove that formed the basis of the sacrificial offerings in the wilderness (Lev.1:14). The Psalmist cried "Oh for the wings of a dove" Psalm 55:6. The Apostle said; "I saw the spirit come down from heaven as a dove...on Him." John 1:32.

"The peace of God will guard your hearts and minds...in Christ Jesus." Phil.4:6.

Jonathan Jonathon Jon

'Jonathan' means 'The LORD has given' and is linked with 'David' (which means 'beloved').

Jonathan was the son of Saul and his story is told mainly in the chapters 1 Sam.13 to 2 Sam.9. He was a brave and valiant soldier whose troops loved and served him (1 Sam.14:1-14). Jonathan teaches us that loyalty is one of the greatest virtues. He could have inherited the throne but God had made it clear that David was to succeed King Saul. His loyalty to David brought him into conflict with his father but his motto was: God first...

"Jonathan said...Nothing can hinder the LORD from saving, whether by many or by few." 1 Sam.14:6.

Joran – see George

Jordan
Medieval form: Judd

From Hebrew meaning 'to flow' or 'to flow down'. The name of the principal river in Israel.

The Jordan river is unique, it rises in the foothills of Mount Hermon at Lake Huleh and from there flows 120km to the Dead Sea - although its meandering doubles that distance. It feeds the lake of Galilee and waters the Ghor valley as it flows past Beth Shan, Bethel and Jericho (the oldest inhabited city in the world) and finishes 393 metres below sea level, here it flows into the Dead Sea where, because of the heat, it evaporates and leaves a high salt content.

"...all the people...Confessing their sins...were baptized in the river Jordan." Mark 1:5.

Jos - see Jocelyn Joseph Josephine

Joseph Jo Joe Jos

The name 'Joseph' means 'the LORD added'. Here are three of the important Josephs in the Bible.

Joseph - the son of Jacob (Gen.30:22 to 50:26). The story of this Joseph is one of the most exciting in the Bible. He was the favourite eleventh son of Jacob. Through many adventures he rose to the highest position in Egypt.

Joseph the foster-father of Jesus. Accounts in the gospels of Matthew, Luke and John . Matthew traces his ancestry back to David and Abraham. He must have been a God-loving man because he took Jesus to the feasts in Jerusalem and also preserved His life by fleeing to Egypt.

Joseph of Arimathea (Luke 23:50-51, John 19:38 and Mt. 27:57-60). This man was a rich man and a member of the Sanhedrin. He was a secret disciple because he was afraid of the Jews.

"The LORD was with Joseph and he prospered." Gen.39:2.

Josephine Jo Jos

Josephine means 'the LORD added'. (A name from 'Joseph')

The first Joseph in the Bible is the eleventh son of Jacob. Through many adventures he rose to the highest position in Egypt. His story is seen as in some ways prophetic of the life and resurrection of the Lord Jesus Christ. It culminates in the triumphant declaration "Joseph is still alive! In fact, he is ruler of all Egypt." Gen.45:26.

"I know that my Redeemer lives, and that in the end He will stand upon the earth." Job 19:25.

Joshua Josh

Female form: Jesusa

Joshua or Yeshua (Yehoshua) is the Hebrew name of Jesus and it means; 'the LORD the Saviour'.

Moses made Joshua his personal assistant at the exodus, though he was still only a young man (Exodus 17). It was Joshua who backed Caleb's proposal to invade the promised land (Num.13-14). He 'kept watch' in the tent when Moses went up into the mountain to receive the Torah (teaching) and he was a man who 'waited on God'. (Ex.24, 32, 33 and Num.11). Joshua

fought the Canaanites, and established Shiloh.
*"...choose for yourselves...as for me and my household - we will serve the LORD!"
Josh.24:15.*

Josiah

*The name 'Josiah' means 'God heals'. The boy-king who led Judah's greatest
spiritual and moral revival.*
Some years before Josiah's birth the writer of Proverbs had said: "I love
those who love me, and those who seek me find me." Prov. 8:17. Josiah
began to seek God at an early age and when the word of God was brought
to him he repented and turned his people back to God.
"Neither before nor after Josiah was there a king like him who turned to
the LORD as he did   with all his heart and with all his soul and with all his
strength, in accordance with all the Law of Moses." 2 Kings 23:25.
"Josiah...did what was right in the eyes of the LORD..." 2 Kings 22:1-2.

Joy

*From Latin 'gaudere' which means 'to rejoice'. It is in the Bible many times
describing the feelings of those who love God.*
The words 'rejoice', 'joy', 'joyful' or 'joyfully' occur over 400 times in the
bible and there are as many in the Old Testament as there are in the New
Testament. Joy is different from happiness. It has been said that 'JOY is not
the absence of suffering but the presence of God'. So Paul and Silas could
sing when they had been beaten and thrown into prison (Acts 16). They
knew they were doing what was right! Perhaps the secret of JOY lies in the
acrostic: Jesus first, Others second, Yourself last...
"...weeping may endure for a night, but joy cometh in the morning." Ps.30:5 KJV.

Joyce - see also Jocelyn

*Joyce has both French and Latin origins and was the name of a 7th century
hermit-saint.*
The 7th century saint was the Breton hermit called Jodoc. The Norman
form of Josce meant 'lord' and came from the Old English 'Jose'. This
name begins with 'joy'. 'Joy' in the Bible is a description of the feelings of
those who love and follow God. The words 'rejoice', 'joy', 'joyful' or
'joyfully' occur over 400 times in the bible. A good acrostic for 'Joyce'
might be; Jesus first, Others second, Yourself last; Creates heaven on Earth!
*"Rejoice in the LORD and be glad, you righteous; sing, all you who are upright in
heart!" Ps.32:11.*

Judd – see Jordan

Jude

The name in Hebrew means 'in praise of the LORD' (Gen.29:35). In the Bible as Judah, Judas and Jude.

There is only one Jude in the Bible and he is the author of the final epistle before Revelation at the end of the New Testament. This Jude was the brother of Jesus and like his other brothers and sisters only realised who Jesus was after He had died and risen again (see John 7:5). The epistle of Jude was written to warn of the dangers of following false teachers.

"To Him who is able to keep you from falling...the only God our Saviour be glory, majesty, power..." Jude 24-25.

Judith Jodie Jody Judy

From Hebrew and today means 'a Jewess'. One of Esau's wives.

If you want to read about Judith you will also read about the naming of the town Beersheba in Genesis 26. The problem then (as now) was water and Abraham named the well "Beer-sheba" (Be-er: 'well', sheba: 'oath').

There is also a story in the Apocrypha called 'Judith'. It is frank fiction written around the 2nd century BC.

"He came to Derbe and then to Lystra, where a disciple named Timothy lived, whose mother was a Jewess and a believer." Acts 16:1.

Jules - see Julian

Julia - see Juliana

Julian Jolyon Jules Leanne Lianne

The name means 'compassionate and sensitive'. It was the name of the first Emperor of Rome and of the man who escorted the Apostle Paul on his journey to Rome (Acts 27).

Gaius Julius (whose family name was Caesar) was the first Roman Emperor. In his letter to the Philippians (written from prison in Rome) Paul mentions that there were believers in 'Caesar's household' (Phil.4:22). So it seems that somewhere on his journey or in Rome, Paul had led members of the family to the Lord Jesus Christ. I wonder if this Julius was the first? They were clearly good friends - see Acts chapter 27:3. Perhaps this was one Roman soldier who lived up to his name!

"Julius, in kindness to Paul, allowed him to go to his friends..." Acts 27:3.

Juliana Jill Julia Julie Juliet - see also Julian

The name means 'compassionate and sensitive'. Her husband was 'a lover of the word'.

Paul sent his loving greetings to both 'Philologos and Julia' (Rom.16:15). The name Philologos (her husband) is Greek for 'a lover of the word'.

The escort that Paul had for his journey to Rome in Acts 27 may have lived up to his name because during the voyage he took an opportunity to save Paul's life. To be both compassionate and sensitive is a rare and valuable combination in any person. The Lord Jesus Christ sets us an example and we have a record of His dealings with people in this way.

"The LORD, the LORD, the compassionate and gracious God, slow to anger, abounding in love and faithfulness..." Ex.34:6.

June

The name of the sixth month and the summer solstice. Name given in honour of a 'woman of stately beauty' from the old Latin calendar.

"Summer is a'comin-in" according to the old song about this time of the year - and it is always very welcome - it is the month of bright flowers and long days.

Ovid indicates that this month was given the name 'June' in honour of 'Juno' a Roman goddess who was a woman of outstanding natural beauty and grace. She was the goddess of marriage and the wife of Jupiter.

"...your strength will equal your days." Deut.33:25.

Juno - see Una

Juanita - see Joan

Justin Justine

From the Latin 'Justus' which means 'obedience and devotion to the Law'. There are three people with this name in the New Testament.

Jesus-Justus of Col.4:11. It comes as a surprise to some people that there were a large number of men called Jesus in New Testament times. The addition of another name helped to identify them individually.

Titius-Justus of Acts 18:7. When Paul's preaching split the synagogue his home became the centre for Paul's ministry. He may be the recipient of the book in the Bible addressed to 'Titus'.

Joseph-Barsabbas Justus of Acts 1:23. He was one of two possible successors to Judas. The name Barsabbas means 'born on the Sabbath'.

"...He is faithful and just and will forgive us our sins..." 1 John 1:9.

Jym – see James

134

Kaine Kane

From the Irish Gaelic 'Kathair' which means 'a fighter'. A city was named after his son south of Hebron.

Our modern 'Kaine' possibly came from the Irish Gaelic but long before that there was a man named Cain in the Bible - he was the first of Adam's sons and he let his father down - probably because his father had let him down! However, God seldom allows a bad situation to become worse and his son Enoch must have been good because they named a city after him! This Cain was also a fighter - as were many that followed him.

"Do not be afraid of them; the LORD your God himself will fight for you." Duet. *3.22.*

Kalab – see Caleb

Kamella

Roman origin - from a legend where she was a great fighter and a swift runner.

A name for a lovely lady whose beauty hides other attributes! As long ago as 1205 the name Kamella was used in Britain. It has a warm friendly feel to it and is an ideal choice for a lady. In addition, most ladies have hidden and sometimes undiscovered talents which only emerge in difficult or trying situations. The male form of Kamella is 'Camillus' and he was a soldier in the Venetian army in 1574. When he incurred an incurable wound he was discharged and left to die. He became a Christian, became well and now is the patron saint of sick people and nurses.

"Fight the good fight with all thy might, Christ is thy strength and Christ thy right......
Run the straight race through God's good grace, lift up thine eyes and seek His face..."
    J.S.B.Monsel

Karen Karon Kate Katy Katharine Katherine Kathleen Kathryn Kathy Katie Katya Kara Karina Keryn Kay Kitty Caron Catharine Catherine Cathleen Cathy Catriona Charon
Gaelic; Kaitlyn Kaitlynn

From Greek 'Katharos' meaning 'pure'. These names came from Princess

Katharine of Alexandra who in the 4th century was martyred for being a Christian.

Many people down through the centuries have died for their faith in the Lord Jesus. It may surprise you to know that more have died during the 20th century than any other - or the TOTAL of all the previous centuries.

You may not be called upon to die for Jesus but all of us are called to 'lay down our lives' for each other. Each day we have the privilege of being a living sacrifice for others (Rom.12:1).

Living like this can be MORE difficult than dying for Jesus, but if we know Him He will help us.

"Greater love has no-one than this, that he lay down his life for his friends." John 15:13.

Karensa Karenza Keren Kerensa Kerenza

'Keren' was the name of Job's third daughter born to him after his troubles ended (Job 42:14).

In the next verse we read: "Nowhere in all the land were there found women as beautiful as Job's daughters and their father granted them an inheritance along with their brothers." Job 42:15. The story of Job is in the Bible to remind us that loving God and living an upright life is no guarantee that you will avoid problems or pitfalls. However, it also illustrates that, in the end, God will raise up those who have been cast down.

"I know that my redeemer lives...I myself will see Him...How my heart yearns..." Job 19:25-27.

Karl - see Charles

Kate Katie Katya - see Karen

Katharine Katherine Kathleen - see Karen

Kathryn - see Karen

Kay - see Karen

Kayleigh Kayley

Old English for 'pure-meadow' (from Kay-lea). A lovely picture.

When you bring together two concepts into one name it creates a beautiful picture. 'Kay' is an old English word from 'Katharos' meaning 'pure' and 'Lea' is Old English for 'a meadow'.

The Psalmist must have had something like this in mind when he wrote; "He makes me lie down in green pastures, He leads me beside quiet waters,

He restores my soul..." Ps.23:2. This reminds us that it is not only external situations that give peace but also an internal sense of rest that we get from the ministry of the Holy Spirit.

"Come to me, all you who are weary and burdened, and I will give you rest." Mt.11:28.

Keaton

From the Old English word 'cyta' meaning 'a kite'. The oldest reference is from 1362 and is of Robert de Keaton of Keaton in Ermington (Devon).

The Old English, Welsh and Breton word 'Cyta' was used to describe a kite - from this we get the word for 'kiting' and thus we have the word Keaton. It is also the word for a member of the Hawk family - the Kite-Hawk a long tailed bird of prey. We have expressions such as "To fly like a kite" or "As high as a kite" meaning someone who is feeling 'high'. The children of Israel felt like that because God said of them and us;

"...I carried you on eagles' wings and brought you to myself." Ex.19:4.

Keir

A popular Scottish name. From the Old Norse place-name of 'Kerr' which means 'rough ground with brushwood'. An outstanding Trade Unionist.

This name originates in the north of England and Scotland where it was the name of a place (e.g 'Kerrera' on the west coast of Scotland). It is also often given in honour and memory of one of Scotland's greatest politicians: James Keir Hardie. He was the first Labour Member of Parliament and he founded the Scottish Labour Party and the Independent Labour Party at the end of the 19th century. He was a loving and lovable Christian man.

"... rough ground shall become level, the rugged places a plain the glory of the LORD will be revealed." Is.40:4-5.

Keiran Keira Kieran Kieron Kyron

From Irish Gaelic and meaning 'dark-haired one'. The name of some 26 Irish saints.

Dark hair was always admired in Scriptural times and white hair was thought worthy of honour. In fact God is said to have white hair in Dan.7:9 and Rev.1:14. The story of how Samson lost his strength when the crafty Delilah tricked him into telling her his secret is told in Judges chapter 16. The fact is, Samson had taken the Nazirite vow never to cut his hair. The Lord Jesus would also have had long, dark hair. *"...the hairs of your head are numbered. Don't be afraid; you are worth more than many sparrows." Luke 12:7.*

Keith

From ancient Scottish history and a name for 'a wood' or 'a windy place'. The town of Keith is named after a famous family of the 15th century or earlier.

Situated 80 km (50 miles) north of Aberdeen and on the road to Elgin is the small country town of Keith. Its charter goes back many hundreds of years. There are two bridges (one is dated 1609) across the river Isla which link 'Old' Keith and 'New' Keith. The Apostle Paul speaks about our 'old' nature and our 'new' nature in Romans chapter 6.

"Therefore, if anyone is in Christ...the old has gone, the new has come!" 2 Cor.5:17.

Kelly

From Irish Gaelic 'Ceallach' which probably meant 'a visitor of churches' or a 'bubbling spring'.

An Irishman, Thomas Kelly wrote some of our best-loved hymns. He was originally destined to become a lawyer but was converted in 1792 and joined the church. He wrote nearly 800 hymns and these included; "Look ye saints! The sight is glorious", "The Head that once was crowned with thorns," and "We sing the praise of Him who died". He had a remarkable ability to say profound things in a simple and meaningful way.

"You will be like a well watered garden, like a spring whose waters never fail." Is.58:11.

Kelsey

From Old English or Norse and meaning 'a ship of victory'. The name of a great explorer who established the Hudson Bay Company.

Henry Kelsey 1667-1724 was a British explorer who played a significant role in the establishment of the famous Hudson Bay Company and he rose to become Governor of that Company from 1718 to 1722. He became proficient in Indian languages and was the first white man to explore Canada's central plains and to trade with the Indians. As a highly competent mariner he lived up to the meaning of his name!

"...no mighty ship will sail them. For the LORD is our judge...the LORD is our king; it is he who will save us." Is.33:21-22.

Kelvin

The name of a river - a tributary of the river Clyde. Originally may have meant 'narrow water'.

Lord William Thomson Kelvin was born in Belfast in 1824 but by the age of 17 he was at Cambridge University and was a professor at Glasgow University for 53 years from the age of 22. He made major contributions to the scientific world in the areas of navigation and communication.

Rivers flow through the Bible. From Genesis to Revelation they are very significant. In Genesis the river "...flowed from Eden..." Gen.2:10. In Rev.22:1 it is "the river of the water of life...flowing from the throne of God..."

"Blessed is the man...he is like a tree planted by streams of water..." Ps.1:1-3.

Kendal

From the name of a lovely town in the beautiful Lake District. It means 'village in the valley of the river Kent'. Once a surname and now an attractive Christian name.

Kendal is the largest town in the county of Cumbria with a population of around 25,000. It lies on a bend in the river Kent and was once famous for its 'Kendal Cloth'. The town motto is "Pannus mihi panis" which means "Wool is my bread". The cloth is no longer made but there is still a carpet and woollen industry. King Richard I granted the town the right to hold a market in the 12th century.

"Come now, let us reason together," says the LORD. "Though your sins are like scarlet, they shall be as white as snow; though they are red as crimson, they shall be like wool. Is.1:18.

Kenneth Ken Kenny

From a Scottish Gaelic 'coinneach' meaning 'handsome'. Also the name of a number of famous people.

From Kenneth MacAlpine the first Scottish king in the 9th century to Kenny Dalglish the 'king' of Scottish football - these 'Kenneths' are everywhere. However, when you read the Bible it becomes clear that being 'handsome' does bring its problems. Think of Joseph, David, Absalom, and Daniel - all people described as 'handsome'.

There is an ancient proverb which says: "Handsome is as handsome does", so whether you are a 'handsome' person or not - remember that God is more interested in what we are like on the inside.

"I the LORD search the heart and examine the mind..." Jer.17:10.

Kenton

From Old English meaning 'a royal manor'. Originally it was a place-name, then a surname, now a fascinating Christian name!

In Switzerland and China we still have 'Cantons' and these possibly have the same root as the word 'Kenton' which has been retained by a number English villages   e.g: Kenton, Devon; 'farmstead on the river Kenn', Kenton, London; 'Estate owned by Mr Cenna' etc. The Old English basis of 'a royal manor' reminds us that we are all heading towards one, or something else!

"Let not your heart be troubled...In my Father's house are many mansions ...I go to prepare a place for you." John 14.1-2.(KJV).

Keren - see Karensa

Kerenza - see Karensa

Keri Kerri Kerrie Kerry - see Ceri

Keryn – see Karen

Kesiah Kesia Kezia

The Hebrew name for a lovely sweet-smelling Cinnamon bark (Cinnamomum cassia Blume). It was one of the ingredients used to make anointing oil (Exodus 30:24), and was desired for its aromatic qualities (Psalm 45:8).
It was also the name of Job's second daughter born to him after his troubles ended. (Job 42:12) A few verses later we read; "Nowhere in all the land were there found women as beautiful as Job's daughters and their father granted them an inheritance along with their brothers." (Job 42:15) The story of Job is in the Bible to remind us that God allows the rain to fall on the righteous as well as the unrighteous. Loving God and living an upright life is no guarantee that you will avoid problems or pitfalls.
"I know that my redeemer lives." Job 19:25.

Kevin Kevan Kevyn

From Irish Gaelic and meaning 'born handsome'. The name of a 7th century Irish saint.
In Wicklow southern Ireland there is a valley called "Glendalough"- it was known as "seven churches" many years ago. The 7th century saint St Kevin lived and died there as a hermit. A nearby castle is also named after him.
When you read the Bible it becomes clear that being 'born handsome' does bring its problems. Think of Joseph, David, Absalom, and Daniel - all described as 'born handsome'.
Whether you are 'born handsome' or not - remember that it is far more important to be 'beautiful inside'.
"for everyone born of God overcomes the world." 1 John 5:4.

Kieran - see Keiran

Kimberley Kim

From Old English meaning 'to be royally bold'. Associated with diamonds and other precious stones.
The town called Kimberley in South Africa was named after Lord Kimberley and is famous for its diamonds. Following the Boer war at the turn of the century many people adopted the name. It is also the name for a part of Australia and the hero in a Rudyard Kipling novel.

The diamond is the 'chief' precious stone. It is the hardest, the most imperishable and the most brilliant. When you link this with the meaning of the name 'to be royally bold' you can understand what Paul meant when he said;

"how much greater is the glory...since we have such a hope we are very bold." 2 Cor.3:11-12.

Kingsley

From Old English; 'the Kings field'. ('lea' was the ancient word for a small meadow). First recorded in the Doomsday Book of 1086. Here is Royal property!
The town of Kingsley in Hampshire is recorded in the Doomsday Book of AD1086 as being 'the Kings field' and, later, the town of Kingsley in Staffordshire is also recorded in AD1210. The name denoted the property of the King and as such received royal patronage and protection. The Apostle Paul was aware that Christians were no longer their own property because Jesus had 'paid a price' for them when he died on the cross. They now belonged to the King of Kings! That is why he said;
"For you have been bought with a price: therefore glorify God in your body." 1 Cor.6:20.

Kiran Kirin

Derived from the Sanskrit word for 'ray of light' such as the rays of the sun or the moon. This name reminds us that God created light and is light.
The Bible is full of LIGHT from Genesis to Revelation.
In Gen.1:16 we are told that God created the sun and the moon. King David sang a song of praise to God and in it he says; "You turn my darkness into light" 2 Sam.22:29. When Jesus came He claimed to be "the light of the world" John 9:5. He went on to say that any who followed Him would not walk in darkness but would have the light of life.
"There will be no more night. They will not need the light of a lamp or the light of the sun, for the Lord God will give them light. And they will reign for ever and ever." Rev.22:5.

Kirby

From an Old Scandinavian word 'Kirkjabee' meaning 'a place with a Church'. Also, the Hebrew word 'kir' meaning 'a walled city'. First recorded in the Doomsday Book of 1086AD.
There are at least nine towns and villages in the British Isles which have 'Kirby' as part of their name - it seems that we have been 'incurably religious' for many years! But the true Church, is not a building - it is a group of people who know and belong to the Lord Jesus Christ. Such people can meet without a building and be the Church.
"...the church of God, which He bought with his own blood." Acts 20:28

Kirsten Chirstie Chirsty Kirstie Kirstin Kirstyn Kirsty

From the name 'Christine' which will always have a very special significance because it comes from the word 'Christian'.

It was Gentiles at Antioch who invented the name 'Christian' as a 'nickname' for those who followed 'the way' as it was then known. The word 'Christian' is used three times in the Bible; Acts 11:26, Acts 26:28 and 1 Pet.4:16.

Anyone who has this name is constantly reminded that it meant 'Christ's - one' and of course this is true for everyone because the God who made us sent the Lord Jesus Christ to die for us on the cross.

"..if you suffer as a Christian, do not be ashamed...praise God that you bear that name." 1 Pet.4:16.

Kitty - see Karen

Kristopher – see Christopher

Kyle

From Scottish Gaelic 'Caol' meaning 'a narrow strip of land'. A place-name and new road to the Isles.

Until the late 20th Century, if you wanted to go to the island of Skye, you would need to catch the ferry across the narrow 500 yard sea lane. This has been the traditional way of crossing for thousands of years but at the end of the 20th century a bridge was built from Kyle of Loch-alsh on the mainland to Kyle-akin on the island. Initially, the bridge met with a lot of local opposition because it threatened to change the character of the whole area and the local 'crofters' were anxious to preserve their way of life.

Many songs have been written about the beauty and the solitude of the area. These include "The Skye Boat Song" which is about the escape to Skye of the Young Pretender (Bonnie Prince Charlie) in the 18th century.

"But small is the gate and narrow the road that leads to life, and only a few find it." Mt.7:14.

Kylie

From an Australian Aboriginal word for 'a boomerang'. Handle with care!

There are two distinct types of boomerang - the return boomerang and the non-return or 'war' boomerang. The boomerang is not just a native of Australia - they have been found in the ancient civilisations of Egypt, India and North Africa. The 'war' boomerang can be a deadly weapon in the hands of an expert - a modified form has been useful as a hunting tool. The 'return' boomerang is largely a toy but has also been used to kill birds etc. It can be as dangerous to the thrower as to the target! The 'return' boomerang

is a picture of life - you will often 'get back' what you 'send out'.
"Give, and it will be given to you." (Jesus) Luke 6:38.

Kym Kim

From Old English meaning 'to be royally bold'. Associated with diamonds and other precious stones!

The town in South Africa called Kimberley was named after the famous Lord Kimberley and following the Boer war and the turn of the century many people adopted the name. It is also the name for a part of Australia and the hero in a Rudyard Kipling novel.

The town in South Africa called Kimberley is famous for its diamonds and other precious stones. The diamond is the 'chief' precious stone. It is the hardest, the most imperishable and the most brilliant.

When you link this with the meaning of the name 'to be royally bold' you can understand what Paul meant when he said;

"...since we have such a hope we are very bold." 2. Cor. 3.12.

Kyron – see Keiran

Laila Layla Leila

Arabic for 'evening' or 'night'. A popular name because of her association with the prophet. Recorded from AD701 and used by writers and poets.

This name is sometimes spelt 'Layla' because the Arabic word 'yea' can be romanised as 'i' or 'y'.

One of the most famous stories is that of Quys (later called Majnun)who was so in love with the beautiful Laila that it drove him insane. This story is found in ancient Persian, Urdu and Turkish folklore and is part of a trilogy called "Treasury of Mysteries".

Jesus said: "Greater love has no one than this, that He lay down His life for His friends." John 15:13.

Lana

An old name from French and Celtic. It is also a Welsh stream (from Alun).

Streams are prominent in the Bible. The Bible opens with the story of creation where "a river watering the garden flowed from Eden..." Gen.2:10 and it closes with "the river of the water of life" Rev.22:1. In Psalm 1 we are told that a righteous man "...is like a tree planted by streams of water..." and in Psalm 23 the writer says; "He leads me beside quiet waters.." Ps.23:2.
"Whoever believes in Me...streams of living water will flow from within him." John 7:38.

Lance Lancelot

Old French for 'servant'. A Knight of fame in the legendary stories of King Arthur.

Almost every child will know the stories of Sir Lancelot. These legends come from some original French poems and have been incorporated into the prose of the Arthurian Tales. The story-line is simple, the strong handsome knight rides to the rescue of the weak, defenseless but pretty lady! We love these plots because they mirror God's actions toward us.
"Praise the LORD. Praise, O servants of the LORD, praise the name of the LORD." Ps.113:1.

Larry - see Laurence

Laura Lara Laurel Lauren Laurette Loreen Loretta Lorette Laurisa

From the Latin 'laurus' (bay laurel or bay tree) - the wreaths made from these were symbols of victory in Rome and in the Greek Olympics. Made famous by the Italian poet Petrarch in the 14th century.

Petrarch pined for the lovely Laura and wrote movingly of her beauty and coldness. Whether she was real or imaginary we will never know. However, we are certain of the victory to be won in the race of life and the Apostle Paul urges Timothy to "...compete according to the rules." 2 Tim.2:5.

"She will set a garland of grace on your head and present you with a crown of splendour." Prov.4:9.

Laurence Laurie Larry Lawrence

From the Latin 'Laurentium' a town named after the bay laurel tree. It was a wreath made from bay laurel which was the crown of victory at the Olympics. Also the name of an early Christian martyr.

Isaiah prophesies that in the future the LORD Himself will be the 'laurel' wreath that men will compete for (Is.28:5).

When speaking of the victory to be won in the race of life the Apostle Paul urges Timothy to "...compete according to the rules." 2 Tim.2:5. In the Bible the Christian life is compared to an athletic event. (1 Cor.9:24, Phil.3:14)

The 3rd century martyr Laurence died because he refused to deliver the 'treasures' of the Church to the authorities.

"Everyone who competes in the games goes into strict training. They do it to get a crown that will not last; but we do it to get a crown that will last for ever." 1 Cor.9:25.

Lavinia

Unknown origin but in Roman mythology she was the wife of Aeneas and he fought for her hand. A lovely classical name used in Britain from early in the 13th century.

The ancient town of Latium 30km south of Rome was renamed Lavinium in memory of the successful conquest by Aeneas. It was excavated in 1874 and relics indicating a long history were found. The name 'Lavinia' became very popular in 18th century Britain because the poet Thomson used it instead of the name of Ruth in the Bible book of the same name. The greatest love-story ever told became centred around 'Lavinia'.

"...Where you go, I will go...Your people will be my people and your God my God..." Ruth 1:16.

Lawrence - see Laurence

Layla Leila – see Laila

Leah

A daughter of Laban married to Jacob. A 'builder of the house of Israel' and mother to half the tribes.

The story of Leah is told from Genesis chapter 29. She is honoured as one who "built up the house of Israel" Ruth 4:11. Clearly, she was a woman of distinction because she bore six of the twelve sons of Jacob who became patriarchs of the tribes of Israel. Secondly, when Jacob went to meet Esau she was given a place of honour in the middle of the procession. Thirdly, she was buried with the patriarchs in Hebron. The name Leah means 'wearied'.

"Come to me all who are weary and burdened, and I will give you rest." (Jesus) Mt.11:28.

Leanne Leane - see Julian

Leanora – see Helen

Lee Leigh

Old English for 'a meadow' (from 'Lea'). The name of a famous American General.

The Confederate General Robert E. Lee is a man who has been surrounded by legend and folklore. The truth is that he was an outstanding Army Commander and one commentator has said: "His high character, his moral courage, his noble nature and his mastery of the art of war, made him a notable figure in history." Like many great Generals in other ages Lee was a man who was aware of another 'Commander-in-Chief'. King David, one of the world's greatest soldiers reminded us that it is not external situations that give peace but a sense of rest through the ministry of the Holy Spirit - ...He restores my soul" Ps.23:3.

'They will spring up like grass in a meadow, like poplar trees by flowing streams." Is.44:4.

Lena – see Helen

Leo Leon - see Lionel

Leonard

Meaning 'as bold as a lion' from Norman French and Germanic origin. A converted nobleman who is the patron saint of prisoners. Used in Britain from the 12th century.

St Leonard was a 5th century Frankish nobleman who became a Christian, renounced his wealth and status and became a hermit at Limoges ministering to the needs of captives and prisoners - for whom he is now the patron saint. There are at least 177 churches in England dedicated to him. The name has been common in registers from the 12th century.

"The wicked man flees though no-one pursues, but the righteous are as bold as a lion." Pr.28:1.

Leonie

Latin feminine form for 'a lion' - the king of the beasts! A converted nobleman. The patron saint of prisoners. Used in Britain from the 12th century.

St.Leonard ('as brave as a lion') was a 5th century Frankish nobleman who became a Christian, renounced his wealth and status and became a hermit at Limoges ministering to the needs of captives and prisoners - for whom he is now the patron saint. There are at least 177 churches in England alone dedicated to him. The name has been common in registers from the 12th century.

"The wicked flees though no-one purues, but the righteous are as bold as a lion." Pr.28:1.

Leroy

From the Old French phrase 'del roy' meaning 'a son (or a servant) of the king'. Very popular in the West Indies and America.

This name has always been more popular in America than in Europe - where it originated! Today it is widely used across the world and is fast growing in popularity.

To be a son or even a servant of the king is a great honour - an even greater honour when that king happens to be the King of Kings! Everyone who knows and loves Jesus has this great privilege.

"Now to the King eternal, immortal, invisible, the only God, be honour and glory for ever. Amen!" Tim.1:17.

Lesley Leslie

A Scottish place-name meaning 'a garden of hollies'. The 'Lords of Leslie'. "Christ's kirk on the Green".

The names Lesley and Leslie come from the Scottish town named 'Leslie' - now more a part of the town of Glenrothes in Aberdeenshire on the east coast of Scotland. It overlooks the Vale of Leven and further west, Loch Leven which is renowned for its fishing. The old church of Leslie claims to be "Christ's Kirk on the Green" from the ancient ballads of that name.

The name is registered from the 18th century and was used by the Lords of Leslie.

"And the LORD God made all kinds of trees grow out of the ground   trees that were pleasing to the eye and good for food." Gen.2:9.

Lester

Named after the ancient Roman town of Leicester - from early in the 11th century.

From 1086 the County Town and City of Leicester has been a vital part of English heritage. Earlier records indicate that it was known as 'Ligera ceaster' (a Saxon version of the Roman name meaning "Town of the tribal people called Ligore"). Being just 145 km (91 miles) north-west of London it was ideally situated on the river Soar to be a junction on the Fosse Way (the great Roman road - now the A46) for traffic to the Midlands and beyond.

"But small is the gate and narrow the road that leads to life, and only a few find it." Mt.7:14.

Letitia Laetitia

From Latin meaning 'gladness'. Popular from the 12th to the 17th century and revived in the last century.

There are records from 1199 to the end of the 17th century indicating that the name was very fashionable, it then fades from the scene until late in the 19th century.

The dictionary defines 'gladness' as "looks, feelings etc marked by, filled with, expressing, JOY".

"Let the heavens rejoice, let the earth be GLAD; let them say...the LORD reigns!" 1 Chron.16:31.

Levi

Hebrew for 'united'. The third son of Jacob and the father of Moses. One of Jesus's twelve apostles. Blue denim jeans!

The leader of a tribe which God appointed to a special responsibility. They escorted the Ark of the Covenant (Duet.10:8) and because of their loyalty a curse was turned into a blessing. In the New Testament Levi is called to follow the Lord Jesus and he is also known by the name of 'Matthew' ('God's gift').

'Levi' Strauss immigrated from Russia to America in the Gold Rush of 1850. He wanted to sell clothes to the miners. He noted that they needed strong, durable trousers so he made some from the canvas which they also used for tents. Later denim was substituted and used by, among others, the American Cowboys!

"...he saw Levi...sitting at the tax collector's booth. "Follow me," Jesus told him...Levi got up and followed him." Mark 2:14.

Lewis – see also Louis

Means 'famous warrior' of Norman-French origin. In its French form of 'Louis' it was the name of 18 Kings of France (8th to 19th centuries).

King David was one of the most famous warriors of all time. When he went out to meet the giant Goliath he only took his sling and five small stones - but one man and God is always a majority.

Many famous Army Commanders and Military men have been committed Christians. Oliver Cromwell established parliamentary rule and General Allenby (a descendant of Oliver Cromwell) liberated Palestine after 500 years of Ottoman rule. They fought in God's strength.

"Therefore put on the full armour of God, so that when the day of evil comes, you may be able to stand your ground." Eph.6:13.

Liam - see also William

Irish Gaelic for 'William' which is thought to come from German meaning 'seeking protection'.

One of the most famous kings was King William III of England, better known as 'William of Orange'. He only reigned for thirteen years but during that time the Bill of Rights and the Act of Settlement were passed.

Yet another William(s) founded the YMCA in 1844. He was born the son of a Somerset farmer and rose to become a Knight of the Realm. He attributed his success to the fact that he had become a Christian through Charles Finney.

"Let all who take refuge in you be glad...spread your protection over them." Ps.5:11.

Lianne - see Julian

Libbie Libby - see Elizabeth

Lilian Lily

From the Latin 'lilium'. Lilies were the traditional Christian symbol of purity. Jesus used them as an object lesson, He is described as 'the lily of the valley'.

'Lilian' and 'Lily' are from the same root and have three main symbolisms in Christianity: Since the 19th century and possibly long before, they have been a symbol of purity. Secondly, Jesus exhorted His followers to "...consider how the lilies grow..." Luke 12:27 when he wanted to encourage them to trust God more. Thirdly, in the book of the Song of Songs, the lover (the Lord Jesus) is described as "the lily of the valley". S.of S.2:1.

"Consider how the lilies grow...Solomon in all his splendour was not dressed like one of these." Luke 12:27.

Linda Belinda Lindy Lyn Lynda Lynn Lynne Lynette

Spanish for 'pretty' and also similar to an Old German word which means 'wise and supple'.

A combination of Spanish and Old German meanings for this name seem to cover everything. If we list them in order of importance:

Wisdom - Solomon was commended by God because he asked for "wisdom and knowledge" 2 Chron.1:10. Someone has said that wisdom is 'education in action' (see Proverbs chapters 1-4 and 8 and 9).

Supple - or bodily fitness. The Apostle Paul says that this benefits - a little! (See 1 Tim.4:8). Pretty - or good looks. Scripture is full of warnings against physical appearance being the sole criterion for judging people - it is more important that we are 'beautiful inside'.

"Your beauty should not come from outward adornment...instead it should be that of your inner self, the unfading beauty of a gentle and quiet spirit..." 1 Pet.3:3-4.

Lindsay Lindsey Linsay Lyndsay Linsey

Originally a word Celtic word which became a Scottish surname. The Danish name for that part of Lincolnshire called 'Lindsey' was 'lindo' meaning 'island of Lincoln'.

The cathedral city of Lincoln is on the summit of the Cliff range of hills. The first historical mention of it is by Bede in AD628 when he says that Paulinus preached there and established a Church. Then the city was called 'Lindsey'.

"You are the light of the world. A city on a hill cannot be hidden." Mt.5:14. Lincoln cathedral can be seen for miles around and Jesus had this sort of prominence in mind when He spoke of our Christian witness and testimony.

"...let your light so shine before men, that they may see your good deeds and praise your Father in heaven." Mt.5:16.

Lionel Leo Leon

From the old French and Latin for 'lion'. Edward III used it in 1273. A popular Jewish name.

The French name 'Leon' is from the Latin root 'leo' meaning 'lion'. Edward III named his third son Lionel (old French and English for a young lion). The name was popular in the 15th century. Long before that Jacob, as he died, declared of Judah (the root of 'Jew' etc) "You are a lion's cub" Gen.49:9.

There are several stories about lions in the Bible, the best known being the one about Samson, who fought and killed a lion with his bare hands, and

his riddle in Judges chapter 14. Part of this riddle was used by a syrup company for many years: "Out of the eater; something to eat, Out of the strong something sweet..."
"the lion of the tribe of Judah, the root of David, has triumphed." Rev.5:5.

Lisa Liz Liza Lizzie Lizzy - see Elizabeth

Lloyd

From Welsh 'Llwyd' meaning 'grey'. A 'market' for Underwriters and a prosperous Bank.
The history of this name is shrouded in mystery - much like its meaning! For all that, it is a good name which cannot be shortened (although the Americans, unable to pronounce the double 'L' invented 'Floyd' from it).
The famous 'Lloyds of London' Insurance Market, the prestigious 'Lloyds Bank' and the man everyone's father seemed to know, David Lloyd George (the famous Welsh politician 1863-1945), have made this name popular.
"The glory of young men is their strength, grey hair the splendour of the old." Prov.20:29.

Lois

From Greek meaning 'better'. Timothy's grandmother and the mother of Eunice (2 Tim.1:5).
The first recorded use of the name 'Lois' in England is in a Lincolnshire Parish Register in 1583.
Timothy, one of the apostle Paul's co-workers was the product of a Christian home - his mother and grandmother had taught him the Scriptures. Timothy was imprisoned for the faith and nothing is known of his final fate, but his testimony and that of his godly mother and grandmother has been read by millions through the years.
"Because your love is better than life, my lips will glorify you. I will praise you as long as I live." Ps.63:3-4.

Loraine Lorraine

From German French meaning 'The place of a famous army'. A French District which has been the subject of conflict ever since the 9th century.
When Charlemagne's empire disintegrated this area in north-east France became the object of disputes between France and Germany up to the end of the second World War when it was returned to France. Formerly known as 'Lotharingia' today it is part of Alsace-Lorraine with the German-speaking population located around Alsace and the French-speaking people in Lorraine.
At the beginning of time there was a conflict over territory known as the Garden of Eden. Man was finally banned and, as a result, the word of God

tells us that "all creation" awaits our redemption (Rom.8:22-23).
"Creation itself will be liberated from its bondage...into the glorious freedom...of God."
Rom.8:21.

Loreen - see Laura

Loretta Lorette - see Laura

Lorna

A name created in 1869 by R.D.Blackmore for his novel "Lorna Doone". It is possible he was inspired by the 'Firth of Lorne' in Argyll. An Old English word 'needing to be found' as in 'love-lorn'.

Blackmore was a barrister and the son of an Anglican Minister. He wrote many novels but is remembered exclusively for 'Lorna Doone'. The story is set in the West Country and is a work of singular charm, vigour and imagination. The book was immediately recognised as a leader in the romantic revival.

Perhaps an even greater love story is the book of Ruth in the Bible, this too appeared at a crucial time and played a part in changing the world. From Ruth came Jesse, from Jesse came David and from David's line the Lord Jesus was born.

"The Son of Man came to seek and to save that which was lost." Luke 19:10.

Lorraine - see Loraine

Louis Lewis

Means 'famous warrior' from Norman-French origin. It was the name of 18 Kings of France.

King David was one of the most famous warriors of all time. When he went out to meet the giant Goliath he only took his sling and five small stones - but one man and God is always a majority.

Many famous Army Commanders and Military men have been committed Christians. Oliver Cromwell gave Britain parliamentary democracy and General Allenby (a descendant of Oliver Cromwell) liberated Palestine after 500 years of Ottoman rule. These men and many others, fought in God's strength. "Fight the good fight...Christ is thy strength and Christ thy might". J.S.B.Monsell.

"They were brave warriors, famous men, and heads of their families." 1 Chron.5:24.

Louisa Louise

From Norman-French meaning 'famous warrior'. The male form 'Louis' was the

name of 18 French kings - not all of whom were fighting men.
One of them LOUIS 14th became known as the 'Sun King' because his reign resulted in a great flowering of European culture. His luxurious palace at Versailles was a great venue for all the leading musicians and artists of his day. Famous musicians performed and beautiful paintings adorned the walls. Among other things he founded academies of Painting, Sculpture, Science and Architecture. At around this time in nearby Germany, Handel and Bach were growing up. It would be hard to over-estimate the effect that Louis 14th had on our European culture.
"May the LORD make the woman who is coming into your home like Rachel and Leah...famous in Bethlehem." Ruth 4:11.

Lowena Lurlene Lurline

The 'middle' Cornish word for 'joy'. This is a lovely name and a description of the feelings of those who love and follow God.
The ancient Cornish Celtic language is divided into 'old' Cornish, (pre-AD1300) 'middle' Cornish(1300 to 1600) and 'late' Cornish (from 1600). Cornish is in some ways, similar to Breton or Welsh - in fact some 'late' Cornish has borrowed words from both of these languages.
The words 'joy', 'joyful' or 'joyfully' occur nearly 250 times in the bible and there are as many in the Old Testament as there are in the New Testament. Joy is different from happiness. It has been said that 'JOY is not the absence of suffering but the presence of God'. So Paul and Silas could sing when they had been beaten and thrown into prison (Acts 16). They knew they were doing what was right! Perhaps the secret of JOY lies in the acrostic;
Jesus first, Others second, Yourself last...

Lucas - see Luke

Lucy Lucia Lucinda Lulu

From Latin and meaning 'light'. During Roman times if you were born in the early morning you might well be given this name.
'Children of light' is not a new concept - God's first act in the creation of the world was to create light (Gen.1:3). So it was appropriate to use this name for children born early in the day.
When Jesus came He was called 'the light of the world' and the promise was that those who follow Him would not walk in darkness (John 8:12). We are told that heaven will be filled with light - from the glory of God (Rev.21:23).
"...you were once darkness, but now you are light in the Lord. Live as children of light." Eph.5:8.

Luke Lucas

From Greek meaning 'light-giving' or perhaps 'a man of Lucania' which is in southern Italy. Doctor, Writer and Missionary Traveller.

Luke wrote both the gospel and the book of Acts and was a companion to the Apostle Paul on some of his missionary journeys. His gospel is the longest of the four gospels and contains some additional detail of the progress of Jesus from Galilee to Jerusalem. He also includes a number of 'medical' facts and stories - such as the account of Jesus' birth and the woman with the issue of blood.

The book of Acts is a record of the movement of God in and through the early church. Many passages contain the words "we" which indicate that Luke was a personal witness to the events described.

"Our dear friend Luke, the doctor..." Col.4:14.

Lurlene Lurline – see Lowena

Lulu - see Lucy

Luther

From Old German and meaning 'the people's warrior'. The leader of the Reformation. A great American Civil Rights campaigner.

Martin Luther (1483-1546) was the leader of the Reformation movement which gave birth to the Protestant church in Europe. During his early life he was a devoutly religious person and rose to become Professor of Theology but he also became deeply concerned about his own salvation. Through his study of the scriptures he came to realise that salvation was through Christ alone and formulated the doctrine of justification: "sola fide" (faith alone), "sola gratia" (grace alone) and "sola Scriptura" (the Bible alone).

The Rev. Martin Luther King was a famous Christian American Civil Rights Campaigner who was assassinated in 1968.

"...therein is the righteousness of God revealed...as it is written, The just shall live by faith." Rom.1:17 KJV.

Lydia

The name means 'from Lydia', a district of Asia Minor that was highly cultivated and very fruitful.

It is said that both die (dice) and coinage were invented by the Lydians. They also had a great interest in music.

There is only one 'Lydia' in the Bible and she lived in Thyatira. Her story is in Acts 16:13-15. She was an educated and wealthy woman trader in the famous Lydian purple cloth. She invited Paul and his companions to stay at her home. Her experience has been shared by multitudes since then "...I felt my heart strangely warmed...I felt I did trust in Christ, Christ alone for salvation." John Wesley 24th May 1738

"...the Lord opened (or warmed) her heart to respond to Paul's message." Acts 16:14.

Lyn Lynda Lynn Lynne Lynette - see Linda

Mabel

From Latin meaning 'lovable'. First recorded in 1189. Popular in the late 19th and early 20th centuries.

The name Mabel has a long history, it was originally from Amabel but quickly became established as a name in its own right. C.M. Young (1884) records; "It is still used among the northern peasantry"(!) This does reinforce the fact that the name was very 'common' in the Yorkshire area about that time.

'Lovable' is defined by the dictionary as 'deserving love' and whilst we cannot always claim this - the Lord Jesus certainly can. Frances Ridley Havergal (1836-79) wrote: "Take my love; my Lord, I pour At Thy feet its treasure store:"

"But let all who take refuge in you be glad...those who love your name may rejoice in you." Ps.5:11.

Mackenzie Mckenzie

An ancient Scottish name which means 'son of Coinneach', a Gaelic name which is usually anglicised as 'Kenneth'.

Originally a Scottish surname and in surnames the prefix 'Mac' or 'Mc' means 'son of'. The equivalent to 'son-of' in Aramaic would be 'bar' - as in 'bar-abbas' 'son of his father'. We can all claim to be the son or daughter of our father.

The anglicised version 'Kenneth' means 'handsome'. However, when you read the Bible it becomes clear that being 'handsome' does have its problems. Think of Joseph, David, Absalom, and Daniel - all people described as 'handsome'. There is an ancient proverb which says: "Handsome is as handsome does" and whether you are a 'handsome' person or not - remember that it is far more important to be 'beautiful inside'.

"He was ruddy, with a fine appearance and handsome features." 1 Sam.16:12.

Madeline Madelaine Madeleine Madelena Madelyn Magdalene

From Hebrew meaning 'a woman of Magdala'. Used in the UK from the 12th century. Often pronounced the French way which means 'sentimental'.

The town of Magdala is just to the north of Tiberias on the sea of Galilee between Tiberias and the Mount of Beatitudes (where Jesus preached the famous 'Sermon on the Mount'). Mary came from this area and she had cause to be grateful to the Lord because He had healed and blessed her - she in turn ministered to Him. Some scholars think that she is the woman who washed the feet of Jesus and anointed them with the precious perfume - "...the house was filled with the fragrance..." John 12:3.
"Mary Magdalene went to the disciples with the news: 'I have seen the Lord!'" John 20:18.

Mae Mai - see Mary

Madge Maggie - see Margaret

Madison

Norman/French and Germanic origin meaning 'strong in the battle'. From the 11th century when it was used as a surname for 'the son of Maud'. A lovely name for a fighter!
The name was introduced by William I when he married Matilda the daughter of Baldwin V of Flanders. It was often reduced to 'Maud' which was used in Tennyson's Poem in 1855 (from that time all three names have grown in popularity). 'Maud's-son' became 'Madison'. This name is the reason why 'Magdalen' in Oxford is pronounced 'Maudlin'! The biblical origin was the town of Magdala on the shores of the sea of Galilee. This is from a Hebrew word which means 'tower'. Now we have the saying "a tower of strength". The Bible has a lot to say about 'battle';
"...the battle was God's..." 1 Chron. 5.22.

Magali – see Margaret

Magda – see Madeline

Magdalena Magdalene – see Margaret

Maia

A lovely name from Greek mythology - a goddess who was the daughter of Atlas and the mother of Hermes. Her 'day' is the 15th May and that month is named after her!
This lady should have everything - her father was reputed to be one the strongest men who ever lived - her son is variously depicted as a 'messenger of the gods', a successful businessman and a brilliant athlete!

Sadly, mythology is not real life and reality rarely endows us with so many attributes. Only one thing is possible for all of us - it is possible to be strong and beautiful inside!

"Your beauty should not come from outward adornment...Instead, it should be that of your inner self, the unfading beauty of a gentle and quiet spirit, which is of great worth in God's sight."   1 Peter 3:3-4.

Maida

A name from a battle in Italy, a street in north London and a shelter from the Great Plague.

At the battle of Maida in Southern Italy in 1806 Sir John Stuart defeated the French under Gen. Regnier. In memory of this the houses being built on the Edgware Road were called 'Maida Hill' and then 'Maida Avenue'. The whole area is now known as 'Maida Vale'. It was this area together with Hampstead to the north that escaped the Great Plague of London. There is also an Arabic Urdu word 'maydan' which means 'an open space'.

If you reverse the two syllables you have 'a maid' which reminds us of a verse in the Bible.

"...as the eyes of a maid look to the hand of her mistress, so our eyes look to the LORD" Ps.123.2.

Maire Mairi Mair Mhairi - see Mary

Maisie - see Margaret

Majid

From Arabic and meaning; 'glorious', 'illustrious', 'noble'. One of the names of God.

This name together with other names such as 'Majdi' and 'Amjad' are popular Arabic names which come from the root word 'Majid'. There are several other names which are variants but they all have the basic meaning of 'glorious'. In the Old Testament the glory of God was exhibited in different ways and at different times - such as the Temple dedication when the glory was such that the priests could not fulfil their functions (1 Kings 8.11.). In the New Testament the glory of God is seen in Jesus Christ (John 1.14.). *"...what is man...that you care for him...you crowned him with glory..."* Ps.8.5.

Malcolm

From the original Irish name of Callum with a Latin source meaning 'a dove'. Adopted by Scotland sometime in the 6th century through St Columba and changed to form the basis of many other names.

In the Bible the dove has always been the symbol of peace and the symbol of the Holy Spirit. It was a dove that Noah sent out from the ark in order

to find out if the waters had receded (Gen.8). It was a dove that formed the basis of the sacrificial offering in the wilderness (Lev.1:14). The Psalmist cried "Oh for the wings of a dove" Ps.55:6. John the Baptist said: "I saw the Spirit come down from heaven as a dove...on Him." John 1:32.
"...be...as innocent as doves." Mt.10:16.

Mallory

Originally from an Old French nickname for someone who had an experience of misfortune. A famous English writer in the 15th century whose writings and identity were both surrounded with mystery!

Sir Thomas Malory wrote the famous prose version of 'Le Morte D'arthur'. An account of the life and work of the legendary King Arthur and his 'Knights of the Round Table'.

Molla Mallory was one of the most famous American tennis players of all time - she won the US singles championship eight times and she is a member of the International Tennis Hall of Fame.

"Misfortune pursues the sinner, but prosperity is the reward of the righteous." Prov.13:2

Mandy

From Latin meaning 'to be loved', 'lovable' or 'deserving love'. Three lovely definitions of one name.

'To be loved' is very easy and enjoyable - we were made by God to receive love and it is a basic human need we all have.

'Lovable' - we all have special features and characteristics that make us attractive. Someone wrote; "If nobody loves you - create the demand!"

'Deserving love' how is it possible? The gospel (good news) is that God loved us when we didn't deserve it.

"He tends his flock like a shepherd: He gathers the lambs in his arms and carries them close to his heart; he gently leads those that have young." Is.40:11.

Manuel - see Emmanuel

Manya – see Mary

Marc Marcus - see Mark

Margaret Margo Eilis Greta Madge Magali Maggie Masie Maisie Margery Marjorie Meg Megan Meghan Peg Peggy Rita

These names are from the Latin Greek 'Margarita' meaning 'a pearl' or 'a child from the light of the moon'. This is because an ancient legend said that pearls were produced by moonbeams.

We know today that pearls are produced by irritants entering the bodies of oysters.

Jesus said that the Kingdom of Heaven was like "one pearl of great price" Mt.13:44-46 KJV. So these names are linked with the greatest treasure known to man - they are associated with heaven.

"The twelve gates were twelve pearls, each gate made of a single pearl." Rev.21:21.

Maria Marian Marie Marisa - see Mary

Marigold

The name of several golden-yellow flowers belonging to the family Compositae. The corn marigold is the most popular and this is dried for hay. The use of the marigold for dyeing began in Germany.

There are also the 30 species of the genus Tagetes of America and Africa. The marigold has strongly scented leaves and these form a cup-shaped base below the flower. The other varieties also come in red and orange.

Jesus spoke of the lilies and the fact that if God takes care of them then He will also take care of us. In the Song of Songs the flowers of spring depict renewal.

"On the walls all around the temple, in both the inner and outer rooms, he carved cherubim, palm trees and open flowers." 1 Kings 6:29.

Marika – see Mary

Marilyn

A combination of two names; 'Miriam' which means 'sweet smell (myrrh) of the sea' and 'bright, shining' from the Greek 'Helen'.

A very modern name popular since the middle of the 20th century. A combination of 'Miriam' and 'Ellen' (from 'Helen'). Miriam was the only sister of Moses. She was the one who watched over him when he was a baby and was hidden in the bulrushes. Moses was a great leader but he would not have survived if a young girl had not been a reliable guardian... Helen means 'light' or 'bright shining' and was the name of the mother of the Emperor Constantine. She went to the Holy Land and located many of the sites where Jesus had preached and performed miracles.

"Pleasing is the fragrance of your perfumes; your name is like perfume poured out." S.of S.1:3.

Marion - see Mary

160

Marjorie Marjory - see Margaret

Mark Marc
Original Latin form: Marcus
Italian and Spanish form: Marco

The name means 'God has shown Grace'. Mark is the name of the second Gospel.

The writer of the second gospel was often called "John Mark" and this is significant because the name 'John' means 'The grace or mercy of the Lord', so whether you use one or both names, his attributes are clear. He wrote the shortest Gospel of just sixteen chapters. There is an urgency in Mark's writing, the King James version makes frequent use of the word 'straightway' and in more modern translations this is translated "as soon as" or "at once". *"The King's business requires haste." 1 Sam.21:8 KJV.*

Marlene

From the German shortening of 'Mary Magdalena'. From the middle of the 20th century.

The town of Magdala is just to the north of Tiberias on the Sea of Galilee between Tiberias and the Mount of Beatitudes (where Jesus preached the famous 'Sermon on the Mount'). Mary came from this area and she had cause to be grateful to the Lord because He had healed her - she in turn ministered to Him. She is the woman who washed the feet of Jesus and anointed them with precious perfume "...the house was filled with the fragrance..." John 12:3.
"When Jesus rose early on the first day of the week, he appeared first to Mary Magdalene..." Mark 16:9.

Marlon

An ancient French translation of the name 'Marc' (with the added 'lon' - a combination of 'el' and 'on') it means 'God has shown Grace'.

In the gospels he was often called "John Mark" and this is significant because the name 'John' means: 'The grace or mercy of the Lord', so whether you use one or both names, his attributes are clear! One of the most descriptive verses in the New Testament is John 1:14. "We have seen His glory...full of grace and truth". There is an urgency in Mark's writing, the King James version makes use of the word "straightway" but in more modern translations this is translated "as soon as" or, "at once".
"...because the King's business was urgent" 1 Sam.21:8.

Martha

From Aramaic and meaning 'a lady'. The sister of Mary and Lazarus. Popular in the UK from the Reformation. The wife of Simon?

This name is unique to the New Testament and is unique to this one person - there are no other 'Martha's' in scripture. Matthew, Mark and John agree that Jesus was anointed in Bethany. Matthew and Mark say that it took place in Simon's home. In Luke Jesus is received into Martha's home and served the supper at which His feet were anointed - so it is reasonable to assume that she was married to Simon.

"Jesus loved Martha and her sister and Lazarus." John 11:5.

Martin Martyn

From 'Mars' the name of the Roman god of battle. 'Martin of Tours' in the 4th Century.

Martin of Tours was born in Hungary and enlisted into the Roman army at 15 years of age by his pagan father. Five years before this he had taken an interest in Christianity. At the age of 18 he saw a poor beggar at the town of Amiens and he divided his cloak with him, shortly afterwards he had a vision of Christ wearing the half-cloak that he had given the beggar. Two years later he was baptised into the Christian faith and later became a Bishop.

"The spirit of the Lord is on me, because He has anointed me to preach good news to the poor..." Luke 4:18.

Martina

From 'Mars' the name of the Roman god of battle. A famous tennis-player. Martins - the most beautiful, agile and tireless of birds.

In the 20th century this name has come into popularity through people like the famous tennis-player Martina Navratilova from Czechoslovakia. It is also the name of some of the most graceful of God's creatures - such as the House Martin and the Sand Martin, birds of the swallow family which were named after St Martin of Tours.

"Even the sparrow has found a home, and the swallow a nest for herself...a place near your altar, O LORD...my King and my God." Ps.84:3.

Mary Mae Mai Maria Marian Marie Marion Marisa Maureen May Moira Miriam
Molly Moyra Polly
Gaelic form: Mari Mairi Maire Mhairi
Russian form: Manya
Polish form: Marika
Short form: Ria

The name Mary means 'sweet smell (myrrh) of the sea' and it comes from the Hebrew Miriam.

There are at least six different Mary's in the New Testament and here are three of them: Mary Magdalene came from the village of Magdala just north of Tiberias on the Sea of Galilee. The Lord cured her of evil spirits (Luke 8:1-3). Mary the sister of Martha. She was the one who, according to the Lord Jesus, "has chosen what is better" Luke 10:42. Mary the mother of Jesus (the Virgin Mary). She believed and trusted God for what He had promised; see the early chapters of Matthew and Luke.

"Mary said: 'My soul glorifies the Lord and my spirit rejoices in God my Saviour'" Luke 1:46-47.

Masie – see Margaret

Matilda
French form: Maud
Norman French and Germanic origin meaning 'strong in the battle'. From the 11th century.

The name was introduced by William I when he married Matilda the daughter of Baldwin V of Flanders.

It was not used very much in the 16th and 17th centuries but Tennyson's Poem "Maud"(1855) was partly responsible for its revival and from that time it has grown in popularity. It features in the Australian song "Waltzing Matilda".

The Bible has a lot to say about 'being strong - in the Lord'.

"Finally, be strong in the Lord and in His mighty power." Eph.6:10.

Matthew Mathew Matthias Mattia Matt
Matthew is the writer of the first gospel in the New Testament. He was Jewish and his name means 'a gift from God'.

He describes himself as "the tax-collector" Mt.10:3 and in his day this would not have been very complimentary because tax collectors survived on the extra money that they were able to extort from people. What a strange occupation for someone with a name which means 'gift of God'. One day Jesus passed by and invited Matthew to "Follow Me." Mt.9:9. He not only forgave Matthew but trained him to lead others to know the Saviour.

One day Matthew sat down to write the story of everything that Jesus had done - a sort of 'story of my life'...

"Follow me,' he told him, and Matthew got up and followed him." Mt.9:9.

Maud - see Matilda

Maureen - see Mary

Maurice Morris

From Latin 'Mauricius' which means 'a Moor'. A Swiss martyr and a lovely lakeside resort. From the 3rd century and used in the UK since the 11th century.

These names have been popular in Britain since 1086 but their history goes back to the 3rd century. In AD286 Maurice, the leader of an Egyptian Christian group, was martyred in Switzerland because he would not worship the pagan gods of the Roman Emperor Diocletian. He and his entire group were massacred at Agaunum - which was renamed St Moritz in his honour. The many thousands who holiday at this beautiful mountain resort may never realize the history of the name.

"They overcame him...by the word of their testimony..." Rev.12:11.

Mavis

The Old-English and French word for 'Song-thrush'. A recent addition to feminine names.

The song-thrush is one of many species of thrush found in the UK and most of Europe. It is one of the finest songsters - loud and musical, each phrase being repeated two or three times. It has a brown back and a speckled breast, its eggs are blue with black spots and it lays up to five, twice a year. When other food is scarce it has a remarkable ability to feed on snails and will often have a favourite stone on which to break them open.

"...in your hands He has placed...the birds of the air." Dan.2:38.

Max Maximilian

Latin meaning 'the greatest'. Maximilian the 1st (1493-1519) was a renowned German 'Holy Roman Emperor' hunter and fighter. His name has become popular in Teutonic countries.

Jesus turned the whole concept of 'greatest' upside down when He said; "...the greatest among you should be like the youngest, and the one who rules like the one who serves." Luke 22:26. This concept of 'ruling servanthood' was new then and is still almost unknown today. He wasn't decrying greatness but He was counselling the right use of authority and the need for humility.

"The greatest among you will be your servant." Mt.23:11.

May - see Mary

Meg Megan Meghan - see Margaret

Melanie Melany

From Greek meaning 'dark-skinned'. Used extensively by the Romans. First used in the UK from the 17th century. Very popular in Cornwall.

'Melania' was the name of two saints in the 5th century - a grandmother and a granddaughter. The younger Melania sold everything, freed her slaves, gave all her money to the poor and retired to the Mount of Olives. Whilst the name was used by the Romans and introduced here in the Middle Ages it was relatively little known until it featured in the film "Gone with the Wind" in 1939. The Greek 'melas' means 'dark' and is also used of the islands of Melanesia.

"Dark am I yet lovely O daughters of Jerusalem...I am dark because I am darkened by the sun." S.of S. 1:5-6.

Melissa Melinda

Latin for 'lemon balm' (melissa officinalis). It may well have been the name for a lovely product known in the Bible as the 'balm of Gilead'. Also the Greek name for 'a bee'.

The humble bee was vital to the survival of God's people for a number of different reasons.

One variety of 'balm' was used in anointing various ailments "Get balm for her pain" Jer.51:8, "...food and drink, and healing balm" 2 Chron.28:15. Jeremiah cried "...is there no balm in Gilead...no physician...no healing?" Jer.8:22 and

"...He took our infirmities...carried our sorrows...by His wounds we are healed..." Is.53:4-5.

Melvin Melvyn

From Anglo-Saxon meaning 'a friend'. A Scottish favourite and a name for a person who will be a companion and good company.

Friendship is a wonderful thing and Scripture has a lot to say about it, for instance; "A friend loves at all times" Prov. 17:17 and "I am a friend to all who fear you" Ps.119:63.

True friendship makes demands. Abraham was called "the friend of God" Jas.2:23 because he heard the voice of God and obeyed it . Jesus underlined this concept when He said "You are my friends if you do what I command." John 15:14. He said that it could entail 'laying down our life' for our friends (John 15:13) - which He did for us.

"...but there is a friend who sticks closer than a brother." Prov.18:24.

Meriel Merrill Merrell Meryl Muriel

From Irish Gaelic meaning 'sea - bright'. First recorded in 1198. Originally from

Normandy and Brittany. King William I is said to have had a half-sister called Meriel.

The origin of these names is lost in the mists of antiquity - it is possible that they came from Irish Gaelic, Breton or Welsh. In the Middle Ages Meriel was popular with Jewesses which means that it may well have been derived from 'Miriam'. For all that, 'Meriel' was first recorded by the Curia Regis Rolls of 1198. There are many verses in the Bible about the sea.
"Mightier than...the great waters, mightier than the breakers of the sea - the LORD on high is mighty." Ps.93:4.

Merlin Mervin Mervyn

From the Welsh 'Myrddin' which means 'a sea fort'. A small falcon and a 'wizard' name!

There is a little uncertainty about the origin of these names - but there is no doubt that they came from Wales and the name 'merlin' means 'a sea-fort' in Welsh. The origin is probably 'Myrddin' with its English pronunciation changed to 'Merlin'. He was the legendary wizard in the fables of King Arthur and his Knights of the Round Table. The Merlin is also a handsome small falcon (falco columbarius) which breeds in the northern UK and Scandinavia; in America it is called the Pigeon Hawk.
"The LORD is my rock, my fortress and my deliverer...in whom I take refuge."
2 Sam.22:2-3.

Merrill Merrell Meryl - see Meriel

Mervin Mervyn - see Merlin

Meta – see Pearl

Meurig - see also Maurice Morris

From Latin 'Mauricius' which means 'a Moor - a North African'. From the 3rd century and used in Wales since the 5th century. A Swiss martyr and a lovely lakeside resort.

The name Meurig (Maurice) has been popular in Wales since the 5th century but its history goes back to the 3rd century. In AD286 Maurice led an Egyptian Christian group which was martyred in Switzerland because they would not worship the pagan gods of the Roman Emperor Diocletian. He and his entire group were massacred at Agaunum - which was renamed St Moritz in his honour. The many thousands who holiday at this beautiful mountain resort may never know the history of the name.
"They overcame him...by the word of their testimony..." Rev.12:11.

Mhairi – see Mary

Michael Michaela Michele Michelle Mick Mickey Mike Mitch Mitchell

The name 'Michael' means 'who is like God?' and it occurs 15 times in the Bible.

Angels are real heavenly beings and a number of books have been written about them by Dr Billy Graham and others. The most famous Michael in the Bible is the Archangel Michael who has a special responsibility for God's chosen people the Jews (Daniel 12:1). Revelation chapter 12 :7 - 9 seem to indicate that Michael will have a part in the final overthrow of Satan. *"Who among the gods is like you O LORD...majestic...awesome...working wonders..." Ex.15:11.*

Mildred Milbrough

From Old English meaning 'gentle'. From the 7th century. Three sisters who all became 'saints'.

During the 7th century there was a king living in Mercia who had three daughters. He called them; 'Milbrough' (gentle defence), 'Mildgyth' (gentle gift), and 'Mildthryth' (gentle strength). It was from the last one that the name Mildred developed. All three sisters were canonised. 'Mildred' was a surname in Shropshire and also among Romany families.

"but the LORD was not in the wind...but the LORD was not in the earthquake...but the LORD was not in the fire. And after the fire came a gentle whisper." 1 Kings 19:11-12.

Miles

From Old Slavonic meaning 'merciful' or possibly from Latin meaning 'a soldier'. Recorded in 1086 and brought to Britain by the Normans.

Taking the Old Slavonic and the Latin together the name would mean 'merciful soldier'. This then would reflect the commands which John the Baptist gave to the soldiers when he met them: "Don't extort...don't accuse falsely - be content with your pay." Luke 3:14. Another soldier who was assigned to carry out the gruesome task of crucifixion said of the Lord Jesus who was on the central cross: "Surely this was a righteous man." Luke 23:47.

"Blessed are the merciful, for they will be shown mercy." Mt.5:7.

Milla - see Camilla

Millicent

From Old German meaning 'a strong worker'. The daughter of Charlemagne was called Millicent. First recorded in England in 1201.

Charlemagne lived in the 8th century and was a powerful ruler. So this name has a long and illustrious history - it was popular with the Lombards and Burgundians. Brought into Britain at the end of the 12th century by the Normans as Milisende, it has grown in popularity ever since.
"All hard work brings a profit but mere talk leads only to poverty." Prov.14:23.

Milly - see Amelia

Miranda

From Latin meaning 'worthy to be admired'. The heroine of "The Tempest" by Shakespeare. Recorded in Britain in 1687 at Rochdale.
When William Shakespeare wanted a really good name for the heroine of his play "The Tempest" he chose 'Miranda' - perhaps he was aware of its old Latin meaning. She was certainly a lady endowed with very many admirable qualities.
Even when we don't feel that WE are worthy to be admired - we can always be thankful that our God always will be.
"You are worthy, our Lord and God, to receive Glory and Honour and Power..." Rev.4:11.

Miriam – see Mary

Mitch Mitchel Mitchell - see Michael

Mohammed Muhammad Ahmad

Arabic for 'the praised one'. Founder of Islam. A very popular name among Middle-Eastern men.
Sadly, Christianity and Islam have always had strained relationships although Islam has always held that Jesus is a prophet. In the past 'Christians' have persecuted Muslims (and Jews) and the Church needs to confess this and repent of it. The great fact which Muslims, Jews and Christians hold in common is the unity and one-ness of God.
"I am the LORD, and there is no other; apart from me there is no God." Is.45:5.

Moira Moyra Molly - see Mary

Monica Monique Monika Mona

From Latin meaning 'to advise'. The mother of St Augustine. First recorded in the UK in 1640.
'Monica of Hippo' was the Christian mother of St Augustine who "pursued him with prayers, tears and admonitions". Her own husband was a pagan with a very bad temper who became a Christian a short while before he

died in AD372. St Augustine testified to the influence of his godly mother in his "Confessions". She had great concern for the future of her youngest son but could never have envisaged the influence that he would have on the Christian world.

Good advice is always hard to find - we tend to ask those who we feel will agree with us. For a totally impartial and completely independent source you could always try the book of Proverbs.

"Listen now to me and I will give you some advice, and may God be with you." *Ex.18:19.*

Molly – see Mary

Morag

A Scottish Irish Gaelic name meaning 'great'. Possibly from The Great Glen or Glen Mor which divides the Central Highlands from the north of Scotland.

The word 'mor(a)' in both Irish and Scottish Gaelic is a diminutive form of the word for the sun. There are other associations which are lost mysteriously in the mists of time. Our English word 'great' has at least twelve definitions in the Oxford dictionary - in this case it is the sense of being immense - like the sun. Gen.1:16 says: "God made two great lights the greater light to govern the day and the lesser light to govern the night. He also made the stars."

"Then sings my soul, my Saviour God to thee: How great thou art, how great thou art!" Anon. (From a Russian translation of a German poem)

"For great is your love...and your faithfulness reaches to the skies." Ps.108:4.

Moray - see Murray

Moreen

From Irish Gaelic 'Moirin' and meaning 'great'. Common in parts of Ireland and Scotland. Please do not confuse me with 'Maureen'!

This lovely name is quite obviously of Irish origin and shares its roots with names such as 'Mor', and 'Morag'. The very pronunciation of the name brings a vision of the beautiful green of Ireland with its incredible scenery and warm-hearted people. Why such a lovely place should have so sad a history is a mystery and previous centuries have also seen their problems - such as the potato famine in 1847. The UK Government made huge grants totalling £10m and many Irish folk made their home on the mainland as a result - bringing with them such lovely names as these.

"He calls His own sheep by name and leads them out."(John 10. 3.)

Morgan Morghan

Irish Gaelic for 'sea-bright'? First known record in 1198. Originally from Normandy and Brittany. A very pleasant name!

The origin of the name 'Morgan' is lost in the mists of antiquity - it is possible that it came from Irish Gaelic, Breton or Welsh! It is a lovely name which was first recorded by the Curia Regis Rolls of AD1198.

There are many verses in the Bible about the sea, here is one of them;

"Mightier than the thunder of great waters, mightier than the breakers of the sea - the Lord is mighty." Ps. 93.4.

Morris - see Maurice

Morwena Morwenna

From Old Cornish and Welsh - meaning 'a maiden'. A fifth century saint and the daughter of a prince!

This lovely name comes from two main sources; Welsh and Old (Celtic) Cornish. The first part 'mor' is the Welsh word for 'the sea' and it could also be linked to the Welsh word for 'a maiden' which is 'morwyn'. We know very little about St Morwenna except that she was the daughter of Prince (St) Brychan - and from his name we get the name of the 'Brecon' Beacons etc. She is immortalised in the name of the beautiful tiny Cornish village of Morwenstow ('the holy place of St Morwenna') which overlooks the Atlantic Ocean.

"Mightier than the thunder of great waters, mightier than the breakers of the sea   the LORD is mighty." Ps.93:4.

Moses Mosy

From Hebrew. The man chosen by God to lead the Israelites out of Egypt. A leader, a prophet, a lawgiver, an author and a fine example of God's grace!

The name 'Moses means 'to draw out' and may be of Egyptian origin. He was the man whom God elected to lead His chosen people out of captivity in Egypt but he had many lessons to learn before he was able to do it! At the end of his life God instructed him to go to Mount Nebo where he could view the promised land - he would not be able to enter it because he had failed God at one critical point. However 1,500 years later, when the Lord Jesus was transfigured it was Moses, representing the law with Elijah representing the prophets, who stood with Him - grace had triumphed and Moses was IN the promised land!

"Moses his chosen one" Psalm 106:23.

Moyra - see Mary

Muhammad - see Mohammed

Muriel - see Meriel

Murray Moray

From Gaelic and meaning 'sea'. Possibly from 'Moray Firth' which is in northeast Scotland. The half-brother of Mary Queen of Scots was called Moray.
The Moray Firth is one of the most beautiful areas of Scotland. Coming in from the northeast and the North Sea the firth narrows at two points, firstly at Fortrose and then again at Inverness. The views from the sides of the firth are breathtaking - to the north the Sutherland and Caithness highlands, to the south the Cairngorms and the Grampian highlands. There are many verses in the Bible about the sea, here is one of them:
"Mightier than the thunder of great waters, mightier than the breakers of the sea - the LORD is mighty." Ps.93:4.

Myra

From Latin meaning 'admired' or 'to admire'. Chosen by the famous Lord Brooke as the name of his heroine in love poems. A fragrance of myrrh?
In the 17th century when Lord Brooke (Fulke Greville) wanted a name which sounded like 'admired' for the heroine of his love poems, he chose 'Myra'.
It is also thought that the name may have originated from the word myrrh - a sweet smelling herb which was one of the gifts given to Jesus by the Magi - Mt.2:11.
It is also the name of the port where Paul changed ships on his way to Rome for his final trial before Caesar - see Acts 27:5. It is one of the six largest cities of Lycia in southeastern Asia Minor located on the River Andracus about 5 km (3 miles) from the sea. The site of the ancient ruins is called Dembre today.
"My name will be great among the nations, from the rising to the setting of the sun. In every place incense and pure offerings will be brought to my name, because my name will be great among the nations," says the LORD Almighty. Mal.1:11.

Myrtle

From Greek meaning 'victory'. One of the prettiest and most popular of the flower names. In the 19th century it was a traditional element in a bride's bouquet.
Myrtle bushes have fragrant evergreen leaves and scented white flowers. The myrtle is mentioned in Neh.8:15, Is.41:19 & 55:13, and in Zech.1:8-11.

'Victory' is one of the sweetest words to the human ear. Scripture is very clear that victory belongs to God. This is summed-up by David when he says "the battle is the LORD's" 1 Sam.17:47.

Remember that a 'lost battle' is not always a 'lost war'.

"For the LORD your God is the one who goes with you to fight for you against your enemies to give you victory." Deut.20:4.

Nadia Nadine

From Russian meaning 'hope'. One of the three great Christian virtues from 1 Cor.13. "...faith, hope and love..."

The dictionary definition is; "look forward to with expectation and desire". The Christian hope is all of this and more. All of us, because we are made by God, have a basic necessity to hope - it is something which has been planted in our very nature and character. Even when there is little prospect we will still hope.

"And hope does not disappoint us, because God has poured His love into our hearts by the Holy Spirit..." Rom.5:5.

Nancy

Means 'God has graciously favoured me' (once a form of 'Ann' from the Hebrew source 'Hannah').

Nancy means 'God has graciously favoured me' and the source of the name is also an illustration of what it means. Hannah was a woman of prayer and one day after she had been praying and weeping in the Temple she promised God that if He gave her a son she would dedicate him to God. God granted her wish - see 1 Sam.1. Her son became the great prophet Samuel who turned Israel back to God.

"O LORD, when you favoured me, you made my mountain stand firm; but when you hid your face, I was dismayed." Ps.30:7.

Nahum

Short form of the Hebrew word 'Nehemiah' which means 'the compassionate God'. Ninth in the lineage of the Lord Jesus. A poet and a prophet!

Nahum lived in the days of the good king Josiah and all we know of him is in his book - one of the so-called 'Minor' prophets. But Nahum was a mighty writer and a powerful prophet. He foretold the downfall of Nineveh - but before that wrote about the greatness of the God he loved and served. His name is preserved in the names of towns such as Capernaum - literally 'the village of Nahum'. The true meaning of his name is summed-up in a verse in the first chapter of his book;

"The LORD is good, a refuge in times of trouble. He cares for those who trust in him..." Nahum 1:7.

Naomi

Hebrew for 'my delight' and one of the heroines of the book of Ruth (the greatest love story ever told).

Naomi was a citizen of Bethlehem but she lived there hundreds of years before Jesus and a little while before King David. Because of the famine she decided to go with her husband across the Dead Sea to the land of Moab. Sadly her husband died and also her two sons who had married local girls. One of the daughters-in-law went back to her own people but the other one called Ruth decided to return with Naomi to Bethlehem and to become one with the people of God. Some time later Ruth married Boaz and was the Great Grand-mother of King David. So Naomi's daughter-in-law Ruth is included in the ancestry of the Lord Jesus Christ.

"The women said to Naomi: 'Praise be to the LORD, who this day has not left you without a kinsman redeemer'." Ruth 4:14.

Nasief

Arabic for 'servant'. A picture of the Lord Jesus Christ who, according to prophecy would be 'the suffering servant'.

The ministry of 'servants' is largely unknown in the west today - but there are still those who have a 'servant spirit' and a heart to serve others. When the apostle John wrote his gospel he spoke of his namesake - John the Baptiser calling people to repentance because there was one coming after him "...the thongs of whose sandals I am not worthy to untie..." (John 1.27.) The truth was that there was one servant lower than the one who untied the sandals - and he was the one who washed the feet! Jesus was prepared to go lower in his servant role. (See John 13.1-17.)

"Guard my life, for I am devoted to you. You are my God; save your servant who trusts in you." Ps.86:2.

Natalie Natalia Natasha Tasha

From Latin: 'of' or 'from one's birth'. Originally given only to children born on Christmas Day.

People fortunate to have this name should try to remember that once it was given to record the fact that someone had been born on the day when Christ's birth was celebrated. Mary set an example when she said: "My soul...and my spirit rejoices in God my Saviour, for He has been mindful of the humble estate of his servant." Luke 1:46-48.

"Born, to raise the sons of earth; Born, to give them second birth..." Charles Wesley.

"From birth I was cast upon you; from my mother's womb you have been my God." Ps.22:10.

Nathan

Hebrew meaning 'given'. A man of great courage when denouncing King David's sin.

Nathan was a prophet of God and in 2 Sam.12 we are told of his fearless approach to King David. David had 'stolen' Bathsheba the wife of Uriah and then put Uriah in the front line of battle so that he would be killed. Nathan told David a parable about a man who stole another man's sheep - when David said that the man should be put to death, Nathan replied; "You are the man" 2 Sam.12:7. David repented and Psalm 51 is a result.

"Be on your guard; stand firm in the faith; be men of courage; be strong. Do everything in love." 1 Cor.16:13-14.

Nathanael Nathaniel Nathalie Nat Nate

This name means 'a gift from God' and the only record of him with this name is in John 1:43-51.

According to Jesus he was an Israelite in whom there was "nothing false" John 1:47. It may be that Nathaniel was studying the word of God when Jesus saw him - the phrase "Under the fig" may be a symbolic term describing someone reading the Tanach (Old Testament). If this is the case then it reinforces all that Jesus said about him - he was a young man seeking God and trying to live a 'good' life. Although we will never reach God through our own 'goodness' God has promised that those who seek Him will find Him.

"...but the gift of God is eternal life in Christ Jesus our Lord." Rom.6:23.

Necko

Necko is a Greek word which means 'lame'. Although he was lame he rose to be one of the great Pharaohs of Egypt who recognised the God of Israel.

Necko was a wise ruler who lived around 600 years before Christ. It was he who began the canal linking the Nile with the Red Sea. He also appointed Eliakim as King of Judah in place of the wicked Josiah and he renamed him 'Jehoiakim' which means 'Yahweh will establish' - so he had a real knowledge of God!

God has a wonderful way of taking His former enemies and using them to his glory. A.T. Pierson had this in mind when wrote; "He maketh the rebel a priest and a king, He hath bought us and taught us this new song to sing; Unto Him who has loved us and washed us from sin, unto Him be the glory for ever, Amen!"

"Necko said...God has told me to hurry; so stop opposing God, who is with me..." 2 Chron..35:21.

Ned Neddy - see Edward

Neil Nelson Niall Nigel

From Irish Gaelic meaning 'champion'. First recorded in the 11th century.
The actual origin of these names has been the subject of much discussion. They possibly began life in Ireland and then moved to Iceland where it was 'Njal', from there they appeared in Scandinavia and France and were Latinised as Nigellus etc. Both the Danes and the Norse had a form of Neil before they appeared here in 1086. Nigel, Nial and Nelson (Neil's-son) all share the same roots. So, Admiral Lord Nelson (1758-1805), President Nelson Mandela and Neil Armstrong are all 'namesakes'. These, in their own way, were all 'champions'.
"The heavens declare the glory of God...the sun...like a champion rejoicing to run his course." Ps.19:1-5.

Nell Nellie Nelly

From Greek meaning 'a bright one' or 'light'. In use in the UK from the 12th century.
Nell originally came from 'Helen' and 'Eleanor' which is 'bright shining one' in Greek.
Everyone thinks of Nell (Eleanor) Gwyn the orange-selling mistress of Charles II. She has been much misunderstood and among her many creditable achievements was the establishment of the Royal Chelsea Hospital on Chelsea Bridge Road. It was designed by Christopher Wren and built in 1682 with the purpose of providing a home for elderly and wounded soldiers known as Chelsea Pensioners.
Today Nell is a name in its own right with an illustrious history.
"I am the light of the world. Whoever follows me will never walk in darkness..." John 8:12.

Nelson - see Neil

Netta - see Jane

Neville Nevil Nevile

From the French 'Neu-ville' meaning 'new town'. Surname brought over by William the Conqueror.
This name belonged to a large and powerful French family before it was brought to England in 1066 by William the Conqueror. For some years it was used as a surname and only since the 17th century has it been a Christian name. Among the users in the 20th century were the novelist Nevil Shute and the Prime Minister, Neville Chamberlain.
"Behold, I will create new heavens and a new earth." Is.65:17

Niall - see Neil

Niamh

Irish Gaelic meaning 'beauty' or 'brightness'. From Irish folklore - she fell in love with Oisin and took him away to the land of the young.

A number of very popular names have their origin in Irish legends and this is one of the more fascinating ones. It should be pronounced neev or nee-av. Oisin, the son of Finn MacCool was carried away over the waves to the land of 'Tir na nOg' ('the land of the young') by the beautiful Niamh, there to have every wish fulfilled and to live happily ever after.

Sadly, in reality we don't have such magical powers - most of us have to WORK to make our 'dreams' come true.

"The king is enthralled by your beauty; honour him, for he is your lord." Ps.45:11.

Nicholas Nichola Nicola Nicole Nikki Nikolas Nickolai

From Greek meaning 'victory to the people' or from the Italian 'Nicoletta'.

The most famous 'Nicolas' is 'Saint Nicholas' or in German 'Nikolaus' who is known in Britain as 'Santa Claus'.

Saint Nicholas who lived during the fourth century was said to be the patron saint of Russia, sailors and children. The legend is that he gave gifts to children on the 6th of December and this date has become his 'feast day'. In places on the Continent such as Switzerland his day is celebrated separately from Christmas Day. Although originally from 'Nicholas' these other names are now names in their own right.

"Thanks be to God for His indescribable gift."(Jesus) 2 Cor.9:15.

Nicola Nicole Nikki - see Nicholas

Nigel - see Neil

Nimrod

This Name means 'a rebel'. He was a hunter warrior. His story is told in Gen.10:8-12.

Nimrod lived in Babylonia and he was the founder of the cities of Nineveh and Calah in Assyria and there was a country close by called "the land of Nimrod" Mic.5:6. Several areas still bear his name both in Assyria and Babylon. There are many legends connected with him in secular ancient writings and it is possible that other mythological figures have been credited with his exploits. A ruined Crusader castle in the north of Israel called L'Asibebe is built over the spot where Nimrod is reputed to have been buried.

"...Nimrod grew to be a mighty warrior on earth." 1 Chron.1:10.

Nina – see Anthony

Nita - see Joan

Noah

From a Hebrew root meaning 'to rest and comfort'. The hero of the flood and the last of the ten great Patriarchs. A great man of faith!

The story of Noah and the great flood is told in the book of Genesis chapters 5 to 9. Other parts of the Bible comment on Noah and his trust in God. He is included in the lineage of Jesus and Jesus himself speaks about Noah when he is describing the 'last days' (Mt.24:37-39). Sadly, the flood did not destroy man's inherent sinfulness and even Noah "a preacher of righteousness" fell and let God down - illustrating that everyone needs to put his faith and trust in God's forgiveness... The writer of the book of Hebrews says that "without faith it is impossible to please God" and begins his list of men of faith with Noah (Heb.11:6-7).

God...protected Noah, a preacher of righteousness..." 2 Pet.2:4-5.

Noel Noelle

From Old French 'nouel' and the Latin 'natalis' which means 'his birthday'. First recorded in the 13th century. Once chosen automatically for children born on the 25th December.

These names are now often given to children whether they are born on Christmas Day or not. In the Middle Ages it was assumed that if you had a boy or girl born on the 25th December you would automatically use one of these names - most people preferred this to being called 'Christmas' - as was sometimes the case after the Reformation. Children were also called Pentecost, Easter or Mid-winter if they were born on the appropriate day!

"Glory to God in the highest, and on earth peace to men on whom his favour rests." Luke 2:14.

Nola - see Fenella

Noreen – see Honour

Nora Norah - see Honour

Norman Norm Norma

Viking names meaning 'a northerner' i.e. a 'Norwegian' or 'North-man'. It has always been popular in Scotland and in particular with the clan Macleod.

It was the people from the north - the Scandinavians who settled in Gaul and founded Normandy. They adopted the French culture and language. From there they set out to conquer new fields and of course just across the channel was England.

The Norman Conquest of Britain gave the nation a new unity, changed the course of history and additionally, gave every child a date to remember - 1066. But as with every culture, it is not who you conquer - but who conquers you that is important.

"No, in all these things we are more than conquerors through Him who loved us." Rom.8:37.

Oengus - see Angus

Olga

From 'Helga' a Norse word meaning 'holy'. Helga was a Scandinavian who founded the Russian monarchy.

The name Olga evolved from Helga in Russia and the earliest record of the name in the UK is from the 10th century. St Olga was the first Russian convert to Christianity and is reputed to have founded and encouraged the faith in Russia.

The name means 'holy' - but what is 'holy'? As far as the Bible is concerned 'holiness' means 'to be separate' or 'set apart'. So we have "holy land", "holy Sabbaths", a "holy nation", a "holy place" etc. So 'holiness' is belonging to or being part of something that is chosen by God and is reserved for His exclusive use.

"Holy, holy, holy, is the LORD Almighty; the whole earth is full of His glory." Is.6:3.

Oliver Olive Olivia

For thousands of years Oriental people have regarded the olive and the olive tree as a thing of beauty, strength, divine blessing and prosperity.

When the dove returned to the ark it was carrying an olive leaf in its beak and since then these two have symbolised 'peace'. It was olive oil that lit the temple and originated the miracle of the festival of Chanukah that Jesus attended (see John 10:22). It was the Mount of Olives that Jesus loved so much and it was from the Garden of Gethsemane (Gethsemane means 'olive press') at the foot of the Mount of Olives that Jesus went to His mock trial and crucifixion.

"But I am like an olive tree flourishing in the house of God; I trust in God's unfailing love for ever and ever." Ps.52:8.

Olwen Olwyn

From Welsh meaning 'white footprint'. The legend of "Culhwch and Olwen".

The story of "Culhwch and Olwen" was part of one of the Welsh legends surrounding King Arthur. In the story Olwen, a giant's daughter, is wooed by a prince who is set certain tasks in order to qualify for her hand. He has to obtain help from King Arthur for these tasks. Olwen was so-called because wherever she walked she left trails of white flowers.

In reality, the Psalmist knew that there was only one way to leave a trail of blessing.

"Blessed is the person who does not walk in the counsel of the wicked...But his delight is in the law of the LORD...Whatever he does prospers." Ps.1:1-3.

Omar - see Umar

Omead

From an ancient Urdu word meaning 'expectation'. The dictionary definition "...the prospect of future good..."

Have you ever really looked forward to an event and thought that the day would never come...? Sometimes when the day does eventually dawn we are a little disappointed - but even then the anticipation has been fun!

God says that there are going to be things happening in the future and that we can look forward to them with real expectation. The birth of the Lord Jesus Christ was like this and one man was heard to cry '...now I can die in peace!'. (See Luke 2:29).

"The creation waits in eager expectation for the sons of God to be revealed." Rom.8:19.

Onka

From an ancient Sanskrit word meaning 'an auspicious beginning'.

This is from a Hindu word source but can also be found among the Yuraba people of Nigeria. Perhaps it was a home-sick man that named a river in southern Australia Onkaparinga – together with a nearby township. If you know the source of these words please let me know because it is also the first name of the surgeon who inserted my latest CRT (Cardiac Resyncronisation Therapy Device) So now you know!

"Your beginnings will seem humble, so prosperous will your future be." Job 8:7.

Ophelia

From Greek meaning 'help'. Used by Shakespeare in "Hamlet". An important Biblical site.

In Hamlet 'Ophelia' is Hamlet's lover - but where did Shakespeare get the name? He may have been reading his Bible and noticed that Mount Ophel is an important site. It was possibly one of the places David's soldiers camped before they took the city (see 2 Sam.5:6-7). Later we are told that it was here that the servants of the temple lived - they 'helped' in the ministry (Neh.11:21). Paul lists 'helps' as one of the ministries of the body of Christ (1 Cor.12:28).

"...where does my help come from? My help comes from the LORD" Ps.121:1-2.

Oprah

A recent addition to feminine names. The American television personality Oprah Winfrey explained that her name was to be ORPAH which is Hebrew for 'gazelle' but the Registrar made a mistake.

This would not be the first time that a Registrar's slip has resulted in an attractive name emerging. The original name of Orpah occurs in the book of Ruth and when, after a series of disasters Orpah decides to return to her own people, Naomi commends her to God's loving care and a prosperous future:

"May the LORD show kindness to you...may the Lord grant...that you will find rest.." Ruth 1:8-9.

Orpah

From the Hebrew meaning 'a gazelle'. One of the participants in the story of Ruth.

The name Orpah occurs in the book of Ruth. Naomi was a citizen of Bethlehem and she lived there hundreds of years before Jesus and a little while before King David. Because of a famine she decided to go with her husband across the Dead Sea to the land of Moab. Sadly her husband died and also her two sons who had married local girls. One of the daughters-in-law went back to her own people, her name was Orpah. In love Naomi commends her to God's loving care and a prosperous future;

"May the LORD show kindness to you...may the LORD grant...that you will find rest.." Ruth 1:8-9.

Orson

From Norman-French meaning 'little bear'.

The bear is a large carnivorous animal closely related to racoons, pandas and the dog family. Although classified as flesh-eating, most species (other than the polar bear) are mainly vegetarian - but they will eat almost anything. The bear in the Bible is most likely to be the Syrian Brown Bear which is now very rare - the last one in Israel was killed in the 1930s. David killed several bears whilst guarding his father's sheep (1 Sam.17). In the light of these facts one wonders why the (teddy) bear is every child's favourite night-time companion!

"Better to meet a bear robbed of her cubs than a fool in his folly." Prov.17:12.

Oscar Oskar

From one of two sources: Old English 'Osgar' which would be a joining of 'Os' (a god) and 'gar' (a spear), or from Irish Gaelic meaning 'beloved'.

A compound might be: 'a god-like warrior, much-adored'! These are the attributes of the Lord Himself - we can emulate them but never match them. 'Beloved' means to be loved and to be loving. To be loved is very easy - everyone longs for loving and unconditional acceptance. That is the way God made us so that we can receive His love. To love is not always so easy because there are people who we find very difficult to love.

"...God demonstrates His own love for us in this: While we were still sinners, Christ died for us." Rom.5:8.

Osmand Osmund

From two Olde English words; 'Os' which means 'a God' and 'mond' which means 'one who protects'. Recorded in 1086 in the Doomsday Book. The name of an 11th century saint.

This ancient name brings together two words from Olde English both of which have a powerful meaning in themselves. Today we realise that it is not God that needs 'protection' - but us! The psalmist knew the truth of this fact and in Psalm 5 and verse 3 he indicates that these words were on his lips in the morning - that is always a good time to claim God's protection!

"But let all who take refuge in you be glad... that those who love your name may rejoice in you." Psalm 5:11.

Oswald

From Old English and meaning 'god-power'. First recorded in the 7th century. The name of two saints.

'Os' is the Old English for 'a god' and 'weald' the word for 'power'. Oswald, King of Northumbria was born in AD605 and whilst he was a young man in exile he became a Christian through the witness of the monks on the island of Iona. He was determined to spread the faith and asked for help from Iona, and St Aidan responded. The second St Oswald was the Archbishop of York who died in AD992. He was instrumental in introducing and encouraging monasticism and reformed some of the wayward priests of his day.

"...they will see the Son of Man coming...with power and great glory." Mt.24:30.

Othniel

A Hebrew word meaning 'God's time'. The nephew of Caleb who delivered the people of God from a wicked oppressor.

The story of Othniel is the story of a man who was the right man for the right time - God's timing is always perfect!

During the time of Joshua and the initial conquest of Israel the people of God learned to trust and obey God. Fifteen years later when Israel had forgotten God he allowed them to be over-run by their enemies and for eight years they were in bondage to Cushan (whose name means 'double wickedness'). Then Israel turned back to God and Othniel delivered them. He was the first of seven Judges to 'rule' Israel. The story is in Joshua 15:13-19 and Judges 3:8-11.

"...I tell you, now is the time of God's favour, now is the day of salvation." 2 Cor.6:2.

Owen Owain

A popular Welsh name probably from Latin meaning 'well-born'. (There is also a welsh word 'oen' which means 'a lamb'.) A name from Welsh legend and a freedom fighter.

Various spellings of Owen have been recorded from the 11th century. In its current spelling the earliest record in the UK is 1200. The name has featured in Welsh legend and was the name of a famous Welshmen: Owen Glendower who in the 15th century fought for independence from England. The term 'well-born' possibly means to be born of high estate or of nobility but Jesus had something else in mind when He said:

"I tell you the truth, no one can see the kingdom of God unless he is born again." John 3:3.

Paddy - see Patrick

Paige Page

From the ancient usage of 'page' who was a young person in attendance to someone of high rank and was in training to be a squire or a knight.

In Medieval times young men were recruited to serve an 'apprenticeship' to the landed gentry. In exchange they were trained in hunting, shooting, heraldry and all the social 'graces' of their day. They were often later promoted to be squires or knights. Today the sovereign is usually attended by paiges on ceremonial occasions such as the State Opening of Parliament, weddings and funerals. On these occasions they wear their traditional costumes of scarlet and white decorated with gold lace.

"Deal with your servant according to your love and teach me...I am your servant..." Ps.119:124-125.

Pamela Pam

From Greek meaning 'as sweet as honey'. An important and lovely product in the Bible.

This name was used by Sir Philip Sidney in 1590 for his poem 'Arcadia' but it did not come into general use until the eighteenth century when Samuel Richardson titled his novel "Pamela". Honey was vital in the early days of the children of Israel. Some 19 times in the Old Testament they had been promised "a land flowing with milk and honey" e.g. Ex.3:8. It was used for food (Prov.24:13), for cake-making (Ex.16:31), medicine (Prov.16:24), gifts (2 Sam.17:29), as a precious resource (Jer.41:8) and a valuable export (Ez.27:17).

"How sweet are your words to my taste, sweeter than honey to my mouth." Ps.119:103.

Pansy

From French 'Pensee' which means 'a thought'. 'Pansy' was the pseudonym of Isabella Alden who wrote a series of books in the 19th century.

Isabella also wrote "A Life of Christ" (She was a committed Christian). The brilliant French philosopher Blaise Pascal entitled his defence of the Christian life "Pensees" (thoughts); in it he argued for faith in Christ alone for salvation. The pansy is also a lovely flower belonging to the violet family. There are at least four species which grow wild in Britain, including the Wild Pansy the Mountain Pansy and the Field Pansy. The many garden hybrids of the Wild Pansy produce a wide range of colourful flowers over a long period.

"Flowers appear on the earth; the season of singing has come". S.of S.2:12.

Pascal Pascale

The English (paschal) and French word for 'Passover' or Easter'. A famous French Scientist.

The Christian philosopher Blaise Pascal (1623-1662) made his impact on the world of physics, literature and Christianity. His arithmetical machine was built to assist his father in his work as a tax official but laid the basic principles for digital computers that were to come many years later. In 1654 he had a personal experience of Jesus Christ and was an evangelical Christian for the remainder of his short life.

From around 1200 it was a common practice to name your child after the Christian season in which he or she was born. So we have names such as Noel, Nowell, Christmas, Easter, Pentecost, Tiffany, Midwinter, and Loveday. Easter has a very special significance for Christians because, as Paul says in 1 Cor.15:14: "...if Christ has not been raised, our preaching is useless and so is your faith."

"He has risen!" Mark 16:6.

Patricia Paddy Pat Patsy Pattie Tricia

Originally from Latin meaning 'a noble lady'.

Jewish culture raised womanhood to levels of 'eminence'. The Hebrew law said that a mother should be honoured, feared and obeyed (Ex.20:12, Lev.19:3, Deut.21:18) this and many other laws were applied equally to men and women. The attitude of Jesus raised womanhood to new heights of nobility. His mother Mary is described as "...blessed...among women..." Luke 1:42, and on the resurrection morning the greatest message ever told was entrusted to a woman: "...go, tell..." Mark 16:7. There are very many 'noble' ladies in Scripture.

"Finally...whatever is true, whatever is noble, whatever is right, whatever is pure, whatever is lovely, whatever is admirable...think about such things." Phil.4:8.

Patrick Pat Paddy

Originally from Latin meaning 'nobleman'. The Patron saint of Ireland whose life is surrounded with intrigue and controversy.

St Patrick the patron saint of Ireland lived in the 5th century and was born in Scotland. He was the son of a Roman Magistrate and had a deep respect for Rome. He was captured and enslaved for six years by a band of Irish marauders. During this time he drew closer to God and he says: "The Lord opened to me the sense of my unbelief that I might remember my sins and that I might return with my whole heart to the Lord my God." He escaped to Britain and eventually found his way back to Ireland where his life is shrouded with legend. However, he broke the power of heathenism in Ireland and his teaching was both scriptural and evangelical.

"...the seed on good soil stands for those with a noble and good heart, who hear the word, retain it, and by persevering produce a crop." Luke 8:15.

Paul Paula Pauline

The name Paul means 'modest' and it was the name of the great apostle of the early church.

The Apostle Paul changed his name in Cyprus - possibly through the influence of Governor Paulus at Pathos. From that time he used his name frequently. When he came to write the book of Romans he needed to begin it in a way which would illustrate the theme of the book so he chose to start it with his new name.

When we speak of something being 'modest' or 'small' we often equate these words with a lack of strength or influence – the gospel turns this concept on its head. The Apostle whose name meant 'modest' or 'small' wrote:

"God chose the foolish things of the world to shame the wise...the weak things...to shame the strong." 1 Cor.1:27.

Pearl Meta

Means 'a child from the light of the moon'. An ancient legend says pearls were made by moonbeams.

We know today that pearls are produced by irritants entering the bodies of oysters but the ancient legend was held to be true for very many years. Jesus said that the Kingdom of Heaven was like "fine pearls" and when a man finds one of great value he sells all in order to acquire it (Mt.13:45-46). In the 'New Jerusalem' pearls have a very special function - they are the substance from which the twelve gates are constructed. So the name Pearl is linked with the greatest treasure known to man - the heavenly city.

"...the twelve gates were twelve pearls, each gate made of a single pearl." Rev.21:21.

Peg Peggy - see Margaret

Penelope Pen Pennie Penny

A clever woman, known for her faithfulness and shrewdness. From Homer (Greek mythology). She was the wife of Odysseus (Ulysses) during the Trojan war.

The story is a simple one: Odysseus, the son of King Laertes, is a skilful and brave fighter, he goes off to fight the Trojan war and leaves his lovely wife Penelope at home. He returns many years later to find that she is defending his estate and herself against various suitors. With the aid of faithful friends he fights them off and is reunited with his sweetheart.

"Love the LORD, all his saints! The LORD preserves the faithful..." Ps.31:23

Percival Perceval

From the French 'perce-val' which means 'one who pierces the valley'. Recorded in the 12th century. A place in Normandy.

The name 'Percival' was created by the medieval poet Chretien de Troyes as the name of one of the heroic knights of the legendary King Arthur. Originally the name came from a place in Normandy called Percheval.

Valleys are very important, among other things they provide places where people can live in comfort and grow their crops. In the Scriptures they have great significance - they often mark boundaries or great events in the history of the nation.

"...they assembled in the valley of Beracah (meaning 'blessing') where they praised the LORD." 2 Chron.20:26.

Peregrine Perry

From Latin 'peregrinator' meaning 'a pilgrim'. Also the name of a 7th century saint who was a hermit near Modena Italy.

Whenever anyone mentions 'Pilgrims' the first name to spring to mind is John Bunyan and his wonderful allegory "The Pilgrim's Progress". In fact, Bunyan wrote three great works whilst imprisoned in Bedford for his faith. "The Pilgrims Progress", "The Holy War" and "Grace Abounding to the Chief of Sinners". Included in the The Pilgrim's Progress is the hymn: "Who would true valour see - let him come hither.." Another hymn which he wrote is not as well-known, it begins "He that is down needs fear no fall, he that is low, no pride, he that is humble ever shall have God to be his guide".

"Blessed are those whose strength is in you, who have set their hearts on pilgrimage." Ps.84:5.

Peter Pete Petronella Petrina Petronilla
Old French and Old English form: Piers.

The name means 'a rock' or 'stone'. The Apostle Peter is one of the great characters of the New Testament.

He was a man who was capable of rising to the heights and also sinking to the depths. He was called to follow Jesus whilst he was fishing (Luke 5:10) and one of the highlights of his life was the great confession he made at

Caesarea "You are the Christ" Mt.16:16. He was with Jesus at the transfiguration (Mt.17:1-13) but soon after denied Him (Luke 22:57-60). He was restored by Jesus (John 21:15-19) and played a significant part in both Pentecost (Acts 2) and the admission of the gentiles to the church (Acts 10).

"He is the Rock, His works are perfect, and all His ways are just. A faithful God who does no wrong." Deut.32:4.

Petula

From Latin meaning 'a seeker'. The name of a music group in the 1970s. Cromwellian sect that had much to commend it.

'Seekers' is a term still in use by groups such as the Salvation Army who use it to describe those who are actively seeking the Lord Jesus. From the time of Cromwell there was a religious group called 'The Seekers'. They were a small, earnest, peaceable and spiritual group who were eventually absorbed by the Quakers.

"I love those who love me, and those who seek me find me." Prov.8:17.

Philip Phil Phillip Philippa Pip Pippa

From the Greek name meaning 'a lover of horses' and there are at least four people in the New Testament called 'Philip'. The name of the father of Alexander the Great.

The two most famous 'Philips' are Philip the Apostle and Philip the Evangelist.

Philip the Apostle was there when some Greeks arrived who said, "Sir...we would like to see Jesus." John 12:21 and it was Philip and Andrew who brought them to the Saviour. Philip the Evangelist was on his way from Jerusalem to Gaza when he brought the Ethiopian Eunuch to Jesus - the story is told in Acts 8:26-40.

"His pleasure is not in the strength of the horse...the LORD delights in those who fear Him." Ps.147:10-11.

Phoebe

Greek meaning 'the shining one'. A lady commended by the Apostle Paul. This name is also the second name of the Greek goddess Artemis - the goddess of the moon.

When the Apostle Paul began his long list of personal greetings to the folk in Rome he mentions Phoebe first of all and commends her (Rom.16:1-2). It seems likely that she actually carried the letter to Rome for him. She had many good qualities and had obviously been a blessing to him. I wonder if it was her example that inspired hymn-writer Susan Warner to write: "Jesus bids us shine first of all for Him, well he sees and knows it if our light grows dim...".

"In the same way, let your light shine before men, that they may see your good deeds and praise your Father in heaven." Mt.5:16.

Phyllis Phillis Phyl

From the Greek and meaning 'leafy'. In Greek mythology it was the name of a young lady who died for love and was turned into an almond tree. In the Bible, Aaron's rod also grew almonds.

The almond tree is one of the most beautiful flowering trees somewhat similar to the peach tree. It flowers earlier than most - from January to the end of March - so it is susceptible to frost. Its beauty has inspired festivals in its honour. There are 11 references in the Bible to the almond - all of them in the Old Testament. The story of Aaron's rod is in Numbers chapter 17 and is a demonstration of how God deals with grumblers.

"...the tree of life...the leaves...are for the healing of the nations." Rev.22:2.

Piers - see Peter

Pip - see Philip

Pippa - see Philip

Polly - see Mary

Poppy

From Latin 'papaver' and Old English 'popaeg'. A varied and beautiful flower. 150 different species of which some 10 are common in the UK. Can be, and are, used for medicinal or illicit purposes.

Each year the Royal British Legion invite us to wear a poppy in remembrance of those who died in two World Wars - their motto is "Wear your poppy with pride".

It is the humble poppy which provides the medical profession with the opium that it needs for drugs - sadly this opium is also misused.

"The grass withers and the flowers fall, but the word of our God stands forever." Is.40:8.

Priscilla Cilla

From Latin meaning 'former'. First recorded in the UK in 1592. Mentioned by both Luke and Paul.

Both the writer of Acts (Luke) and Paul in his letters to the Romans and to Timothy gave prominence to Priscilla over her husband Aquila. From this we can assume that she had a leadership role in the Church or that she enjoyed a higher social status than her husband. He was a tent-maker like Paul so they had a lot in common. When the Jews were expelled from Rome by the Emperor Claudius they came to Corinth where they met Paul (Acts 18). Their lives were deeply affected by the gospel and from that time they served the Lord. They brought Apollos to a clear understanding of the gospel, and he in turn became a gifted teacher.

"...they invited him to their home and explained...the way of God more adequately." Acts 18:26.

Prudence Pru

From Latin 'prudentia' which means 'forethought' or 'circumspection'. From the 13th century. Appears as a name in Chaucer's books. An outstanding and rare virtue.

The name 'Prudencia' first appears in 1210 in the Curia Regis Rolls. It was very popular after the Reformation and among the Puritans. It gave rise (among other things) to one of the largest Life Assurance Companies in the world.

The dictionary defines the word as "careful to avoid undesired consequences". This is a rare virtue today and people who live up to this name will be sought-after because they have an ability to manage their affairs wisely.

"I, wisdom, dwell together with prudence." Prov.8:12.

Prunella

Latin name for a wild flower commonly known as 'self-heal'. Seven different species. A rockery plant.

Prunella or 'Self-heal' is a hardy perennial. Two of its sub-species have given rise to some delightful rockery plants. One of these has a spike of lovely pale-violet flowers and is called 'Loveliness'.

On one occasion in his home town of Nazareth Jesus pre-empted a challenge and quoted an ancient proverb "Physician heal yourself!" Luke 4:23. There was no other way to secure man's redemption than for the Great Physician to lay down His life and in this way become the great 'wounded healer'.

"...then will I hear from heaven and will forgive their sin and will heal their land." 2 Chron.7:14.

Queenie

The name 'Queenie' began as a nickname for 'Victoria' which is from a Latin word meaning 'Victory'. It became very popular during the 19th century through Queen Victoria.

Victory is not always what it seems - today some of the most prosperous countries seem to be the ones which were defeated in the last world war.

The Bible has many references to 'victory'. Prov.11:14. says; "For lack of guidance a nation (or person) falls, but many advisers make VICTORY sure." 1 John 5:4. says: "This is the VICTORY that has overcome the world...our faith."

"But thanks be to God! He gives us the victory through our Lord Jesus Christ."
1 Cor.15:57.

Quentin Quintin Quinton

From Latin 'Quintus' meaning 'number five'. The 'undeserved favour of God' (grace) is represented by the number five.

In the Bible the figure five often speaks of God's grace - the earth was complete and ready for man's habitation on the fifth day. In order to begin the history of redemption God chose Abram and Sarai and gave them both new names by adding the fifth letter of the Hebrew alphabet (Hei) to their old names. There were five sacrifices for sin according to your ability to pay. Daniel speaks of the fifth Kingdom - God's Kingdom. David slew Goliath with one of five stones (one for Goliath and one for each of Goliath's four brothers!).

"Here is a boy with five small barley loaves...but how far will they go among so many?..."
John 6:9.

Rachel Rachael Rae Rai Raquel   French form: Rochelle
Short form: Wrae

"Lovely in form and beautiful" Gen.29:17. The Hebrew means 'a ewe sheep' - a symbol of gentleness and innocence.

The story of Jacob and Rachel is one of the great love stories of the Old Testament. Jacob falls deeply in love with Rachel and commits himself to work seven years for her father Laban in order to 'earn' her. He is so in love with her that it "seemed like only a few days" Gen.29:20. After the marriage he finds himself married to the older daughter Leah. He then has to work a further seven years to secure Rachel who later died whilst giving birth to Benjamin. In true 'sheep' manner she wandered away from God but always returned to Him.

"I am the good shepherd. The good shepherd lays down His life for the sheep." John 10:11.

Ralph Rolf Rudolf Rudolph

From Old Norse and meaning; 'counsel and wolf'. The first record is from the 11th century when it was pronounced 'rafe', the short 'a' and the 'l' are both from the 20th century.

Wise 'counsel' is often difficult to seek and harder to take. Many counsellors will tell what you want to hear and avoid unpleasant realities. Fortunately, the Lord Jesus Christ is not like that - He will always tell you the truth. In the Old Testament it was promised that the coming Messiah would be a "Wonderful Counsellor" Is.9:6, and in the New Testament Jesus said that this ministry would be part of the work of the Holy Spirit (John 14:16).

There is a promise concerning the wolf: "The wolf will live with the lamb...and a little child will lead them." Is.11:6.

"You guide me with your counsel, and afterwards you will take me into glory." Ps.73:24.

Rae Rai - see Rachel Raymond

Rafael Raphael

A lovely name from two Hebrew words; 'rapha' - 'to heal' and 'el' for 'God'. Literally - God has healed!

The word 'rapha' in its Hebrew form, meaning 'healing' appears 68 times in Scripture. It also appears a couple of times with the meaning of 'a giant'. If you combine these two meanings you have 'a great healer'! The additional word 'el' is a generic title for 'the majestic God'.

Traditionally, Raphael was one of four archangels who wait in the presence of God and do His bidding. Since the 16th century some people have viewed him as the patron saint of travellers.

"Then they cried to the LORD in their trouble, and he saved them...He sent forth his word and healed them." Psalm 107:19-20

Raihannah

A unique combination of two significant names; 'Rai' which means 'to tend and see the path' and 'Hannah' the name of the lady who prayed for a son and to whom God gave Samuel!

The two unique characteristics built into this name give it a wonderful significance.

'Rai' is an Arabic and Persian word which means 'to tend'(A), 'to see and understand' (P) and 'the path'(P).

'Hannah' means 'God has graciously favoured me'. She was the mother of the great prophet Samuel who was the last of the judges and first of the prophets - he anointed both King Saul and King David.

"...he gave her a double portion - because he loved her." 1 Sam.1:5.

Rakhee

From Sanskrit words for 'a full moon'. The great 'lesser light'. Dependable, regular and a sign of the coming King! (Luke 21.25.)

The moon was created by God and in Genesis 1.16. it is called "the lesser light - to govern the night". The Psalmist speaks of God's permanence "as long as the moon" in Psalm 72.5. Because it is so dependable it was used to mark the times and seasons and Scripture often speaks of 'your new moons' etc. From the beginning of civilisation man has sought to worship the created rather than the creator and the moon has been object of veneration by many tribal groups. In particular it was a god in Ur (the city that Abraham moved from) and significantly, a crescent-shaped moon has been found carved on statues of ancient deities.

"And when you look up to the sky and see the sun, the moon and the stars.....do not be enticed into bowing down to them and worshipping things the LORD your God has apportioned to all the nations under heaven." Deut.4.19.

Rama Ram

Sanskrit for 'pleasing' in the sense of 'lovely', 'attractive', 'fortunate'. A popular name in the Orient because of its many associations in ancient classical literature. In Hebrew it means 'high'.

To be 'pleasing' is the deep desire of all mankind and this is something which has been planted in our hearts by God. In the Bible we read that all God had made was "pleasing to the eye" Gen.2:9. Sadly this was also part of man's downfall because we read a few verses later that the fruit of the forbidden tree was also "pleasing to the eye" Gen.3:6.

Many people strive to please their god or gods - not realising that it is far more important that the God and father of the Lord Jesus is pleased with us. In Hebrew it is a 'minor' name sometimes used as a prefix, meaning 'high'.

"I am pleased with you and I know you by name." Ex.33:17.

Rami

From an ancient Sanskrit word meaning 'right'. Occasionally used as a prefix for 'God'.

'To do what is right' has been the pre-occupation of men down through the centuries. Fortunately God has given us a book which gives us plain and explicit rules and guide-lines by which to live. Our problem is not that we don't know what is what is right - our problem is that we often lack the courage to do it!

"And when you look up to the sky and see the sun, the moon and the stars all the heavenly array do not be enticed into bowing down to them and worshipping things..." Deut.4.19.

Ramon – see Raymond

Randal Randall Randle Randolph Randy

Old English meaning 'shield wolf'. Common in the UK from before the Norman Conquest. The source of many surnames. Also popular with Romany families.

This name gave birth to surnames such as Randle with all its variations, Rand, Ranson, Ranking, etc. It was also used by the Romany families of Boss, Lee and Smith. Today we know it as a Christian name and a surname. 'Shield-wolf' denotes both defence and attack and this is similar to the Christian's armour described by the Apostle Paul in Eph.6:10-20 (You will notice that there is NO armour for the back).

"Put on the full armour of God." Eph.6:11.

Raphael – see Rafael

Raquel - see Rachel

Ratan Ratnam

A male name from Ancient Sanskrit from the basic word 'ratna' meaning 'a jewel'.

This word has come from the prakit dialect of ancient Sanskrit – language from central and northern India. The root word means 'a precious jewel'- something beautiful and valuable – which of course, each one of us are. We were created in God's image and He declared that his creation was 'very good' (See Genesis 1;31).

"All who were willing... came and brought gold jewelry of all kinds: an offering to the LORD". Exodus 35;22

Raymond Rae Rai Ray
Spanish form: Ramon

From Old German meaning; 'counsel and protection'. First record is from the 11th century. It was introduced to the UK by the Normans. Similar surnames have evolved from it.

Wise 'counsel' is often difficult to seek and harder to take. Many counsellors will tell what you want to hear and avoid unpleasant realities. Fortunately, the Lord Jesus Christ is not like that - He will always tell you the truth. In the Old Testament it was promised that the coming Messiah would be a "Wonderful Counsellor" Is.9:6, and in the New Testament Jesus said that this ministry would be part of the work of the Holy Spirit (John 14:16). In God's counsel there is protection and total security because He is planning for us in love.

"First seek the counsel of the LORD." 1 Kings 22:5.

Reanne

From an Old Welsh Celtic deity 'Rigantona' meaning 'the great Queen'. She was fond of horses.

This lovely name is a relatively new addition to many other popular names that have come from Wales and the Welsh language - there is no record of it being used before the 20th century.

The Bible contains a number of good 'role models'. There was Queen Esther - her story can be read in the book of the same name. Then there was the Queen of Sheba who travelled over 2,000km in very difficult conditions because she sought the Wisdom of Solomon. Her story can be found in 1 Kings 10. The Lord Jesus commended her for her resolve in Matthew 12:42.

"When the queen of Sheba saw all the wisdom of Solomon...She said to the king...Praise be to the LORD your God" 1 Kings 10:4-9.

Rebecca Rebekah Becca Beccie Beckie Becky Bekki

This is the name of Isaac's wife and it means 'to secure'. Rebecca was a very beautiful woman and the lovely story of how she was chosen is in Genesis 24.

The story of the acquisition of Isaac's wife Rebekah is one of the great love-stories of the Bible. She is described as "very beautiful" Gen.24:16. Even though the way in which she was chosen was somewhat unusual she was totally devoted to Isaac and to her younger son Jacob. As the wife of Isaac and the mother of Jacob she was a founder of the nation of Israel and she provides a vital link in the lineage of the Lord Jesus Christ.

"Let the beloved of the LORD rest secure in Him, for He shields him all day long." Deut.33:12.

Reece - see Rhys

Reginald Reg Reggie Reynaud Reynold

From Old English meaning 'might', 'force', 'power'. Recorded in the 11th century. A popular west-country name.

The origin of these names is a compound of two old English words; 'regen' and 'weald' and both mean 'might', 'force' or 'power' - a strong combination. It was possibly intended for someone as a double complement. Its greatest popularity was in the West Country and it is still common there. It has an Old German counterpart in 'Raganald'.

Down through the ages men (and women) have sought to impose their will on others through human physical force and might. Two thousand years ago a man appeared on the scene to prove that there is another and better way...

"...not by might nor by power, but by my spirit, says the LORD." Zech.4:6.

Regina

The Latin word for 'a Queen'. Used by Queen Victoria in the 19th century and by monarchs since. Sometimes abbreviated to 'R' or 'Rex'. Many coins carry your name!

You would be a very wealthy person if you owned all the coins that have your name on them! Until recently it was the practice to describe the Queen as 'Elizabeth R' or 'Elizabeth Rex' - in fact her majesty signed her name "Elizabeth R". All these various abbreviations are short for "Regina" the Latin word for 'a Queen'. You may not own all the money or even the title but your name teaches us that everyone who knows and follows Jesus is a child of the King of Kings - royalty!

"...he is King of kings and with him will be his called, chosen and faithful followers." Rev.17:14.

Rene Renee

From the Latin 'renatus' meaning 'to be born again'. A name from the 5th century and a truth from the teaching of Jesus.

St Rene was Bishop of Angers from AD426 and the name has been used in Britain from the 17th century.

The teaching comes from the famous words of Jesus in John 3 when he met the leading Pharisee Nicodemus.

Nicodemus seems to be an earnest man in a position of responsibility who didn't want his true feelings to be made public. He could not understand what Jesus meant when He spoke of being 'born again'. Jesus enlightened him and, since that day, many men and women have experienced the new birth for themselves.

"...Jesus declared, I tell you the truth, no-one can see the kingdom of God unless he is born again." John 3:3.

Reuben

From Hebrew meaning 'behold a son'. He saved Joseph from death and had many good qualities. One of the twelve tribes of Israel.

Jacob, before he died described Reuben as "...my might, the first sign of my strength, excelling in honour, excelling in power..." Gen.49:3. It was Reuben who pleaded for the life of Joseph and then returned to the pit where he had been cast in order to rescue him (Gen. 37). Many years after that, it was Reuben who castigated his brothers for getting them all into the mess they were in - but this was only a short while before it was Joseph's turn to rescue him! (Gen.42).

"...Phineas... said to (the tribe of) Reuben; Today we know that the LORD is with us because you have not acted unfaithfully towards the LORD in this matter." Josh.22:31.

Rex

Latin for 'king'. Sometimes it is abbreviated to 'R'. The Hebrew word is 'melek' which has roots in all Semitic languages and whose origins could be 'to reign', 'to possess' or 'to counsel'.

The first King of Israel was Saul - he was chosen because the people wanted to be "...such as all the other nations...". 1 Sam.8:5. Samuel warned them that a King would mean that they paid higher taxes but they persisted and their first choice was a calamity. Their second King, David set the standard for all monarchs who would follow. He had his faults and made some sinful choices but he had a heart for God and he repented and returned to the LORD. Because of his godly example his name is the first and last in the New Testament - with one exception - the King of Kings.

"The king's heart is in the hand of the LORD." Prov.21:1.

Reynaud Reynold - see Reginald

Rhema

An ancient Greek word meaning 'the word'. It occurs 73 times in the New Testament. It has an extra special force when it is used in connection with "the word of God".

It was translated from the Hebrew word 'dabar' which is very important because it relates to 'what God says'. In this way it is an extension of Him and His personality. We read of "...the word of life..." Phil.2:16, "...the word of truth..." Eph.1:13, "the message (word) of salvation" Acts 13:26, "the message (word) of reconciliation" 2 Cor.5:19 and "the message (word) of the cross" 1 Cor.1:18.

"Man does not live on bread alone, but on every word that comes from the mouth of God." Mt.4:4

Rhianna

'A maiden who is favoured by God' - a lovely combination of Welsh and Hebrew. Two of the most beautiful languages in the world!

The first part is from the ancient Welsh word 'Rigantona' meaning a 'great queen' or 'a lovely maiden'. She was a mystic deity in primeval legends.

The second part is from the Hebrew meaning 'to be favoured by God' and refers to the mother of the great prophet Samuel. She promised God that if He gave her a son she would give him back to God. God granted her wish - see 1 Samuel Chapter 1. Her husband was very fond of her and it says; "he gave her a double portion - because he loved her" 1 Samuel 1:5.

"Then (H)anna(h) prayed and said: My heart rejoices in the LORD." 1 Samuel 2:1.

Rhiann Rhiannon Rhyannon

From an Old Welsh Celtic deity 'Rigantona' meaning 'the great Queen'. She was fond of horses.

This lovely name is a relatively new addition to many other popular names that have come from Wales and the Welsh language - there is no record of it being used before the 20th century.

The Bible contains a number of good 'role models'. There was Queen Esther - her story can be read in the book of the same name. Then there was the Queen of Sheba who travelled over 2,000km in very difficult conditions because she sought the Wisdom of Soloman. Her story can be found in 1 Kings 10. The Lord Jesus commended her for her determination in Mt.12:42.

"When the queen of Sheba saw all the wisdom of Solomon...She said to the king...Praise be to the LORD your God." 1 Kings 10:4-9.

Rhoda

Greek, meaning 'a rose'. She announced the arrival of Peter after he had been miraculously released from prison.

Acts chapter 12 tells the amazing story of Peter's release from prison. He knew that the Church had been praying for him so he went directly to the house of John Mark's mother. Rhoda answered the door and she was so

overjoyed at hearing Peter that she left him standing at the door still knocking! Although Rhoda was a slave-girl the story seems to indicate that she was just as excited as everyone else when their prayers were answered.
"As the eyes of slaves look to the hand of their master, as the eyes of a maid look to the hand of her mistress, so our eyes look to the LORD our God, till He shows us His mercy." Ps.123:2.

Rhonwen Rhona Rowena Rowina Rona

From Welsh meaning 'a woman slender and fair'. Or it may be from an old Germanic word meaning 'fame and joy'.
These names are favourite Welsh names and have that lovely Welsh-sound about them. There is a story from Saxon times about a lady called Rhonwen (Rowena) - she was the daughter of Chief Hengist and her beauty brought about the downfall of King Vortigern.
It was also the name chosen by Sir Walter Scott for his heroine in "Ivanhoe".
"the ransomed of the LORD will return. They will enter Zion with singing; everlasting joy will crown their heads. Gladness and joy will overtake them, and sorrow and sighing will flee away." Is.35:10.

Rhys Reece Rees

From Old Welsh and meaning 'warm love' or 'ardour'.
In the English language we only have one word for 'love'. We love our house, our friends, our children, our wives or husbands and we love God. Yet we 'love' each of these with a different type of love. In other languages they use different words to describe different forms of love and this is an example of that. 'Ardour' is the expression of human love between a man and a woman. The Song of Songs is an account of human love but it is also an allegory of God's love for us. God gives us these feelings and they are a reflection of His feelings for us.
"...the Son of God who loved me and gave Himself for me." Gal.2:20.

Ria – see Mary

Richard Dick Dickie Dicky Rick Rickkie Rickie Ricky Rikki

Originates in Anglo-Saxon times. It means 'a strong ruler'. The most famous is Richard the Lionheart.
Richard the Lionheart (Coeur de lion) was Richard I the son of Henry II by Eleanor. He acquired the nickname 'Lionheart' because of his courage in battle - notably the third crusade.
There are several stories of lions in the Bible, the best known being the one

about Samson and his riddle in Judges 14:14. This riddle was used by a syrup company for many years: "Out of the eater, something to eat; Out of the strong, something sweet."

"the lion of the tribe of Judah...has triumphed." Rev.5:5.

Rita - see Margaret

Robert Bert Bertie Bob Bobbie Bobby Rab Rabbie Rob Robbie Robin Robyn

The name means 'bright and famous'. There have been many well-known 'Roberts', 'Robbies', 'Robins' and 'Bobbies' over the years!

Robin Goodfellow or Puck was the mischievous fairy in William Shakespeare's "A Midsummer Night's Dream". Robin Hood on the other hand, robbed the rich to feed the poor. Perhaps one of the best-known 'Roberts' in recent times was a man called Evan Roberts who lived in South Wales. At twelve years of age he went down the coalmine with his father, but when he was twenty-four he felt called into the Methodist Church. For eleven years he prayed intensely for a movement of the Holy Spirit and the Welsh revival of 1904 was the direct result. Over 100,000 people became Christians in Wales and the revival spread all over the world. One man and God can make a difference!

"Who is this that appears like the dawn, fair as the moon, bright as the sun, majestic as the stars in procession?" S.of S.6:10.

Roberta Robina

Means 'bright and famous'. Originally from 'Robert' but now names in their own right.

One of the brightest and most famous birds is the Robin Redbreast which lightens the cold damp English winters. Only in Britain has the European Robin become tame enough to develop a close association with man as a common garden bird. The robin is one of the very few birds that sing all the year round - on the dreariest of days the robin will appear bright and jaunty and will fill the air with his loud, cheery song.

"...the birds of the air, and the fish of the sea, all that swim the paths of the seas. O LORD, our Lord, how majestic is your name in all the earth!" Ps.8:8-9.

Roderick Rod Roddy Rorie Rory

From Old German and meaning 'famous ruler'. First recorded in the 8th century. In Russia it is 'Rurik', in Spain 'Rodrigo' and in Scotland and Ireland 'Ruaridh' or 'Rory'.

A 'famous ruler' would of course, have a sceptre or 'rod'. There are nine different types of rod or staff in Scripture - among them a symbol of authority (Judg.5:14), a weapon for punishment (1 Cor.4.21 KJV) and a support (Gen.32:10).

A shepherd would use his rod to count his sheep and ensure that they were all there. As they 'passed under the rod' he would also have an opportunity to check that they were fit and well.

"...your rod and your staff, they comfort me." Ps.23:4.

Rodney

From the name of the Somerset village RODNEY STOKE, first known habitation of man in the UK. A Famous Admiral of the 18th century.

If you travel toward the Mendip Hills from Junction 21 or 22 of the M5 on your way to Wookey Hole Caves or to the ancient town of Wells you will pass through Rodney Stoke. Should you be tempted to think that Rodney Stoke is just another, albeit attractive, Somerset village remember this: it was here in this lovely countryside that man was first recorded in the UK.

Admiral Baron Rodney lived from 1718 to 1792. He was one of Britain's greatest sailors and among other things, Jamaica owes its present status to a decisive battle which he won against the French in 1782.

"O LORD, what is man that you care for him, the son of man that you think of him? " Ps.144:3.

Roger

From the original Anglo-Saxon word 'Rothgar' which means 'a famous spear'. The name of a legendary King. In the Middle Ages the name for a farm labourer.

One of the most famous spears of the Bible is the one which Goliath carried when he met the shepherd-boy David. It is said that his spear weighed 7 kilos (around 15 lbs.). If you go to the British Museum in London you may be fortunate enough to see one of the most ancient manuscripts in existence. It is dated around AD1000 and is in the form of some poems about the legendary King of Denmark called Hrothar (Roger).

"You come against me with sword and spear and javelin, but I come against you in the name of the LORD Almighty..." 1 Sam.17:45.

Roisin - see Rose

Roland Roly Rowland Rowley

From Old German meaning 'a famous land'. Charlemagne's great warrior. Recorded from the 11th century - originally introduced by the Normans.

As an Old German (Norman-French) name it came over with the Normans and is recorded in 1086 in the Doomsday Book. In those days it was written "Rolland", in the 12th century it became "Rolandus", in the 13th century it was "Rouland" and in the 16th century it became "Rowland". 'Roland' was a famous French soldier under Charlemagne. His exploits were celebrated in the Chanson de Roland. The most 'famous land' in the world is the land of Israel.

"I will give them praise and honour in every land...at that time I will bring you home. I will give you honour and praise among all the peoples of the earth." Zeph.3:19-20.

Rolf - see Ralph

Roma

The Latin and Italian word for 'Rome' - the 'eternal' city and the empire which ruled the world for over a millennium! Also a productive and fruitful area of 800 square miles.

The Campagna di Roma is the vast plain surrounding the city of Rome. Once an area of malarial swamps, it is now a cultivated and beautiful district - as is the town named after it in Queensland, Australia.

The influence of Rome is still felt in Britain today - our roads, ancient baths, town names and fortressed cities constantly remind us that we were uncivilised until Rome arrived! Its influence in the Arts remains and its beauty still inspires poets and writers.

"For here we do not have an enduring city, but we are looking for the city that is to come." Heb.13:14.

Ron - see Ronald

Rona - see Rhonwen

Ronald Ron Ronnie

From Old Norse meaning 'Counsel and power'. A popular name, including that of an American President, Ronald Reagan from 1980 to 1988.

When the great King Solomon was asked by God to choose a gift he asked for "wisdom and knowledge" 2 Chron.1:10-12. So he became one of the wisest counsellors and most powerful men in the world. In this respect he was a 'shadow' of the Lord Jesus. The prophet Isaiah speaks of 'counsel and power' when he speaks of the coming Messiah.

"...He will be called Wonderful Counsellor, Mighty God, Everlasting Father, Prince of Peace..." Is.9:6.

Rorie Rory - see Roderick

Rosaleen Rosalin Rosalind Rosalinda Rosalyn
Spanish form; Roslyn

From the Spanish 'Rosa-linda' which means 'a pretty rose'. Roses have been described as "the gift of angels". Norman, French or German historians equate these names with horses, chariots and armour.

The rose is the most popular and most widely cultivated flower in the world - known for its beauty and lovely fragrance. Other members of the rose family include: almond, apple, apricot, cherry, nectarine, pear, peach and quince. Roses require good, well-drained soil and plenty of sunlight - much like the human spirit. However, some very beautiful plants are found in unusual places. In the same way, we need to blossom where we have been planted.

"I am a rose of Sharon, a lily of the valleys." S.of S.2:1.

Rosanna Rosannah - see Roseanne

Rosamond Rosamund

From Latin or possibly from Old German and meaning 'pure rose of the world'. Used from the middle ages. A legendary beauty from Oxfordshire.

The origin may well have been from two Old German words meaning 'someone who guards horses' but the preferred meaning from the Middle Ages has been the Latin 'rosa-munda' which was one of the titles given to the virgin Mary. The mistress of King Henry II was called Rosamond Clifford and she lived at Woodstock in Oxfordshire in the 12th Century. She was reputed to be very beautiful.

"I am a rose of Sharon, a lily of the valleys." Song of Songs 2:1

Rose Roisin Rosalie Rosie Rosy

Known for its beauty and its fragrance. The rose was the ancient symbol of the virgin. Over 3,000 different varieties. A flower that blooms in the right sort of surroundings.

The rose is the most popular and most widely cultivated flower in the world - known for its beauty and lovely fragrance. Little wonder that it has been called "the gift of angels". There are over 3,000 different species and every year new ones are produced. Some 70 different genera are cultivated for timber, food and ornamental purposes. Other members of the rose family include: almond, apple, apricot, cherry, nectarine, pear, peach and quince. Roses require good, well-drained soil and plenty of sunlight - much like the human spirit.

"I am a rose of Sharon, a lily of the valleys. Like a lily among thorns..." S.of S.2:1-2.

Roseanne Roseanna Rosanna Rosannah

A combination of Rose and Ann; Rose being the ancient symbol of the virgin and Ann being derived from 'Hannah' - 'one whom God has graciously favoured'. Brought to the UK by the Normans.

Here are two ancient and highly treasured names brought together into one lovely combination. The rose is one of the loveliest garden plants and has been called the 'gift of angels'. It not only looks beautiful but smells sweet and is grown and cultivated for its fragrance. Beauty can be only 'skin-deep' so it is important to have that 'inner-beauty' which those who know and love God have been 'graciously favoured' with.

"Greetings, you who are highly favoured! The Lord is with you." Luke 1:28.

Rosemary Rosemarie

The name has TWO possible sources: From the Latin 'ros marinus' meaning 'sweet dew of the sea' or a combination of Rose and Mary; a rose being the ancient symbol of the Virgin Mary.

Botanically, Rosemary is a culinary herb of the mint family originally from the Mediterranean area. It is a small evergreen shrub with flowers in little clusters. Its leaves are dark green on the upper side and whitish below. It has a distinct perfume and has been used for very many years in medicine and aromatic treatment. In olden days it was thought to have the power to help the memory and it was also used as a sign of friendship. Small but beautiful.

"You will be a crown of splendour in the Lord's hand, a royal diadem in the hand of your God." Is.62:3.

Rosie - see Rose

Rosalinda

From the Spanish 'Rosa-linda' which means 'a pretty rose'. Some early Norman, French or German historians equate it with horses, chariots or even armour! Roses have been called "the gift of angels".

The rose is the most popular and most cultivated flower in the world - known for its beauty and lovely fragrance. There are over 3,000 different species and every year new ones are produced. Some 70 different genera are cultivated for timber, food and ornamental purposes. Other members of the rose family include; almond, apple, apricot, cherry, nectarine, pear, peach, plum, prune, quince and loganberry. Roses require good, well-drained soil and plenty of sunlight!

"I am a rose of Sharon, a lily of the valleys." Song of Songs 2:1.

Rosnah

A lovely Malay name which is common in South East Asia. It is a combination of the English 'Rose' and the ancient Malay word 'nah' (here it is!).

Known for its beauty and its lovely fragrance the rose was the ancient symbol of the virgin. It is the most popular and most cultivated flower in the world - little wonder that it has been called "the gift of angels". There

are over 3,000 different species and every year new ones are produced. Some 70 different genera are cultivated for timber, food and ornamental purposes. Other members of the rose family include; almond, apple, apricot, cherry, nectarine, pear, peach, plum, prune, quince and loganberry. Roses require good, well-drained soil and plenty of sunlight!
The Malay word 'nah' means "here it is!"
In the Song of Songs Jesus (the lover) is compared to the ROSE of Sharon! Song of Songs 2:1.

Ross
Gaelic for 'headland' or 'of the peninsula'. Inventor/maker of the 'Stars and Stripes'. A famous name of people and places.
As a surname 'Ross' is well-known. There is a town called 'Ross', a Scottish county called 'Ross' and a number of well-known people who are called 'Ross'. One of the latter is a lady who lived in Philadelphia. She owned an upholstery shop and one day thought that she should make a flag for her country - and so the 'stars and stripes' were born. People are surprised to learn that one of God's names is 'flag' - Moses fought a great battle in Exodus chapter 17 and called the place Yahweh-Nissi which means 'The LORD my flag'.
"He has taken me to the banquet hall, and His banner (flag) over me is love." S.of S.2:4.

Rosy - see Rose

Rowan Rowanne - see Roy

Rowena Rowina - see Rhonwen

Rowland Rowley - see Roland

Roxane Roxana Roxanne
From a Persian root meaning 'the light of dawn'. Alexander the Great had a wife called Roxane - they were deeply in love.
"Have you ever given orders to the morning, or shown the dawn its place?" Job 38:12. "He will make...righteousness shine like the dawn." Ps.37:6. The colours of dawn are purer and colder than the sunset colours because there is less dust in the atmosphere. From deep red to orange then to gold and then to yellow as the sun slowly appears. The most wonderful thing that ever happened took place at dawn - the resurrection of the Lord Jesus (Mt.28:1).
"If I rise on the wings of the dawn, if I settle on the far side of the sea, even there your hand will guide me, your right hand will hold me fast." Ps.139:9-10.

Roy Rowan Rowanne Ruadhan

From the Gaelic 'Ruadhan' which means 'red'. The name of an Irish Saint. A many-faceted word.

The word 'red' has at least six different meanings in the dictionary and they are as different as "the colour of blood" to "a party affiliation" and "a rag which excites someone". It originated from the name 'Rohan' but is now a well-established name in its own right. The Bible has a lot to say about 'red' - here is just one of the verses:

"Though your sins are like scarlet, they shall be as white as snow; though they are red as crimson they shall be like wool." Is.1:18.

Ruby

The most valuable of all precious stones - a thing of great beauty, elegance and attraction. Mogok in Burma is the source of some of the best rubies.

This precious metallic stone has been a thing of value for thousands of years. The queen of Sheba presented Solomon with "...spices...gold...and precious stones..." 2 Chron.9:1. The Temple which Solomon built was also "...adorned with precious stones..." 1 Chron.29:8. In the New Testament we are warned to ensure that we build with "...gold...silver and precious stones..." because every man's work will be "...tried by fire..." 1 Cor.3:12-14. *"Fashion a breastpiece...in the first row there shall be a ruby..." Ex.28:15-17.*

Rudolf Rudolph - see Ralph

Rufus

From the Latin 'rufus' which means 'red-haired'.

Rufus was the brother of Alexander and the son of Simon - the man who carried the cross for Jesus (Mark 15:21). In Rom.16:13. it is clear that his mother (Simon's wife) had also become a Christian. The day that Simon carried the cross must have been a really dark one for him - but imagine all the blessings and benefits which have come from it for this one family - Scripture indicates that both his wife and two sons Alexander and Rufus became Christians.

"Greet Rufus, chosen (choice) in the Lord, and his mother..." Rom.16:13.

Rukhsana

This beautiful name is from ancient Persian and means the one who is the 'Illuminated one', or the 'shinning one' or 'glittering one'.

Enlightened people have a 'glow' or an attraction which seems to make them stand out from the crowd. Many folk down through the ages have claimed to be 'enlightened' but sadly, their so-called 'lights' have been extinguished. Only one person seems to have been what he claimed to be "The light of the world". His promise was they "...would not walk in darkness" but have "the light of life" - they would be really enlightened!

"...I pray also that the eyes of your heart may be enlightened in order that you may know the hope to which he has called you, the riches of his glorious inheritance..." Ephesians 1:18.

Rupert

The name means 'bright and famous'. 'Rupert' is the English form of the German name 'Rupprecht'.

Prince Rupert of the Rhine was the name of a nephew of Charles Ist. He was a brave and brilliant General who came to Britain during the civil war in order to support the Royalist cause. He left his name behind and it has been a popular and well-liked one ever since. Down through history many other famous men have been called Rupert.

"LORD I have heard of your fame: I stand in awe of your deeds O LORD." Hab.3:2.

Russell Russ Rusty

From Norman French 'rousel', a nickname for someone with red hair. Also the family name of the Duke of Bedford since Henry VIII. One of England's great philosophers.

Sir Bertrand Russell (1872-1970) was one of England's greatest philosophers and also a passionate supporter of nuclear disarmament and pacifism. There is a theory that red-headed people have fiery tempers, but the truth is that everyone has a temper. The ancient Rabbis have a saying which goes like this: "You can tell a man's character from his temper (ka-as), his pocket (kees) and from his drinking habit (kos)."

"Better a patient man than a warrior, a man who controls his temper than one who takes a city." Prov.16:32.

Ruth

Hebrew for 'companion' or 'friend', the eighth book in the Bible and one of the greatest love-stories of all time.

The story begins in Bethlehem - like two other great stories (King David and the Lord Jesus). Naomi and her husband decide to go to the land of Moab in search of food. They took their two sons with them. Sadly both Naomi's husband and her two sons die and she is left with her two daughters-in-law. One named Orpah returns to her own people but the other called Ruth will not leave Naomi. Later, after her return to Bethlehem Ruth courts and marries Boaz and they become the great grandparents of King David. Ruth is included in the lineage of the Lord Jesus in Matthew 1:5.

"Your people will be my people and your God my God...the LORD deal with me be it ever so severely if anything but death separates you and me." Ruth 1:16-17.

Ryan

Of uncertain origin but probably from old Irish meaning 'a modest king'. May also have been from an ancient water god - for example the river 'Rhine'.

He was not a king but he was one of the greatest men who ever lived and he changed his name from 'Saul' to 'Paul'. There were several reasons for this but one of them was that, in Greek, 'Paul' has the sense of being 'modest'. Additionally, the change of name meant that he could better carry out his ministry of bringing the gospel to the gentiles.

John the Baptist had the same attitude when he said: "He must increase and I must decrease" John 3:30 KJV.

There is something about following Jesus that makes people feel small - but actually makes them great.

"What is man that you are mindful of him?...you crowned him with glory and honour" Heb.2:6-7.

S

Sabina Sabine

From the Latin 'a woman of the Sabines' (a people of ancient Italy). In the UK from the 12th century. In its Irish phonetic it means 'sweet'. A saint and an early Christian martyr under Hadrian.

This was originally a Roman name used by both males and females. St Sabinus was a 4th century Bishop of Spoleto and St Sabina was martyred by Hadrian. There is also a French version 'Sabine'. The name means 'sweet' from its Irish spelling and pronunciation. The dictionary gives at least NINE definitions of the word 'sweet'. Normally we tend to think of the sweet taste or sweet nature - the Bible brings these together in one verse.

"How sweet are your words to my taste, sweeter than honey to my mouth." Ps.119:103.

Sabrina

Means 'a princess'. According to ancient legend the river Severn was called Sabrina after the daughter of a Welsh King. John Milton (1608-74) used the name in "Comus".

The river Severn is Britain's longest river. It rises in the Welsh hills and runs through Shrewsbury and Worcester. When it reaches Gloucester it begins to widen into the tidal Bristol Channel and there are few crossing points.

Rivers run through the Bible - from Genesis chapter 2 where "a river flowed out from Eden" to Revelation chapter 22 where an Angel "showed me the river of the water of life, clear as crystal, flowing from throne of God..." According to the Bible the person God makes righteous is:

"...like a tree planted by streams of water..." Ps.1:3.

Sacario

Possibly from Hebrew meaning 'God remembered'. It is more likely an ancient Latin word meaning 'Exchequer' - the one in charge of all the accounts!

Zacharias (the Greek version of the Hebrew name Zechariah) was the father of John the Baptist and the word is so similar that there must be a connection in the dim recesses of time! The more likely history is from around AD1230 when it was used in an ancient document called the 'Liber Rubeus de Sacario' (The red book of the Exchequer). This was an attempt to sort out all the feudal rents and rates. A man called Halls translated it in 1896 and it is now the name of a very popular 'Rap' singer!

"...Do not be afraid, Zechariah (Sacario); your prayer has been heard." Luke 1:13.

Sacha - see Sasha

Sadie

It means 'a Princess' or 'a princess of multitudes, my Lady'. Originally evolved from 'Sarah'.

First recorded in 1895 this name is thought to have evolved from Sarah who was the wife of Abram - they lived in a town called Ur which was probably somewhere in southern Iraq. God called Abram out of Ur and Sarai went with him. At this time God changed both their names. Abram became Abraham (father of many) and Sarai became Sarah (Princess). Sarah is recorded in the role of honour in Hebrews chapter 11 because she required great faith to believe all that God promised to do for her and her husband. So 'Sadie' has a noble and fascinating history!

"Is anything too hard for the Lord?" Gen.18:14.

Sally - see Sarah

Salema

From an Arabic word which can mean 'healthy' and 'safe' or 'secure'. A town in Russia and a surname in the USA!

This lovely Arabic (and Pharsi) word is well-known and has a number of different uses. The small town near Marijampole, Lithuania and the New Jersey USA surname share one common feature in that no-one knows where they originated! Most people know that true health, safety and security come from God. The prophet Isaiah tells us that; "...by his wounds we are healed." Isaiah 53:5. Then the psalmist says; "...I will dwell in the house of the LORD forever." Psalm 23:6. Here is the secret of real health, safety and security!

"Keep me safe, O God, for in you I take refuge." Psalm 16:1.

Salome

From the word 'shalom' which is a Hebrew word meaning 'God's peace and wholeness'. A lovely name which has a double history in the Bible.

It could be called "The tale of two Salome's". The first one was the daughter of Herod who danced before him and as a 'prize' requested the head of John the Baptist (Mark 6:21-29). The other Salome was a follower of the Lord Jesus who ministered to His needs and was present at both the crucifixion and the resurrection. She saw and accepted the Saviour for herself. (Mark 15:40 and 16:1). 'Shalom'- PEACE is a lovely word - it means more than just a cessation of conflict - it means God's wholeness.

"The LORD bless you and keep you; the LORD make his face shine upon you and be gracious to you; the LORD turn his face toward you and give you peace." Num.6:24-26.

Samantha Sam

Means 'heard by God'. It developed from the name 'Samuel' - he was the last of the 'Judges' and the first of the 'Prophets'.

Samuel's mother was a good example of the meaning of his name. She prayed for many years to have a son and vowed that if God answered her prayer she would dedicate him to God. Her son Samuel was not a very good example of the meaning of his name - God called him eight times before he recognised the voice of God and responded appropriately. The story is in the first three chapters of 1 Samuel. Some Churches which do not practice infant baptism have a Service of Dedication instead and base it on the story of Samuel and his dedication to God by his parents.

"Speak, LORD, for your servant is listening" 1 Sam.3:9.

Samara

The winged-fruit of the ash or sycamore tree. A region, town and river in Russia.

The town of Samara changed its name for a brief period between 1935 and 1991 in honour of a Soviet leader but it has now reverted to its 16th century title. It is an industrial centre and leading grain-producer in south central Europe where the Volga and Samara rivers meet.

The sycamore-fig tree of the Bible and the middle east is a variety of the common fig tree and is quite different from the European sycamore, which is a kind of maple. The sycamore-fig tree was important to the economy and they were plentiful. This was the tree used by Zacchaeus when he wanted to see Jesus (Luke 19:1-9).

"He is like a tree planted by streams of water, which yields its fruit in season and whose leaf does not wither. Whatever he does prospers..." Ps.1:3.

Samina

Originally from an Arabic word which means 'highly valuable or expensive'. The name of a river in Liechtenstein.

This lovely name evolved from the Arabic word 'sami' which means 'high and beautiful', this word in turn came from the word 'sama' which means 'to be given height'.

It is also the name of a river in the tiny principality of Liechtenstein which is situated between Switzerland and Austria. Here three great valleys drain into this lovely river in one of the most beautiful parts of Europe.

"Then an angel showed me the river of the water of life...flowing down from the throne of God..." Rev.22:1.

Samuel Sam

From Hebrew 'heard by God'. The last of the Judges and the first of the Prophets.

Samuel lived at a critical and decisive time in the history of Israel. After forty years wandering in the wilderness the new nation-state had arrived in the promised land and now demanded a king so that they would be like the other nations around them. He anointed Saul and then David as kings and fulfilled many other roles during his lifetime. His thrilling life-story is told in 1 Sam.1-25 and it teaches us that to be 'heard by God' we must first of all 'hear God'.

Samuel was the product of prayer and early in his life he was dedicated to God but he had to receive God's call for himself and respond appropriately: "Speak, for your servant is listening." 1 Sam.3:10.

"This poor man called, and the LORD heard him; he saved him out of all his troubles." *Ps.34:6.*

Sandra - see Alexandra

Sanjay

From a Sanskrit word meaning 'victorious' or 'triumphant'. A prominent character in ancient India vedas and epics. Name of the son of Indira Gandhi.

Mrs Indira Gandhi was Prime Minister of India 1966-1977 and 1980-1984, and her son was named 'Sanjay'. He was also her Chief Political Adviser but sadly he died in an air accident in 1980.

Victory is not always what it seems - today some of the most prosperous countries seem to be the ones which lost the second world war. The Bible has many references to 'victory'. "For lack of guidance a nation (or person) falls, but many advisers make VICTORY sure."Prov.11:14.

"The horse is made ready for the day of battle, but victory rests with the LORD." *Prov.21:31.*

Saphena Saphina

Greek meaning 'clearly visible' - also from 'Sapphire' the most beautiful of the precious stones. A 'life-line' for many.

The first recorded use of the word 'Saphena' is in 1398 where it is used to describe two of the most prominent veins in the leg - the internal and the external saphena (it is the latter which is utilised in heart bypass operations). The assumption is that, as the veins are blue and exceptionally valuable, they were associated with the beautiful blue sapphire stone. The Sapphire is mainly found in Sri Lanka and parts of Thailand - although less valuable stones have also been found in the USA and Australia. All of us are 'clearly visible' to God - precious and valuable.

"For by Him all things were created...visible and invisible..." Col.1:16.

Sandy - see Alexander

Sarah Sally Sara Shara Sharah

There is only one Sarah in the Bible. It means 'a Princess'.

Sarai was the wife of Abram and they lived in a town called Ur which was probably somewhere in the area of southern Iraq. God called Abram out of Ur and Sarai went with him. At this time God changed both their names to Abraham (father of many) and Sarah (Princess). Sarah was a very beautiful woman and this gave them problems as they travelled. The story begins in chapter 11 of Genesis and concludes in chapter 25 when Abraham is buried beside his wife at Hebron. Sarah is recorded in the roll of honour in Hebrews chapter 11 because she required great faith to believe all that God promised to do for her and her husband.

"Is anything too hard for the LORD?" Gen.18:13.

Sasha Sacha - see also Alexander

Originally Russian for 'Alexander' meaning 'a strong helper' and 'protector of men'. Now recognised in the West as either a male or a female name.

The Russian form of the Greek name Alexander. In the Bible there is an account of a man called Simon who had two sons - one called Alexander (Sasha) and the other called Rufus. Simon was the man who carried the cross for Jesus (Mark 15:21). Can you imagine what it must have been like for 'Sasha'? His father would have told both the boys and his wife the story about the day he carried the cross. It's not surprising that 'Sasha', his brother and his mother all became Christians - Simon had played a vital part in the last moments of the Saviour's life. We know that they were part of the Church many years later because they are mentioned in the epistles e.g. Rom.16:13.

"The Lord is my helper; I will not be afraid. What can man do to me?" Heb.13:6.

Satya

A Sanskrit word for 'truth'.

Pontius Pilate asked: "What is truth" John 18:38 and down through the centuries men and women have repeated that question in one form or another. Strangely, the one who had said "I am the way, the truth and the life" John 14:6 was standing in front of him at that moment. The Psalmist says; "Teach me your way O LORD and I will walk in your truth" Ps.86:11. It is interesting to note that in the Old Testament 'truth' is often equated with a person's character see the story of Joseph's brothers in Gen.42:16 "...that your words may be tested to see if you are telling the truth".

In the New Testament Jesus says that His Holy Spirit: "... will guide you into all truth" John 16:13.

" I tell you the truth, if you have faith...it will be done." Mt.21:21.

Saul

From Hebrew meaning 'a requested (prayed-for) child'. The first King of Israel. The Jewish name of the Apostle Paul.

Saul the first King of Israel was chosen because the people wanted to be like the nations round about and God gave them what they asked for. Generous and brave, Saul fell victim to his position and three times abused it. In the New Testament it is the Jewish name of the great apostle Paul. His name was Saul and he was converted on the Damascus road (Acts 9). Following this he suffered much for the gospel. His name was changed at Cyprus to the Greek or gentile version 'Paul' (Acts 13:9). We have him to thank for a large part of the New Testament.

"I want to know Christ and the power of His resurrection and the fellowship...of His sufferings..." Phil.3:10.

Scott Scot

Means 'a Scot'. The name of many famous men in history.

Scotland is a very beautiful country of some 5 million people who are warm-hearted and generous. From north to south the mainland measures some 440 km (274 miles) and is 245 km (154 miles) wide but nowhere can you be more than 65 km (40 miles) from the coast. It includes 186 islands, many 'Lochs', mountains and remote heather-clad rolling hills.

Few names stir the heart more than Robert Falcon Scott - Scott of the Antarctic. He was the first man to try to reach the South Pole in 1904 and again in 1912. After the longest sledge journey in history he made it only to find that he had been beaten by Amundsen. His party perished on the return journey - just 18 km (11 miles) from their base camp.

"The good man brings good things out of the good stored up in his heart" Luke 6:45.

Seamas Seamus - see James

Sean Shane - see John

Sebastian

From Latin meaning 'a man from Sebasta' which means 'Majestic' and was a city in Asia Minor. A very handsome young Roman soldier who was a 3rd century martyr.

St Sebastian was a young Roman soldier who was martyred by being shot to death with arrows. He is buried in the Catacombs on the Appian Way near Rome. His death was the subject of many paintings because he was apparently a very handsome young man. He is the patron saint of archers, soldiers and pin-makers. The name was initially very popular in Spain and in France and has, since the 16th century, been a favourite in the UK.

"O LORD, our Lord, how majestic is YOUR name in all the earth!" Ps.8:1.

Selda

An abbreviation of 'Griselda' which is from Old German meaning; 'Christ's soldier'. In Boccaccio and Chaucer she is 'the loyal, patient wife' who is rewarded for her fidelity.

Few modern wives would survive the tests that her insecure husband set up in order to check her true affection for him. First of all he secretly arranged for the children to be 'fostered' and told her that he had killed them. Then he later told her that he was going to divorce her and marry an attractive younger lady - who actually turned out to be their oldest daughter! When (Gri)selda proves her loyalty she is rewarded and they live happily ever after!

The translation 'Christ's soldier' or 'fighter' is the most likely Old-German meaning because He invites us all to 'battle' for Him in a world that rejects Him.

"...the LORD saves; for the battle is the Lord's..."   1 Sam.17:47

Selina Celina Celine Seline

From Latin for 'heaven' (there is also a similar word in French). A very famous and lovely Countess.

Selina Countess of Huntingdon (1709-1791) became a Christian and joined the Methodists in her early thirties. A few years after the death of her husband she became very prominent in the Evangelical Revival. Her principle aim was to reach the upper classes of society with the gospel and to this end she built chapels and instituted a liturgical form of worship. There are still a number of chapels which bear the inscription "The Countess of Huntingdon's Connexion". Her name means 'heaven' and heaven was her goal!

"Whom have I in heaven but you? And earth has nothing I desire besides you."   Ps.73:25.

Seth

Hebrew meaning 'placed' or 'appointed'. The fourth man on earth who lived to a great age. The ancestor of Noah - and all of us.

When Cain killed Abel God gave Eve another son whom she called 'Seth' because she said, "God has granted me another child in place of Abel, since Cain killed him." Gen.4:25. The very next verse says that Seth had a son called Enosh. Between those two verses 105 years elapsed and Seth went on to live to 912 years (sin had only just begun to ruin the life of man). God 'appointed' the human race to run through Seth - where would we have been without him?

"The LORD brought me forth...I was appointed from eternity." Prov.8:22-23.

Seumas - see James

Shane - see John

Shara Sharah – see Sarah

Shannon

Meaning 'senior' and the name of a place. A name from the 'emerald isle'.
The river Shannon rises at the foot of the Cuilcagh Mountain and passes through some of the most beautiful scenery in Ireland and the British Isles, finally flowing into the Atlantic Ocean in southwest Ireland. It is 354 Km (220 miles) long and links many rivers and canals. It also supplies much of Ireland's power through a Hydro-electric plant.
Rivers flow through the Bible. From Genesis to Revelation they are very significant. In Genesis the river "...flowed from Eden..." Gen.2:10. In Revelation it is "...the river of the water of life - from the throne of God..." Rev.22:1.
"How beautiful...like gardens beside a river, like aloes planted by the LORD" Num.24:5-6.

Sharon Shaeron

Hebrew meaning 'a plain', 'a field' or 'a song'. A venue for rich, natural beauty.
In the Song of Songs Jesus (or the 'beloved') is prophetically described as "the lily of the valley, the rose of Sharon" S.of S.2:1. 'Sharon' is the rich alluvial plain in Israel roughly between Mount Carmel and Tel Aviv. It is mentioned a number of times in Scripture. In the centre of the plain of Sharon today is the town of Petach Tiqva which means 'a door of hope'. Hosea says; "I (God)...will make the Valley of Achor a door of hope." Hos.2:15.
"Sharon will become a pasture...the valley of Achor a resting place...for my people..." Is.65:10.

Shaun - see John

Sheena - see Jane

Sheralee

From the French word for 'darling' or 'dearest'. There is also a Spanish word which sounds very similar and means 'dear'.
'Dear' or 'Dearest' are words which we normally reserve for people very close to us - our "nearest and dearest". It can be just a form of greeting -

such as the one we use when we start a letter. The word 'darling' is an extra special word normally reserved for one particular and special person who is the sole object of our affection and trust.

The word is mentioned 9 times in the Bible and all 9 are in the Song of Songs. It would appear that most are a prophetic description of the Lord Jesus Christ.

"How beautiful you are, my darling! Oh, how beautiful! Your eyes behind your veil are doves." Song of Ss 4:1

Shareefa Shareefah

From the Arabic word meaning 'noble', 'virtuous'. The one time title of the governor of Mecca. (There is also a Pharsi word which means 'custard apple'!)

This beautiful name comes from an ancient Arabic word and the earliest record we can trace is the 9th century. When the Apostle Paul wrote to the Corinthian Christians he said: "Not many of you were wise by human standards; not many were influential; not many were of noble birth." 1 Corinthians 1:26. We are thankful he said "not many" - he didn't say "none"! There have been some Christians of 'noble' birth and they have made a considerable impact upon their world. Shareefa means 'noble' and everyone who is a child of God is a 'child of the King' - born into a 'royal' family. *"On his robe...he has this name written: KING OF KINGS AND LORD OF LORDS." Revelation 19:16.*

Sheila
Gaelic form: Sheelagh Shelagh

From the Irish form of St 'Cecilia' a 3rd century martyr. The Patron saint of all musicians.

Cecilia was a pagan woman who became a Christian and then brought her husband to Christ. As a result they were both martyred together sometime in the 3rd century. She was a very fine singer and so became the patron saint of musicians. Many people down through the centuries have died for their faith in the Lord Jesus. It may surprise you to know that more have died in the 20th century than in any other - or the TOTAL of all the previous centuries. You may not be called upon to die for Jesus but all of us are called to "lay down our lives for our brothers." 1 John 3:16. Each day we have the privilege of living for others and this can be MORE difficult than dying for Jesus. *"Greater love has no-one than this, that He lay down His life for His friends." John 15:13.*

Sheldon

An Old English surname with a number of different meanings depending on the area! A writer who walked "In His Steps".

The Old English name 'Sheldon' is common in Devon, Derbyshire and the West Midlands - the original word is lost in the mists of antiquity but it probably comes from the Saxon word 'scelf', or 'scylf' for a ledge or shelf.

The American writer C M Sheldon may have had this in mind when he wrote the all-time best seller "In His Steps" - for sixty years it was top of the book lists and sold over eight million copies. It is the story of a town where people determined to live like Jesus for a year!

"I have considered my ways and have turned my steps to your statutes." Psalm 119:59.

Sherene – see Cher

Shey – see James

Shelley

From Old English meaning 'meadow by a cliff'. An ancient surname. A famous poet and made popular in the 20th century by a film star.

Whenever you see the phrase 'ley' or 'ly' or 'lea' in a name or surname you can be almost certain that it refers to the Old English word for 'meadow'. With the name 'Shel-ley' you possibly have a meadow by a cliff, there may even be the sea or a flowing stream at the foot of the cliff and this makes a very peaceful and picturesque scene. Isaiah likens this to the movement of the Holy Spirit among God's people as they begin to fulfil their prophesied future.

"They will spring up like grass in a meadow, like poplar trees by flowing streams." Is.44:4.

Sholto

From the Scottish Gaelic word 'Sioltach' meaning 'a fruitful sower'. The middle name of the ninth Marquess of Queensbury who formulated the rules of modern boxing!

The rules of modern boxing were first published in 1867 under the sponsorship of John Sholto Douglas, ninth marquess of Queensberry, from whom they take their name. The meaning 'a fruitful sower' reminds us of the parable that Jesus told in Luke chapter 8.

"But the ones that fell on the good ground are those who, having heard the word with a noble and good heart, keep it and bear fruit with patience." Luke 8:15.

Shirley

From 'Shire-lea' Old English for 'a bright meadow'. A male and female name in the past.

When you bring together two concepts into one name it creates a beautiful picture. 'Shire' is an Old English word for 'a rural area' bright, open and inviting. 'Lea' means 'a meadow'. It has always been God's great desire to take care of his children in the same way that a shepherd takes care of his flock - we have many pictures of this in the 'shepherd psalms' and in other places such as John chapter 10. He will lead us to the 'green pastures' if we will let him.

"How then can the LORD pasture them like lambs in a meadow?" Hos.4:16.

Shona - see Jane

Sian - see Jane John

Sibyl Sybil

Greek 'Sibylla'. Brought to Britain by the Normans. The name of a woman who was said to be 'the voice of God'. In 1845 Benjamin Disraeli chose 'Sibyl' as the name of his political novel.

In classical times 'Sibyls' were prophetesses and it is suggested that some even foretold the coming of Christ 600-800 years before the event. In and after the 2nd century BC alleged "Sibylline Oracles" were written by Jews and later by Christians but they were never accepted as Divinely inspired and do not form part of the Bible.

"For the word of God is living and active, sharper than any double-edged sword..." Heb.4:12.

Sidney Sydney

From Old English meaning 'a wide water meadow'. Royal links in England and a city in the antipodes.

The origin of the name 'Sidney' could be from St Denis in France (St-de'-nee) because Henry II was from Anjou and his father was Count of Anjou. This is one of the earliest records of the name. The city of Sydney in Australia was named after Thomas Townshend the 1st Viscount Sydney in 1788 by Captain Arthur Phillip. It is now a prosperous State capital of some 4 million people with a huge natural harbour and a famous opera house.

The Old English meaning of 'a wide water meadow' gives a very peaceful and picturesque scene.

"I will grant peace in the land, and you will lie down and no one will make you afraid." Lev.26:6.

Silas Silvanus Silvester Sylvester

From Latin 'Silvanus' - 'one who lives in the woods'. A fellow-traveller with the Apostle Paul.

There is a legend which says that St Sylvester (Silas), the first of three popes with that name, cured the Emperor Constantine of leprosy. In return, the legend says, Constantine gave the pope the city of Rome and its environs. The New Testament speaks of an earlier Silas (Silvanus) who was the Apostle Paul's travelling companion on his second missionary journey. He is also mentioned as the man who was sent by the Church at Jerusalem to welcome into fellowship the first Gentile converts through the Church of Antioch.

"With the help of Silas, whom I regard as a faithful brother..." 1 Pet.5:12.

Silvia - see Sylvia

Simon Cymon Simeon Simone

'A listener' from the Hebrew 'shama' - to hear. The famous Simeon who saw the child Jesus and exalted God in a song of praise (Luke 2:29-32) and Simon Peter the Apostle.

Someone once said that God gave us one mouth and two ears - because He wanted us to listen twice as much as we spoke. The fact is, not many of us listen more than we speak so consequently we find ourselves having to retract things said in haste and apologise for not hearing all the facts. Jesus constantly warned us to "Consider carefully what you hear" Mk.4:24. One of the other dangers of talking so much is that we fail to hear God when He speaks to us.

"Speak, LORD, for your servant is listening." 1 Sam.3:9.

Siobhan Siobhon - see Jane

Sion - see John

Sophie Sonia Sonya Sophia

From Greek meaning 'wisdom'. The great cathedral at Constantinople has this name as part of its dedication.

'Holy Wisdom' (Hagia Sophia) is a regular dedication on very many orthodox churches throughout the Middle East. Wisdom is a constant subject in the Bible. When God challenged Solomon to ask for any gift he (wisely) chose to ask God to give him "wisdom and knowledge" 2 Chron.1:10 and he is known as the wisest man who ever lived.

The difference between knowledge and wisdom is the ability to apply wisely what knowledge we have gained.

"The fear of the LORD is the beginning of wisdom and...understanding." Prov.9:10.

Spencer

From Olde English - the name of one who 'dispensed'. Someone who gave and

gave and gave... Also the name of a great English family!
You would have to go back a very long time in English history to find the origin to this excellent name. If you were born into a royal or noble family then you might well have had a 'dispenser' in your household. His task was to dispense - that is, to distribute all the things needed to run a large household. The 'Spencers' were one of Englands oldest and most aristocratic families and it is likely that their name was passed down through the years from this origin. You would need to go back even further in time to meet the greatest giver of all - his name was Jesus and it is true that He gave and gave and gave...
"...the Son of God, who loved me and gave himself for me." Galatians 2:20.

Stacey Anastasia Annastazia

Originally from a Greek word 'anastasis' meaning 'resurrection'. A 4th century Christian martyr.
Anastasia was the daughter of the Emperor Constantius Chlorus at the turn of the 4th century. Her name indicates that there was a Christian presence in the Imperial household at that time. She gave her name to a later saint who was martyred in Dalmatia. The resurrection of Jesus is the main subject of 1 Cor.15, in which Paul concludes: "...if Christ has not been raised, our preaching is useless and so is your faith." 1 Cor.15:14.
"Jesus said...I am the Resurrection and the life...do you believe this?" John 11:25.

Stanley

From Old Anglo-Saxon and meaning 'a stony field' (stane-lea). It was originally a surname but the exploits of the great explorer in the 19th century influenced its use as a popular Christian name.
Sir Henry Morton Stanley was the man who found David Livingstone in Africa when all the world feared that he was dead. On November 10th 1871 he uttered those famous words "Dr Livingstone I presume?" He was one of the great African explorers when the continent was unknown and "the white-man's grave". Of his meeting with Livingstone he said words to the effect that had he stayed one further day with David Livingstone then he himself would also have become a Christian...
"..So this is what the Sovereign LORD says: "See, I lay a stone in Zion, a tested stone, a precious cornerstone for a sure foundation; the one who trusts will never be dismayed." Is.28:16.

Stefan - see Stephen

Stella

The Latin word for 'star' which might also be described as 'a heavenly being'!
One of God's major creations on the fourth day. "He also made the stars."
Gen.1:16.

When God promised Abraham that "I will...make your descendants as numerous as the stars in the sky and as the sand on the seashore." Gen.22:17, Abraham must have thought there was no real comparison - he could only see a few hundred stars and he could hold that number of grains of sand in one hand. Today astronomers know that there are possibly more stars than grains of sand on all the sea shores of the world. But like people each one is different. The Apostle Paul says; "The sun has one kind of splendour...the stars another; and star differs from star..." 1 Cor.15:41.
"I, Jesus...I am the Root and the Offspring of David, and the bright Morning Star."
Rev.22:16.

Stephen Stefan Steven Stephanie Steve Stevie

From Greek for 'a crown'. There is only one person named Stephen in the Bible - the first Christian martyr.

The story of Stephen is told in the book of Acts chapters 6 and 7. There is an interesting sequel in Acts 8:1-4.
Stephen was chosen as one of the first deacons because he was full of faith and full of the Holy Spirit (Acts 6:5). It wasn't very long before he upset the synagogue and was brought before the Sanhedrin where he mounted a long and spirited address in defence of all that he had been saying. When he accused them of murdering Jesus they were furious. He cried "I see heaven open and the Son of Man..." Acts 7:56. At this he was stoned to death. He was the first of many thousands of men and women who have died for Jesus.
"They chose Stephen, a man full of faith and of the Holy Spirit.." Acts 6:5.

Stewart Stuart

From Old English 'sti weart' who was the Manager of a large household or farm. The origin of our word 'steward'. A Scottish royal family from William the Steward in the 14th century.

William the Steward was in fact the co-founder of the Scottish royal family with the name 'Stuart'. He married the king's daughter and his son later became king - thus beginning a line of Scottish, and later, British kings.
The principle of 'being a steward' originates in the Bible (Gen.43:19). It is a Christian's responsibility to be a good steward of the things that God has entrusted to him (Luke 12:42-48). The words 'steward' and 'manager are interchangeable.
"...the Lord said, Who then is that faithful and wise steward...?" Luke 12:42 KJV.

St John (Often pronounced: Sin-gen)

A name given in honour of St John the Apostle. It means "the grace or mercy of the Lord". There are two well-known people in the New Testament with the name 'John'.

'John the Baptist' was a fiery preacher announcing the Kingdom of Heaven and demanding that all men repent and believe the gospel.

'John the Apostle' was different in character. He could be high-spirited (see Mk 3.17. & Luke 9.49.) But he could also be loving and it was to his care that Jesus committed his mother when he was on the cross. (John 19. 26-27.). He also wrote the Fourth Gospel, the Epistles of John and the book of Revelation.

Some of the favourite 'grace and mercy' verses are; "For God so loved the world..." John 3.16.,

"....the blood of Jesus purifies.." 1 John 1.7. "Behold I stand at the door...." Rev.3.20.

Susanna Sue Susan Susanne Susie Suzanna Suzanne

From the Hebrew 'Shoshannah' which means 'a lily'. 'Susanna' was a member of the support team for the Lord Jesus.

When you join the attributes of a beautiful flower with a servant spirit you have a useful team member. The story of Jesus' itinerant ministry team is in the first 3 verses of Luke chapter 8 and Luke is the only writer who mentions them. Being a doctor he would be more aware than most of the need for support services.

Some people are called to be the 'front' people while others are called upon to support them - to pray, give and serve.

Susanna had received healing and blessing from Jesus and she was now in a position to help minister that to others.

"My beloved is mine, and I am his: he feedeth among the lilies." S.of S.2:16 KJV.

Summer

From the Old English 'sumor'. In the west a time of ripening harvest and long, warm, sultry days. In scripture a 'sign of the times'.

"Now learn this lesson from the fig tree: As soon as its twigs get tender and its leaves come out, you know that summer is near." Mt 24:32. In the days of Jesus the 'fig tree' was a synonym for the Pentateuch (the first five books of the Bible) also for the people of Israel - so when Jesus saw Nathaniel 'under the fig tree' - he was probably studying the word of God (John 1:48). Now read all the other passages which talk about the 'fig tree'!

"He told them this parable: "Look at the fig tree...you can see for yourselves and know that summer is near...you know that the kingdom of God is near." Luke21:29-31

Sybil - see Sibyl

Sydney - see Sidney

Sylvester - see Silas

Sylvia Silvia

From Latin meaning 'a woman of the forest'. The mother of the founder of Rome and a saintly mother of a saint. A poem by Shakespeare, later set to music by Schubert.

Rhea Silvia was the mother of the twins Romulus and Remus - their lives are shrouded in legend and fantasy but it appears that Romulus killed Remus and went on to establish the great city of Rome.

St Gregory the Great was one of 16 popes to be called 'Gregory' and he lived in the 6th century. His mother was called Silvia and clearly she had a good influence on him because he became a renowned Bible expositor.

"...from infancy you have known the Holy scriptures which are able to make you wise for salvation through faith in Christ Jesus." 2 Tim.3:15.

Talan

Old Cornish and from the 10th century. This man should be a 'hi-brow'! 'Hao' is 'Hello' in Talan - a modern German language.

Old Cornish and Breton have many similar words - and this is one of them. In both Old Cornish and Breton the word is from the word 'Tal' meaning 'forehead' and is first recorded in the Bodmin Manumissions. More commonly known as the 'Bodmin Gospels' they can be viewed today in the British Museum.

Talan is also a modern (German) language and, as we have shown, many words are strangely familiar.

"...a reminder on your forehead that the law of the LORD is to be on your lips. For the LORD brought you out..." Exodus 13:9.

Talitha

Aramaic for 'damsel' or 'young lady' used by the Lord Jesus when He raised Jairus' young daughter from the dead.

The words of Jesus in Mark 5:41 are "Talitha koum!" and this can be translated: "Young lady, arise". The word for 'young lady' is an affectionate term from a root word which could be equated with our 'lambkin' in English.

This was yet another demonstration that Jesus has power over life and death - even when it came to His own death He said that He had authority to lay down His life and authority to take it again (John 10:18).

"Arise, shine, for your light has come, and the glory of the LORD rises upon you." Is.60:1.

Tamar Tamara Tamarah

Hebrew for a 'date palm' which is a symbol of prosperity and righteousness.

There are three people and one town with the name 'Tamar' in the Old Testament: a daughter of David, the wife of Er, and a daughter of Absalom. There is also a town near the Dead Sea which is now known as Palmyra. (See Ez.47:19 and 48:28).

Dates and date palms were signs of prosperity and righteousness (Ps.92:13-14). At the Feast of Tabernacles the Children of Israel were instructed to take the leaves and rejoice before the Lord (Lev.23:40). When the Lord

Jesus entered Jerusalem on 'Palm' Sunday it was the branches of the date palm that they took as they went out to meet Him.

"...standing before the throne...wearing white robes...holding palm branches in their hands..." Rev.7:9.

Tamsin

The name means ' a twin' and is a contracted form of 'Thomasina' which is the female form of 'Thomas'. She will always be linked with the famous 'doubting Thomas'.

Two facts are often missed: Firstly, Jesus put in a 'special personal appearance' for Thomas and gave him the opportunity that no-one else has ever had. Read about it in John 20:24-31. Secondly, Thomas made one of the greatest statements a human being has ever made. When he saw Jesus he said: "My Lord and my God!" John 20:28.

The name Tamsin may mean 'a twin' - but in God's eyes every twin is unique.

"A woman who fears the LORD is to be praised." Prov.31:30.

Tanya Tania Tonya

From the Russian 'Tatiana', a 3rd century martyr. She is venerated in the Russian Orthodox Church.

The Russian Church dates from the first century but it was not until AD955 when Princess Olga was converted that it began to grow. In 1925 a new era of persecution by Stalin began with his purge of the Christian Churches. The example set by Tatiana in the third century has been repeated very many times and thousands have died for their faith. In spite of its persecution the Russian Church has survived and continues to grow.

"...on this rock I will build my church, and the gates of Hades will not overcome it." Mt.16:18.

Tara

From Hebrew and meaning 'to pause'. One of the camp-sites for the children of Israel soon after they left Egypt. From the father of Abraham.

This name has a long and illustrious history! It may have originated as an adaptation of the name of Abraham's father who was called Terah. Its meaning is to 'pause' or 'stop' - and the children of Israel had many opportunities to do just that before they were to reach the promised land! We sometimes need to pause on our journey of life.

"Be still, and know that I am God; I will be exalted among the nations, I will be exalted in the earth." Ps.46:10.

Tasha - see Natalie

Tasneem Tasnim

From Arabic meaning 'a fountain of Paradise'.

A name containing two fascinating words in its original translation. A fountain is a source of life and a thing of beauty - very few inanimate objects can make this claim. The Psalmist says; "For with you is the fountain of life; in your light we see light" Ps.36:9. Paradise is a synonym for heaven. God created a paradise on earth in the garden of Eden where man and woman had all they could desire - but they still wanted more and finally had to be excluded. God promises to restore Paradise. Jesus promised the dying thief that he would be with Him in Paradise that day.

"On that day a fountain will be opened to...cleanse them from sin and impurity." Zech.13:1.

Tariq

From Arabic and meaning 'one who knocks at a door' or 'one who calls late at night'. Also the name of the morning star and the name of a famous rock!

This name shares some of the attributes of the Lord Jesus who, long before, was called 'the one who knocks at the door' (see Rev.3:20) and hundreds of years ago was called 'the bright Morning Star' (see Rev.22:16).

In AD711 the 86th Surah crossed the sea to Spain and conquered a piece of land which still bears his name - Jabal-Tariq - you and I know it better as Gibraltar!

"God is my rock in whom I take refuge....He is my stronghold, my refuge and my saviour..." 2 Sam.22:3.

Ted Teddy - see Edward

Tegen

From ancient Cornish meaning 'a beautiful, rare and precious jewel'. It is also a Dutch word meaning 'over-against'.

The Dutch word 'tegen' is included in the title of a famous book by a Dutch poet who became a Christian early in the 19th century. His name was Isaac Da Costa and the book he wrote was entitled "Objections (tegen) to the spirit of the age". He could write a similar book today! The Cornish word has a further application when it is used as a 'nick-name' for the 'ring-finger'. Here it is pronounced 'Tykky-deu' which can also mean 'God's butterfly'!

"...Gold there is, and rubies in abundance, but lips that speak knowledge are a rare jewel." Proverbs 20:15.

Terence Terry

From a Latin family name used by the Romans: 'Terentius'. Also an Irish

Gaelic name which means 'one who initiates an idea'. Recorded from the 3rd century St Terentius.

Before the third century St Terentius there was a Latin comic dramatist whose name was also Terentius (called Terence in English). He had been brought to Rome as a slave from N. Africa but was made a 'freeman' and in gratitude took the name of his master.

'One who initiates ideas' or has 'brainwaves' could be a heavy burden to carry. We all get 'ideas' from time to time - the trouble is that someone else has usually got there before us or we don't have the means to put our ideas into practice.

"...if you call out for insight and cry aloud for understanding...then you will understand the fear of the LORD...For the LORD gives wisdom...knowledge and understanding." Prov.2:3-6.

Teresa Theresa Therese Tess Terri

From Greek - the name of the island 'Thera' which means 'a harvest'. The origin could also be Latin, Italian, Spanish, German or French because they all have similar names.

The history of this name is shrouded in the mists of antiquity - it has been known on the continent from the 5th century but was clearly in existence before that. In AD395 Paulinus of Nola became a Christian through the influence of his wife Therasia. Together they left a life of affluence and joined a monastery . They concentrated on building hospitals and waterworks for the poor of the area. In AD409 Paulinus was made Bishop of Nola. There are three 'Harvest Festivals' in the Jewish calendar - heralding the great harvest of souls at the end of time.

"The harvest is the end of the age, and the harvesters are angels." Mt.13.39.

Thea

From the Greek for 'the gift of God'. Originally 'Dorothea' but now an attractive and engaging name in its own right!

The Greek word 'Theos' is the word for God and it forms the basis for many of our English words. The Greek word was added to the Latin 'Doron' making the male name 'Dorotheos' from which we have the names 'Dorothy' and 'Dorothea' - now female names (also the reverse 'Theodora'). There were many early saints with variations of this name but 'Dorothy' as a female name did not become popular in Britain until the Middle Ages. Your name predates many of the other varieties and takes us back to the ancient Greek word which they all sprang.

"....the gift of God is eternal life in Christ Jesus our Lord." Rom 6.23.

Thelma

From Greek meaning 'wish' or 'will'. A 19th century heroine.

When Marie Corelli in 1887 needed a name for her heroine she chose 'Thelma' - perhaps she had in mind the Greek meaning behind it. There is no record of the name being used before then but many have chosen it since.

'Will power' can be a force for good or evil because God has given us the ability to 'make up our minds' about almost every issue. That is why the hymn writer says in the famous hymn of consecration: "Take my will and make it thine, it shall be no longer mine: Take my heart - it is thine own; it shall be thy royal throne." Frances Ridley Havergal (1836-79)

"Yet not as I will, but as you will." Mt.26:39.

Theresa - see Teresa

Thomas Tom Tommy
Welsh form: Tomos

From Aramaic and Greek meaning ' a twin'. He will always be linked with the famous 'doubting Thomas' - but that phrase tells only half the story.

Two facts are often missed: Firstly, Jesus put in a 'special personal appearance' for 'doubting Thomas' and gave him the opportunity that no-one else ever had. Read about it in John 20:24-31. Secondly, Thomas made one of the greatest statements a human being ever made. When saw he Jesus he said: "My Lord and my God!" John 20:28.

Thomas teaches us that the Lord Jesus never rejected people with honest questions. The name may mean 'a twin' - but every Thomas is unique.

"Because you have seen me, you have believed; blessed are those who have not seen and yet have believed." John 20:29.

Tiernan

From Irish Gaelic 'tighearna' meaning 'lord', or from the Latin 'tertia' meaning to be 'in order'.

The Irish King Tiernan O'Ruark lived in the 12th century and is partly responsible for the Anglo-Norman invasion and conquest of Ireland by England! He was king of Breifne (now the general area of Cavan and Leitrim) when his wife was abducted by the king of Leinster - when Tiernan objected to the abduction the king of Leinster sought help from King Henry II of England - so who said that the Irish problems were new?

It's nice to have a name which means 'lord' - but there is only ONE real Lord!

"...the good news of peace through Jesus Christ, who is Lord of all." Acts 10:36.

Tiffany

From the Greek and meaning 'epiphany' (manifestation). This is a reference to the visit of the wise men to the infant Jesus. A 'seasonal name'.

From around 1200 it was a common practice to name your child after the Christian season in which he or she was born. So we have names such as Pascal (Passover), Noel, Nowell, Christmas, Pentecost, Easter, Midwinter, Loveday and others. 'Epiphany' is an important season in the Christian calendar because it symbolises Christ's 'manifestation' to the world - when He was publicly declared God's Messiah. It was the time when the Gentile wise men or 'magi' visited the baby Jesus. In the west we remember this on the 6th January.

"He was chosen before the creation of the world, but was revealed in these last times for your sake." 1 Pet.1:20.

Timothy Tim Timotheus Timmy
French form: Timothee
Russian form: Tyoma

The name means 'honoured' or, 'one who honours God'. He was a convert and companion of the apostle Paul. The product of a Christian home - his mother taught him the Scriptures.

Paul had a great love and respect for him although he was not a strong person and needed an occasional encouraging word (see 1 Cor.16:10-11, 1 Tim.4:12 and 2 Tim.1:7). Like Paul, Timothy was imprisoned for the faith and nothing is known of his final fate but his testimony has been read by millions through the years. He has been truly 'honoured'.

"I am not ashamed - I know whom I have believed and am convinced that He is able..." 2 Tim.1:12.

Tina

The name 'Tina' began as a contraction of the longer name Christina and it will always have a very special significance because it in turn, comes from the word 'Christian'.

It was Gentiles at Antioch who invented the name 'Christian' as a 'nickname' for those who followed 'the way' as it was then known. The word 'Christian' is used three times in the New Testament; Acts 11:26, Acts 26:28 and 1 Peter 4:16. Anyone who has this name is constantly reminded that it meant 'Christ's - one' and of course this can be true for everyone because the God who made us sent the Lord Jesus Christ to die for us on the cross.

His name means; Lord; Supreme Ruler, Jesus; Saviour, Redeemer, Christ; The promised Messiah.

Tirzah

This lovely Hebrew name means 'pleasant', 'well-pleasing'. She was the youngest daughter of the daughters of Zelophehad. It was also the name of the capital city of the northern Kingdom.

Both the girl Tirzah and the city were evidently very beautiful and this was taken up by William Blake in 1794 when he wrote a famous poem entitled "To Tirzah". The city of Tirzah was captured by Joshua (Joshua 12:24) and was close to the present town of Nablus. After the death of Solomon it was the capital of the northern kingdom.

"You are beautiful, my darling, as Tirzah, lovely as Jerusalem, majestic as troops with banners." S.of S 6:4.

Titus

A Latin name of uncertain meaning and history - possibly meaning 'honoured'. He was a companion of the apostle Paul and the recipient of an epistle from him.

'To honour' is to recognise the worth of something and give it that recognition in a tangible way. The apostle Paul 'honoured' Titus by taking him on some of his journeys (the reason he is not mentioned in Acts may be because he was the brother of Luke the writer). Paul also commissioned him with a number of delicate tasks - such as resolving the problems in the Church at Corinth (see 2 Cor.8:6).

"As for Titus, he is my partner and fellow-worker among you" 2 Cor.8:23.

Toby Tobias

The Greek version of the Hebrew name 'Tobiah' which means 'the goodness of the Lord God'.

Originally from the Apocryphal book "Tobit" where Tobiah (the son of Tobit) goes on a long journey with his dog 'Toby'. The story is frank fiction but the name lives on in real life.

Even more of a reality is the 'goodness of the Lord God' - from the beginning of time men have found joy in praising God for His loving kindness. "How good is the God we adore, our faithful unchangeable friend, whose love is as great as His power and knows neither measure nor end!" J.Hart.

"I will cause all my goodness to pass in front of you, and I will proclaim my name, the LORD, in your presence." Ex.33:19.

Tom Tomas Tommy - see Thomas

Toni Tony - see Anthony

Tonya - see Tanya

Toria - see Victoria

Tracey Tracy

From the French place-name 'Traci-Bocage' in Normandy. Very popular in the USA. Perhaps originally from the Greek word for 'harvest'.

After Hebrew and Greek one of the most popular name-sources is the French province of Normandy just across the English Channel. This is because many names were 'brought over' by William the Conqueror in 1066.

If the original source was the Greek word for 'harvest' then any owner of this name should be justly proud. In every culture harvest-time is revered and celebrated. Jesus spoke of the 'harvest-field' being "ripe for harvest" John 4:35. By this He meant the souls of men and women were 'ripe' to receive Him and His word.

"The harvest is plentiful, but the workers are few. Ask the Lord of the harvest, therefore, to send out workers into his harvest field." Luke 10:2.

Travis

Originally from the French word 'traverser' which means 'to cross-over'. The name given to any man who was a collector of tolls.

'Toll-collectors' are not very common in Britain today except at the major river-crossings such as the Bristol Channel and the Thames crossing at Dartford.

A 'toll' is the price paid for a service which someone gives. So we have the expression "it took its toll" meaning - there was a price to pay.

Jesus paid the 'toll-price' for us when He died on the cross and if we wish to 'cross-over' onto His side then, because of this, we have nothing to pay.

"I tell you the truth, whoever hears my word and believes him who sent me has eternal life and will not be condemned; he has crossed over from death to life." John 5:24.

Trevor Trefor

From the Welsh place-name meaning 'large home-dwelling'. 'Trefor' is the original.

Places in Denbighshire, Anglesey and Caernarfon all used this name in the days when it described mini-towns or large villages. Today they are well-liked Christian names.

In olden times, as today, a house does not make a home. The Psalmist says "Unless the LORD builds the house (home) its builders labour in vain."

Ps.127:1. God's original intention was that every home should reflect the nature and character of His home but this can only happen when He is central.

"If the home is deserving, let your peace rest upon it..." Mt.10:13.

Tricia - see Patricia

Tristan Tristen Tristam Tristram

From Celtic meaning 'noisy'. Recorded in the UK from the 12th century. The noble hero of a sad love story. An island paradise waiting to erupt again?

The name has French links because the first part 'triste' means 'sad' and there are a number of similar French names. There are also versions in French of the medieval love story of "Tristan and Isolde". Love and sorrow are often mixed in real life because they are emotions felt at critical times.

Tristan da Cunha is a group of four islands in the Atlantic Ocean - the main island is, in fact, a volcano.

It appears that the Temple was quite a noisy place at times - one has only to read Psalm 150 to imagine the volume!

"...Listen, a noise on the mountains...The LORD Almighty is mustering an army for war." Is.13:4.

Trey

Old English word for 'three' also for the trunk of a tree - something really firm, strong and reliable!

This name was first recorded in the Doomsday Book of AD 1086 because it was the name of a town in Sussex - 'Treyford'. So called because it was the name of a ford marked by a giant treetrunk!

It was also the Old English word for 'three' (and the present Irish too!).

When you put these two together you are immediately reminded of the Trinity - firm, strong and reliable.

"...his delight is in the LORD...He is like a tree planted by streams of water...whatever he does prospers." Ps.1.

Troy

The name of an ancient Greek city surrounded by legend and forever linked to the wooden horse. Also from the surname and French city of Troyes. Any assayist can tell you what you are worth.

The "Legend of the Wooden Horse of Troy" captures the imagination of every young person - there must be some truth in the original. Today 'Troy' is a well-liked name and also a measure of fine metals such as gold and silver. An assayist is a man who tests the quality of metals and he will tell you that any human body is only worth a few pounds when it is reduced to its basic constituents. Fortunately, God doesn't look at our metallic worth - He values us much more.

"...you know that it was not with perishable things such as silver or gold that you were redeemed ...but with the precious blood of Christ..." 1 Pet.1:18-19.

Trudi Trudie Trudy - see Gertrude

Tyla

From the ancient Latin word 'tegere' meaning 'to cover'. This is the root source of our word 'tile' but it also includes 'a door-keeper'.

The 'door-keeper' was not there just to prevent people from entering - in the original meaning of the word he was also part of the security of the individual and a guardian of his secrecy. No intruder could get to the man who had a 'tegere'. Later the word became the old English word 'tigele' meaning 'to cover' and was the source of our word 'tile' and 'tiler' and this, in turn, was the origin of the lovely name 'Tyla'.

Then Jesus said... "I am the door. If anyone enters by Me, he will be saved..." John 10:7-9.

Tyrone

From Irish meaning 'Eoghan's land' and formerly the name of a county in Northern Ireland.

In the fifth century Tyrone was a principality of one of the sons of Niall - his name was Eoghan and the land was called Tir Eoghan which has gradually become Tyrone. There are very many raths (ancient hill-forts) in the county and it is steeped in history. Like most of Ireland it is very beautiful. To the north you have the Sperrin mountains and the Mourne and Blackwater rivers. It has been part of the United Kingdom since the 17th century but, since 1973, it is no longer a separate county, it is now divided into the districts of Strabane, Omagh, Dungannon and Cookstown.

"I lift up my eyes to the hills where does my help come from? My help comes from the LORD, the Maker of heaven and earth." Ps.121:1-2.

Ulysses

Irish Gaelic form: Ulick

Latin for 'Odysseus', the Greek hero in Homer's "Iliad". He created the 'wooden horse of Troy'.

Ulysses was a warrior in the ancient poems of the Iliad and the Odyssey. In it he was a reluctant hero who was brave and cunning in battle. At one stage the Greeks are besieging the city of Troy and build a wooden horse. When the citizens of Troy think that the Greeks have left the horse they drag it into the city not realising that soldiers are hiding inside. During the night the soldiers come out and open the gates - and the city is captured.

"Finally , be strong in the Lord and in His mighty power." Eph.6:10.

Umar Omar

Arabic for 'flourishing' or 'most high'. The dictionary definition: "to grow vigorously, thrive, prosper, be successful, to be in one's prime, to be in good health..."

The name of a chief mentioned in Gen.36:15 where it means 'a man of his word' - a man who can be trusted or a man who has something to say, this name has an excellent meaning and it encapsulates the dreams of any young person. Sadly, dreams are not reality and it is sometimes difficult to change an aspiration into fact. Help is at hand and in the psalms we have two recommendations. Firstly, dwell in the presence of God. Secondly, trust in His love.

"...I am like an olive tree flourishing in the house of God, I trust in God's unfailing love for ever." Ps.52:8.

Una Juno

From the Irish Gaelic for 'a lamb' ('uan'). Possibly from the Latin for 'one'. Originally influenced by the Roman Queen of the Gods called 'Juno'.

Sean O'Casey in his play "Juno and the Paycock" (1924) used the Roman name for the Queen of Gods but still pronounced it "oona", whereas the Elizabethan poet Spenser in "The Faerie Queen" used the Latin meaning of 'one' or 'unity'. The best meaning is the Irish Gaelic 'a lamb' because this is found in more ancient forms such as 'Oonagh' and 'Oona'. When John the Baptist proclaimed: "Look, the Lamb of God, who takes away the sin of the world!" John 1:29 he had in mind the sacrificial lamb that was the sin offering, and the other John wrote:

"See, the Lion of the tribe of Judah...has triumphed...then I saw a lamb..." Rev.5:5-6.

Unice - see Eunice

Ursula

From Latin meaning 'the small she-bear'. A 4th century martyr and saint.

The 4th century St Ursula is shrouded in mystery and legend - but these confirm the antiquity of the name.

The bear is a large carnivorous animal closely related to racoons, pandas and the dog family. Although classified as flesh-eating, most species (other than the polar bear) are mainly vegetarian - but they will eat almost anything. The bear in the Bible is most likely to be the Syrian Brown Bear which is now very rare - the last one in Israel was killed in the 1930s. One wonders why the (teddy) bear is every child's favourite night-time companion!

"He gathers the lambs in his arms and carries them close to his heart." Is.40:11.

Valerie

Latin 'Valere' 'to be fit and healthy' and the Roman family name 'Valeria'.
The Romans followed the Greeks by placing great emphasis on physical health and well-being as the Olympic Games demonstrate. Physical prowess was worshipped and those who proved themselves were greatly honoured.
In comparison, the Bible has little to say about physical attributes but much to say about the health of the spirit.
"For physical training is of some value, but godliness has value for all things holding promise for both the present life and the life to come." 1 Tim.4:8.

Vanda Vonda Wanda

From Old German 'vand' which possibly means 'stem' or 'stock'. It could have been an ancient tribal name. Its modern use has been traced from Poland early in the 19th century.
People are becoming more conscious of their ancestry and history because they feel that they need to know where they have come from. (Perhaps it is more important to know where we are going!). When we have discovered our 'stem' or 'stock' we may feel that it is not very special. However there are things that we ALL have in common. The Bible says that we all come from the same 'stem' or 'stock' in the respect that we come from Adam who began life sinless and then fell into disobedience. We have all inherited that sinful nature and need the Saviour God has provided.
"I had planted you like a choice vine of sound and reliable stock." Jer.2:21.

Vanessa

Invented by the brilliant satirist Jonathan Swift(1667-1745) who took the first part of a surname 'Van' (Dutch, meaning 'of') and the nick-name 'Essa' (from Esther) and made 'Vanessa'.
Jonathan Swift was the subject of attention by a lovely lady called Esther Vanhomrigh. Swift was incapable of loving anyone other than 'Stella' (Hester Johnson) but he gave this name 'Vanessa' to Esther Vanhomrigh.
Two beautiful butterflies have the name Vanessa in their Latin names - Vanessa atalanta, the Red Admiral and Vanessa cardui, the Painted Lady.
"...praise the name of the LORD...His splendour is above the earth and the heavens." Ps.148:13.

Vaughan Vaughn

From the Welsh 'fychan' which means 'modest'. One of the 20th century's religious composers.

Ralph Vaughan Williams who died in 1958 was possibly the most significant twentieth century religious composer. He was born the son of a clergyman in 1872 and in his early days was a church organist. He wrote a number of oratorios and also assisted in the editing and compilation of The English Hymnal, Songs of Praise and The Oxford Book of Carols. One of his most outstanding works was the festival setting based on the hymn "All hail the power of Jesus' name". He also wrote works based on The Pilgrim's Progress culminating in an "Operatic Morality".

"The time has come...for rewarding your servants the prophets and your saints and those who reverence your name, both small and great..." Rev.11:18.

Vera Verena

Vera means 'true' in Latin and Verena includes the Russian for 'faith'.

Pontius Pilate asked: "What is truth?" John 18:38 when the One who had said "I am the...truth" John 14:6 stood in front of him! The Psalmist says; "Teach me your way O LORD and I will walk in your truth" Ps.86:11.

Faith is a gift from God (see Eph.2:8) and the word is recorded 254 times in the New Testament. Someone has said that FAITH means Forsaking All I Trust Him.

"Jesus replied, 'I tell you the truth, if you have faith...it will be done.'" Mt.21:21.

Verity

The Old English word for 'truth'. Popular since the Puritans in the 17th century.

Pontius Pilate asked "What is truth?" John 18:38 and down through the centuries men and women have repeated that question in one form or another. Strangely, the One who had said "I am the way, the truth and the life" John 14:6 was standing in front of him. This was a further occasion when the Lord Jesus was openly declaring that He and God were one - the Psalmist had said "...O LORD, the God of TRUTH." Ps.31:5.

"God is spirit, and His worshippers must worship in spirit and in truth." John 4:24.

Vernon

From a French place-name which means 'an alder grove'. A 'de Vernon' was companion to William the Conqueror.

The name Vernon originated from the town of Vernon in the Eure - halfway between Le Havre and Paris. Richard de Vernon was a companion of William the Conqueror so it is assumed that the name was brought over with him in 1066.

The meaning of Vernon is 'an alder grove' and the alder tree normally

grows on river banks. Trees are very prominent in the Bible from the "tree of life" Gen.2:9 in the garden of Eden to the "tree of life" Rev.22:14 at the entrance to the gates of the eternal city. Halfway between the two the Psalmist says of a righteous man:
"He is like a tree planted by streams of water...whose leaf does not wither." Ps.1:3.

Veronica

From the Latin meaning 'a true image' (vera-icon). The name given to the legendary woman who wiped Christ's brow when He was on the way to the cross.
Also a flower better known as 'Speedwell' which has some 300 different species most of which are bright blue.
When you bring the 'true image' of Christ and the beauty of a popular flower together you have a lovely picture for this name. St Veronica (as she became known) performed a very compassionate act when she ministered to Christ. In this way she portrayed the beauty of her nature and character.
"Your attitude should be the same as that of Christ" Phil.2:5.

Vickie Vicki Vikky Vicky - see Victoria

Vickram

An ancient Sanskrit name meaning 'Power' or 'Strength'
A king with this name was famous some 60 years before Christ and in ancient classical stories had the reputation of fighting Demons – and winning! It is said that he demanded and was given as much of the universe as he could cover in three giant steps. Whilst these are mythological tales there is one person who has not only conquered the universe but he helped create it first – his name is Jesus.
"...all things were created by him and for him... and in him all things hold together." Col 1:16-17

Victor Vic

Latin for 'Conqueror'. The dictionary definition is "the one who wins in a battle or a contest".
The Bible constantly speaks of conquest and of victory - the basic assertion being that, as David said: "The battle is the LORD's" 1 Sam.17:47. The Bible also reminds us that a battle is not the war - and it is possible to lose a battle and then win the ultimate war. In Christ the victory is assured - because He has conquered - we shall conquer!
"...we are more than conquerors through him who loved us." Rom.8:37.

Victoria Vickie Vikki Vicky Toria

The name 'Victoria' is the Latin word meaning 'Victory'. It became very popular

during the 19th century through Queen Victoria.
Victory is not always what it seems - today some of the most prosperous countries seem to be the ones which lost the second world war. The same often seems true in our own lives, the psalmist in Psalm 73 became quite perplexed by this seeming incongruity - until he went into the presence of God (Ps.73:17).
The Bible has many other references to 'victory': "For lack of guidance a nation (or person) falls, but many advisers make VICTORY sure." Prov.11:14. "This is the VICTORY that has overcome the world...our faith." 1 John 5:4.
"Here is my servant...the one I love...He leads justice to victory..." Mt.12:18-20.

Vijay Vijaya

The name 'Vijay' is from a Sanskrit word which means 'absolute victory'.
Victory is the defeat of one's enemies and this is promised to the Christian. However two points need to be borne in mind: Firstly, a defeat for God's people can mean a victory for Him. The classic case of this is told in Joshua 6 & 7. The Israelites had conquered Jericho and then went on to capture Ai - which seemed small in comparison. They suffered defeat and Joshua was concerned for God's glory. There was sin in the camp and that had to be dealt with first. Secondly, a lost battle does not mean a lost war and the cross at Calvary is the best illustration of this.
"Shouts of victory resound in the tents of the righteous: The LORD's right hand has done mighty things!" Ps.118:15.

Vikesh

An Indian name which means 'the moon'. One of the 'two great lights' created by God. (Gen.1:16).
The moon is a natural satellite of the earth and its diameter is 3,480 km or 2,160 miles, that is roughly a quarter of the size of the earth. For the moon to complete one lunar phase takes 29 days, 12 hours, 44 minutes and 2.8 seconds. The moon's phases and gravity produce the tidal movements here on earth.
Some ancient civilisations worshipped the sun, moon and stars - the created rather than the creator - and Paul speaks about this in Rom.1:18-23.
"And when you...see the sun, the moon and the stars...do not be enticed into...worshipping things the LORD your God has apportioned to all the nations under heaven." Deut.4:19.

Vinay Vinaya

Of Indian origin and meaning 'educate to act in a correct way'. (Appropriate for one following an ascetic way of life).

Education and training are vital in the maturation process. We need to be taught basic 'life skills' which will ensure that we are accepted in the society to which we belong. Every culture has its own practices and norms and it is good to learn these and so provide a sound basis for adult life. Sadly, neither education nor aspiration can help us to act in a way which will be pleasing to God. The Bible teaches us that our inclination is to do the things which displease God and not do the things which He wants us to do. *"For it is by grace you have been saved, through faith and this not from yourselves, it is the gift of God." Eph.2:8.*

Vincent Vince

Latin meaning 'conquering'. An ancient name which was also the name of many 'Saints'.
Vincent de Paul was a man who rose from poverty to poverty! Born in 1581 to peasant farmers in France he was captured and made a slave in Tunisia. He then became a Christian and rose to minister to both Louis XIII and Louis XIV (the 'Sun King', so-called because of his love for and promotion of the arts). In 1617 he joined a monastery and the rest of his life was spent in service to the poor, founding many orphanages and also organising retreats for ordinands and conferences for clergy. He is now the patron saint of those charities which he inspires.
"...who through faith conquered kingdoms, administered justice, and gained what was promised." Heb.11:33.

Violet Viola

One of the popular names chosen from plants and flowers. Used by great writers.
Shakespeare used this name in 'Twelfth Night' as did Gower in 'Confessio Amantis' (c1380).
The Sweet Violet is a very beautiful flower of the Viola family with blue-violet or white flowers. Because of this it has given its name to the colour at one end of the spectrum - a mixture of red and blue.
The name's earliest known use in Britain was in the first part of the 14th century - it was the name of the wife of Sir John Chandos whom he married around 1330.
"See! The winter is past; the rains are over and gone. Flowers appear on the earth; the season of singing has come, the cooing of doves is heard in our land." S.of S.2:11-12.

Viral

From India meaning 'without price' or 'priceless'. Emphasizing the truth that everyone is a precious and valuable asset.
Different cultures have different values but in all cultures there are things which are more highly prized than others - for example, health, good looks,

fidelity, old age. God puts a value on a man's soul which far exceeds all of these. The Lord Jesus said "What good is it for a man to gain the whole world, yet forfeit his soul?" Mark 8:36. So great was the value that God placed on man's salvation He sent His own son to secure it.

"How priceless is your unfailing love! Both high and low among men find refuge in the shadow of your wings." Ps.36:7.

Virgil

From 'Virga' meaning 'a rod, stick or staff'. Name of the great Roman poet who lived shortly before the birth of the Lord Jesus Christ. Originally spelt 'Vergilius'.

Virgil was born 'Publius Vergilius Maro' on the 15th October 70BC near Mantua Italy. He became one of the most influential writers of all time. He was patronised by Augustus who later became Emperor and he affected every classical writer up to and including the Middle Ages. His greatest work was the Aeneid - a 12 volume epic which took him the last ten years of his life. Some see it as a great philosophical work, others see it as prophetical - even to the point of foretelling the coming of the Lord Jesus Christ.

"...God chose the foolish things of the world to shame the wise; God chose the weak things of the world to shame the strong. He chose the lowly things...so that no-one may boast before him." 1 Cor.1:27-29.

Virginia Ginni Ginny

From an ancient Roman family 'Virginius'. Sir Walter Raleigh, Nth America and Queen Elizabeth I.

The name Virginia became popular in the 16th century when Sir Walter Raleigh discovered north America and called it Virginia after Queen Elizabeth I the 'Virgin Queen'. The first baby to be born there was called 'Virginia'.

The word virgin is also applied to nations and place-names such as "the virgin daughter of Zion" Is.37:22.

"The virgin will be with child and will give birth to a son, and they will call Him Immanuel." which means, 'God with us'." Mt.1:23.

Vishal Vishala Vishalakshi

From India meaning 'immense, spacious'. A sense of vastness and capaciousness.

The Psalmist must have had this thought in mind when he wrote; "When I consider your heavens, the work of your fingers, the moon and the stars, which you have set in place, what is man that you are mindful of him?" Ps.8:3.

There are many things in life which baffle us by their huge size or by their delicate minuteness - what a wonderful God we have. The hymn writer must have felt this when he wrote; "O Lord my God! When I in awesome wonder, Consider all the works thy hand hath made, I see the stars, I hear the rolling thunder, Thy pow'r throughout the universe displayed, Then sings my soul my Saviour God to thee; How great thou art, how great thou art!" Anon. (From a Russian translation of a German poem).

"How awesome is the LORD Most High, the great King over all the earth!" Ps.47:2.

Vivian Viv Vivien Vivienne

From Latin meaning 'alive'. Originally it was the Roman family name Vivianus. The source of our word 'vivacious'.

The Bible is 'the book of life'. The gospel of John speaks about 'life' and 'living' on over 70 different occasions.

God is the author of life - it is His alone to give and to take life in creation. In redemption God also gives life and Jesus said; "I am the way, the truth and the life." John 14:6.

"Whoever is thirsty, let him come; and whoever wishes, let him take the free gift of the water of life." Rev.22:17.

Vonda - see Vanda

Wallace Wallis

From the 13th century Scottish surname which is Old English for 'Welsh' (Walsh).

The earliest record of this name is from the 13th century Scottish patriot Sir William Wallace who fought against the English and was executed as a result in 1305. Around the end of the 19th century his surname began to appear as a Christian name, firstly in Scotland, then in the Americas and now universally as a male or female name.

"Trust in the LORD with all your heart and lean not on your own understanding; in all your ways acknowledge Him and He will make your paths straight." Prov.3:5-6.

Walter Wat

From Old German meaning 'a ruler of people'. A favourite Norman name, brought over by them in the 11th century.

One of the most famous owners of the name was Sir Walter Raleigh - he chose to call his son 'Wat'.

We have the Norman Conquest to thank for many of our names and this was one of the more popular ones that they brought with them. It is made up of two words in Old German; vald 'rule' and harja 'folk' and although it was similar to the Old English name of Wealdhere its true origin has never been in doubt. 'Walter' means 'a ruler of people'.

"what is man...You made him a little lower than the heavenly beings and crowned him with glory and honour. You made him ruler over the works of your hands; you put everything under His feet." Ps.8:4-6.

Wanda - see Vanda

Warren

From the Old German 'Varin' (the name of a tribal group) and brought to Britain by the Normans who had a similar name for a 'game-park'. The name 'Warinus' is also listed in the Doomsday Book of 1086.

Tribal names and identity were very important in ancient times because each had its own significant differences. Even today we tend to link certain characteristics with certain countries and peoples. God has made us all unique - although we may share some common traits, the fact is, there is no-one else quite like me anywhere in the world. In Ezekiel 47:22 God has given very clear guide-lines regarding our treatment of those who belong to other 'tribal groups' - in this passage Israel is given the responsibility of treating all as equal.

"Here there is no Greek or Jew...barbarian, Scythian, slave or free, but Christ is all, and is in all." Col.3:11.

Warwick

Old English for the 'the dairy farm by the weir'. (waer wer-wic). Destroyed by fire in 1694 it is today a pleasant country town in the West Midlands.

This name was probably taken from a surname which in turn had been taken from the name of the town. Warwick has a population of around 20,000, a mediaeval castle, a beautiful Norman Church (St Mary's) and the Birmingham City Museum and Art Gallery. It is built mainly to the north of the river Avon on higher ground to avoid flooding. In 1694 it was almost totally destroyed by fire but was subsequently rebuilt retaining some of the ancient houses which survived.

"...long before your time, from the day God created man on the earth...Has any other people heard the voice of God speaking out of fire, as you have?" Deut.4:32-33.

Wat - see Walter

Wayne

From the Old English word for a skilled carpenter who made carts. In some areas they are still called 'wain-wrights'.

Carpentry is one of the world's oldest - and noblest professions. In ancient Britain a skilled wainwright was always in great demand and the popularity of the cart-maker gave rise to a number of proverbial sayings such as "putting the cart before the horse", "cart-loads" and a "cart-track".

Wood is a fascinating substance to work with and it comes as no real surprise that Jesus was also a wain-wright.

The sign outside one church read "Carpenter from Nazareth requires joiners".

"Isn't this the carpenter? Isn't this Mary's son..." Mark 6:3.

Wendy

A 20th century name invented by a childhood friend of the writer J.M.Barrie and used in his famous "Peter Pan".

When J.M.Barrie wrote Peter Pan in 1904 he needed a name for the 'little mother' and so he chose 'Wendy'. This had been part of his own nickname when he was a child. His youthful companion called him 'friendy-wendy' and so the name was born. Barrie may have been influenced by the Old

English word 'wend' which is still used in expressions such as "to wend one's way", meaning 'to make one's way carefully and/or slowly'. This, in turn, came from an Old High German word.

"A friend loves at all times..." Prov.17:17.

Wesley

From Old English and meaning 'west field' (west-lea). The name of the founder of Methodism and one of the world's greatest preachers. A man used by God to transform the moral character of the nation.

It was on the 24th May 1738 that John Wesley found his heart 'strangely warmed' as he sat in a meeting in Aldersgate Street, London. That experience was to transform his life and the lives of hundreds of thousands through the great Methodist movement. His brother had a similar experience just three days before and his contribution was to write over 7,000 hymns for the revival which swept through the UK as a result of Wesley's preaching. He was born and brought up at Epworth near Scunthorpe but his Chapel and home in London are at 49 City Rd (close to the Old Street tube station) - both are open to the public on a daily basis.

"as far as the east is from the west, so far has he removed our transgressions from us." Ps.103:12.

Wilfred Wilfrid

From the Old English meaning 'wanting peace'. Recorded as early as the 7th century.

The 7th century Bishop of York St Wilfrid had anything but a life of peace - he was regularly falling out with the king and he was eventually dethroned.

Peace is a constant theme in the Bible and today seems as elusive as ever. There are more conflicts in the world today than at any time in human history and there is little prospect of improvement. When God speaks of peace (shalom) it is more than a cessation of violence - it has the concept of 'wholeness'.

"Peace I leave with you; my peace I give you. I do not give to you as the world gives. Do not let your hearts be troubled and do not be afraid." John 14:27.

William Bill Billie Billy Will Willie
Female form: Wilma

William is a very old name thought to come from German and meaning 'seeking protection'. There are very many famous 'Williams' in history.

One of the most famous was King William III of England, better known as 'William of Orange'. He only reigned for thirteen years but during that time the Bill of Rights and the Act of Settlement, laying down the principles of Britain's constitutional monarchy, were passed.

Yet another William(s) founded the YMCA in 1844. He was born the son of a Somerset farmer and rose to become a Knight of the Realm. He attributed his success to the fact that he became a Christian as a young man through the preacher Charles Finney.

"Let all who take refuge in you be glad...spread your protection over them." Ps.5:11.

Winifred Win Winnie – see also Gweyneth

Anglicised Welsh 'Gwenfrewi' meaning 'a friend of peace'. A Welsh princess and saint. From the 7th century.

St Winifred is said to have lived in North Wales in the 7th century. She was a princess who spurned the advances of a heathen suitor. He beheaded her and the legend says that where she fell dead a spring of water gushed out. Today the place is known as Holywell (holy-well) close to the north Wales coast.

The legend may not be true but what is true is that Jesus called peacemakers "sons of God" Mt.5:9.

"Grace and peace be yours in abundance through the knowledge of God and of Jesus our Lord." 2 Pet.1:2.

Winston

Originally from an ancient English place-name, 'Winstone' (Wynna's-stone) a small village between the town of Cirencester and the city of Gloucester. The name of a great statesman.

The Churchill family have used the name 'Winston' since 1620 and, it seems, have plans to continue to do so. This name has also been very popular in the West Indies.

The village of Winstone in the Cotswolds is named in the Doomsday Book of 1086 and it was then understood to be a stone (stan) marking the boundary of the land owned by 'Wynna'.

"Do not move an ancient boundary stone or encroach on the fields of the fatherless, for their defender is strong..." Prov.23:10-11.

Wrae – see Rachel

Xaime – see James

Xanthe

Greek meaning 'Bright yellow'.

An attractive and unusual female name. The dictionary definition says; 'Bright', "Shining, full of light, vivid, clear , cheerful, vivacious, clever, illustrious, hopeful, having good prospects". Is that you? If it is you are fortunate indeed. We all strive for these attributes but few of us secure even one of them! But there is a man who was 'full of light' in fact it is said of him; "He was…The true light that gives light to every man was coming into the world."

"The path of the righteous is like the first gleam of dawn, shining ever brighter till the full light of day." Prov. 4:18

Xenia Zena Zina

From Greek 'hospitality'. An early command to the people of God.

'Hospitality' was to be a mark of God's people and a testimony to the tribes living in and around the land - see Lev.19:34, Ez.47:22-23. The word itself is used twice in the New Testament: Acts 28:23 and Phile.22 where it means 'a place of hospitality'.

The apostle Paul says: "Share with God's people who are in need. Practise hospitality." Rom.12:13. Then he gives an illustration: "Gaius, whose hospitality I and the whole Church here enjoy…" (Gaius means 'to rejoice'). Clearly, Gaius was a man who was rejoicing by giving hospitality to the whole church. John in his third epistle gives the reason why we should practice hospitality.

"We ought therefore to show hospitality…so that we may work together for the truth." 3 John 1:8.

Xavier

Name of a Spanish Saint and the founder of the Society of Jesus in the 16th century.

Francis Xavier was born into an aristocratic family in 1506. He studied law and theology in Paris where, together with five associates founded the Society of Jesus known as the Jesuits. They were committed to poverty and chastity and their aim was to evangelise the heaten. At the request of the Pope in 1537 he was sent to southern India where he successfully established a hospital and churches. But for a short time in Japan he died and was buried in Goa. He was 'canonised by the Pope in 1622.

"For we are God's workmanship, created in Christ Jesus to do good works, which God prepared in advance for us to do." Eph. 2:10.

Yasmin - see also Jasmine

This lovely name is the original Persian word which we usually render 'Jasmine' - it has come to us via Old French! It is also the name of a climbing plant with delicate, beautiful flowers.

The botanical name for Jasmine is 'Jasminum' and there about 100 different species of which we have some 40 or more here in the UK. The white Jasmine blooms from June to October and has a single leaf.

God has created a wonderful world with very many lovely things for our pleasure and enjoyment - we must learn to appreciate them and return thanks.

"O Lord, how majestic is your name in all the earth!" Psalm 8:1

Yetide Yebode Yetunde

This Youraba name together with 'yebode' and 'yetunde' means: 'a loved mother (or a grand-mother) returns'. How to cross the largest man-made lake in the world!

When Lake Volta, the largest man-made lake in the world was created, the ferry crossing grew from a few yards to seven miles! The name of the ferry is 'Yeji'.

The full Youraba word means a return of a loved mother or Grandmother and goes back to the days when some youraba people believed in re-incarnation. It is now accepted to mean that the lovely features of a beloved fore-bear have been inherited by a fortunate child or grandchild.

"...sincere faith, which first lived in your grandmother Lois and in your mother Eunice and, I am persuaded, now lives in you also." 2 Tim.1:5

Yolanda

Greek meaning 'a violet flower'. One of the names chosen from plants and flowers.
The Sweet Violet is a very beautiful flower of the Viola family with blue-violet or white flowers. Because of this it has given its name to the colour at one end of the spectrum - a mixture of red and blue. The earliest known use of this flower-name in Britain was in the first part of the 14th century - 'Violet' was the name of the wife of Sir John Chandos, whom he married around 1330. Yolanda is the Greek name for this lovely flower.

"The creation waits in eager expectation for the sons of God to be revealed." Rom.8:19.

Yohannes – see John

Young
One of those rare English words which is both an adjective and a noun. The dictionary suggests four meanings but generally it is used to describe someone youthful, vigorous, enthusiastic and lively.

Some great men have been described as 'Young', e.g. "The Young Pretender" (Bonnie Prince Charlie in the 18th century), "Pitt the Young(er)" (Statesman who bridged the 18th and 19th centuries), "Teniers the Young(er)" (A Flemish artist of the 17th century). There have also been a number of great men in history whose surname was 'Young'. The word 'young' is mentioned in the Bible 346 times - almost once for every day of the year.

"How can a young man keep his way pure? By living according to your word." Ps.119:9.

Yvonne Yvette
From Old French meaning 'a Yew bow'. The Yew tree looks graceful and beautiful but its beauty hides a deadly secret...

The Yew is a slow-growing, long-lasting evergreen tree of the family Taxaceae. It has dense spreading branches thickly covered with dark green linear leaves in double ranks. Its deadly secret is in its foliage and in its seeds both of which are poisonous particularly if left to ferment!

The wood of the yew is very suitable for bows and was a favourite material for the English 'longbow' for many years.

"I do not trust in my bow, my sword does not bring me victory...but you (God) give us victory..." Ps.44:6-8.

Zachary Zacharias Zak Zaki Zakki Zechariah

From Hebrew meaning 'God remembered'. The penultimate book of the Old Testament. The father of John the Baptist.

Zacharias (the Greek version of the Hebrew name Zechariah) was serving in the temple when he had a visit from the angel Gabriel who told him that, even though he was old, he would have a son and call him 'John'. The angel gave him a sign that this was from God and it all happened as predicted. The full story is in the first chapter of Luke's gospel. Significantly, his name means 'God remembered' and this was another reminder that God always keeps His promises.

"But the angel said to him: Do not be afraid, Zechariah(Zachary); your prayer has been heard." Luke 1:13.

Zahra

From Arabic meaning 'to flower' or 'to achieve splendour'. A traditional name originally used in honour of the prophet Mohammed's mother.

Everyone has certain potential and given the right circumstances we can flourish. Sometimes our background and upbringing will affect the rate at which we realise our ambitions. Education assists us in identifying our strengths and weaknesses but only GOD can help us to really achieve our maximum potential. It is important that each one of us 'blossoms where we have been planted'. We all bear the imprint of the creator and so are capable of reflecting his love and glory whatever the circumstances we find ourselves in.

"So from now on we regard no-one from a worldly point of view...if anyone is in Christ he is a new creation..." 2 Cor.5:16-17.

Zainab - see Zaynab

Zak - see Zachary

Zakki - see Zachary

Zara Zarah

Of Arabic origin meaning 'the brightness and splendour of dawn'. The purest colours.

The colours of dawn are purer and colder than the sunset colours because there is less dust in the atmosphere. From deep red to orange to gold and to yellow as the sun rises over the horizon. "Have you ever given orders to the morning, or shown the dawn its place?" Job 38:12. The Psalmist says: "He will make your righteousness shine like the dawn" Ps.37:6. We use the word to describe the realisation of something, e.g. "it dawned upon me".
"In the morning, O LORD, you hear my voice; in the morning I lay my requests before you and wait in expectation." Ps.5:3.

Zaynab Zainab

A Middle-eastern name meaning 'a fragrant plant'. A story of a woman, a jar and a 'timeless act'.
"Then Mary took about a pint of pure nard, an expensive perfume; she poured it on Jesus' feet and wiped His feet with her hair. And the house was filled with the fragrance of the perfume." John 12:3. The perfume which Mary used was extracted from the roots of a type of camel-grass called Spikenard. This is common in parts of North India and Pakistan. Jesus said that she had done a beautiful thing and indicated that, as He would rise from the dead, there would be no need for anointing after His death. He said that wherever the gospel was preached this story would be told - and it is. See Mark 14:3-9.
"For we are to God the aroma of Christ among those who are being saved...the fragrance of life." 2 Cor.2:15-16.

Zechariah - see Zachary

Zena Zina - see Xenia

Zenobia

A beautiful name from Greek history meaning 'life-giver' or 'gift of life'. Also the name of the lovely and intelligent queen of Palmyra in the first century.
This name is full of classical culture and history! The first part of the name is from Zeus - reputed to be the king of the gods. The second part is from the Greek word for life and together they indicate the meaning 'life-giver' or 'gift of life'. Queen Zenobia of Palmyra ruled large parts of the eastern Mediterranean and Asia Minor - from present day Syria to Egypt but was overthrown by the Roman conqueror Aurelian in 272AD. She married one of her captors and lived out her life in luxury in Italy.
"For with you is the fountain of life; in your light we see light." Ps.36:9.

Zoe

The Greek word for 'life' (the Hebrew equivalent is 'Eve'). 'Zoea' is the name given to a stage in the larval growth of some marine creatures - the emergence of life.

'Life' speaks of activity - being 'alive', being 'lively'. It was God who "...formed the man from the dust of the ground and breathed into his nostrils the breath of life, and the man became a living being." Gen.2:7. So God is the author and originator of life - and many times He is described as "the living God" (e.g. Deut.5:26). Jesus taught that life was a precious gift and that there is nothing a person can give in exchange for eternal life (Mk.8:37). The Gospel of John speaks of life or living in at least 70 places.

"This day I call heaven and earth as witnesses against you that I have set before you life and death, blessings and curses. Now choose life, so that you and your children may live." Deut.30:19

Your name is not an accident. God knows your name. He calls us by name (John 10:3), and, using our name, He invites us to stand before Him (Isaiah 43:1).

He loves you so much that He sent His only Son to die for you on the cross. He is willing and waiting to forgive all your sins and to accept you into His family. Your only requirement is to acknowledge that you need Him and want Him as your Lord and Saviour. I hope and pray that you will make that choice and join His wonderful family.

If I can be of more help to you in any way, please feel free to contact me at one of the following addresses:
David Winter, P.O. Box 10349, Chelmsford, Essex, CM3 4YH, UK, or email me at: iouyeshua@yahoo.co.uk

---

BONUS CONTENT

Thank you for purchasing this valuable book. We are sure that you will spend hours in its pages, looking up the names of friends and loved ones to discover what their names mean.

To say "Thank You" for adding this book to your collection, we want to offer you a **FREE GIFT** to add to your enjoyment of *If A Name Means Anything*.

We have recorded a live interview with David Winter, where he discusses the meaning of modern names, the history behind some famous names, and the impact that your name can have on your life—both now and in the future. We asked David some probing questions…and you are going to be shocked at some of his answers!

You are going to thoroughly enjoy hearing from the author himself, as he draws on decades of research, study and godly wisdom, to share with you insights that only he can give.

For a FREE downloadable copy of this intriguing interview, please visit the webpage below and request your copy.

www.PerissosGroup.com/bonus524

Again, thank you for becoming our valued reader and customer, and we look forward to serving you in the future.

HOW TO SHARE THIS BOOK

If you have enjoyed *If a Name Means Anything,* and you would like to share a FREE SAMPLE of the book with friends, family or colleagues, please direct them to any of the following webpages:

www.IfANameMeansAnything.com/sample

www.PerissosGroup.com/sample524

www.info321.com/sample524

Please feel free to send those links via email, text, social media or any other means possible, so that the wealth of wisdom in this book can be a blessing to as many people as possible.

The sample is absolutely FREE, and it is delivered in digital, downloadable format.

Share it with them TODAY!

ABOUT THE AUTHOR

David Winter has led an exciting and varied life.

He became a Christian at the age of 16, shortly after joining the boys service of the Royal Air Force, where he served in both the Middle and the Far East during his 16 years' service.

Discharged from the armed forces in 1966, he joined the Sun Life of Canada as a Life Assurance Underwriter and married Jennifer, with whom he has 3 children.

David was Honorary General Secretary for a Missionary Society for 11 years, and during that period he was also the UK representative for The European Missionary Association. In this latter capacity, he took hundreds of young people to Switzerland for missionary conferences.

He also sponsored and organized a multimedia presentation entitled "Mission Control" and a Missionary Conference entitled "God's World Congress" at Salford University. In 1976, David led the evangelism teams at the famous Knebworth Park pop concerts for five years.

More recently, he was a presenter on Revelation TV in the UK, where he had a weekly programme called "Voice in the Wilderness" for 4 years.

David now lives with his wife in Essex, England.

ABOUT THE PUBLISHER

WRITE your book.
BUILD your brand.
CREATE your platform.
BROADCAST your message.
EXPAND your reach and income...

Perissos Media helps business owners, speakers, consultants, professionals, sales teams, ministry leaders and inspired individuals to PUBLISH books, audio and video training products and other marketing materials, in order to BUILD your platform and ELEVATE you to Expert Status in your field—with all the financial and lifestyle benefits that come with it.

What is your passion? Are you ready to go from LOCAL to GLOBAL?

Even if you have never written a word, we have resources and services to help you get your message out, one step at a time.

For a FREE gift to help you in building or expanding your platform, and to publish your message to a greater audience, please visit:

www.IWantToPublish.com

We look forward to serving you,

Jerry Kuzma
Director
PerissosMedia.com

PERISSOS MEDIA

If A Name
Means Anything

DAVID WINTER

For more resources,
please visit:

IfANameMeansAnything.com

Printed in Great Britain
by Amazon.co.uk, Ltd.,
Marston Gate.